BORLEY RECTORY: THE FINAL ANALYSIS

The frontispiece overleaf shows the Rev Harry Foyster Bull superimposed upon the summerhouse in the garden of Borley Rectory where he spent so many night hours watching for the spectral nun

BORLEY RECTORY: THE FINAL ANALYSIS

Edward Babbs

assisted by

Claudine Mathias

SIX MARTLETS
PUBLISHING

BORLEY RECTORY: THE FINAL ANALYSIS

First published 2003

First published in the United Kingdom in 2003 by
Six Martlets Publishing
PO Box 7480, Sudbury CO10 9WP

Typesetting, design and production by
Keld Fenwick
Jacket design by Nicholas Fenwick
Printed by
St Edmundsbury Press
Blenheim Industrial Park, Newmarket Road
Bury St Edmunds Suffolk IP33 3TZ
Orders to
Six Martlets Publishing,
PO Box 7480, Sudbury CO10 9WP
United Kingdom

ISBN 0-9544856-0-2

CONTENTS

ILLUSTRATIONS

PREFACE

Seven full-length books have been written about the alleged haunting of, and the witnessing of paranormal phenomena at Borley Rectory, in the former rectory garden and in the church and churchyard across the road from the rectory site.

The first two books on the subject were written by the late Harry Price. They were *The Most Haunted House in England*, published in 1940 and *The End of Borley Rectory*, published in 1946. Both have been re-issued several times and are still easily obtainable. In addition to the two books, Harry Price wrote many newspaper and magazine articles and delivered many lectures and broadcasts about the alleged haunting of Borley.

After Price's death three books and a number of articles were published which questioned vigorously his honesty and integrity. War has waged ever since. The battle lines are drawn between those on the one hand who regard Borley as clear evidence of survival and those on the other hand who regard the matter as a mixture of fraud, trickery and blatant publicity hunting.

At the end of this work we have listed most of the books to do with Borley and with the characters involved. If you read through them, you will be likely to come to the conclusion that psychical researchers are a rather quarrelsome lot! You may gain the impression that they devote a large part of their time to reading each other's books and then tearing them apart, at least figuratively if not literally. You would not be far wrong, either.

We shall try to avoid this conflict and to adopt a different approach in this book. We feel that the trouble is due in part to the fact that some previous researchers and writers have tended to air their own theories and views, when they could have been carrying out much more local investigation. We have tried to address this shortcoming and to make the maximum use of the recollections and first hand testimony of the many people residing still in the Borley and Sudbury area who remember clearly the events and the individuals concerned over the last 70 years and more.

Our credentials for undertaking this work are more than adequate. One of us (EB) is a former member of the Society for Psychical Research and has been deeply interested in the case for nearly 40 years. He resigned from the Society for the sole reason that pressure of work made it very difficult to attend meetings and there has been no question of any disagreement. He takes the view that the Society has earned great respect in its more than a century of existence and that it is anything but the 'farcical organisation' which it has been described as by one sceptical author.

The other half of the team (CM) is the widow of the last rector of Borley and Liston, who took up his duties on 28 July 1955 and who remained in post until 1967. Mrs Mathias lived at the rectories at Liston, firstly in the old one and latterly in the new one (ancient and modern) and knew well the people of both parishes. Both of us live near to Borley and Liston.

Since 1967, these small parishes have been combined with two others and have been administered by a succession of priests residing at Foxearth.

We have to conclude on a sad note; whilst this book was in the advanced stages of preparation, Margaret Finch died on 4 June 2002 at the age of 97. She gave us a great deal of information about life at Borley Rectory. We send our deep sympathy to her family and friends

Edward Babbs
Claudine Mathias

ACKNOWLEDGEMENTS

It is our very pleasant duty to record our appreciation to the many people who have helped us so much in the preparation of this work. We are most grateful to Philip Babbs, Martin Breese, Edward Carter, Gillian Cook, Paul Diner, Stewart P Evans, the late Alfred Finch, the late Margaret Finch, Messrs Gough, Clinton and Broom, the late Gerald Hazell, the late Russell Herbert BEM, Paul Kemp, Kathleen King (née Finch), Dorothy Lane, Olive Marshall, Paul Mathews, Thomas Musk, Frank Nice, the late Canon Leslie Pennell, Ursula Pennell, the late Marie Poore, the late Ted Ritchie, José Simmonds, Alan Wesencraft (who did much more than simply writing the Introduction) and Hilary Wright. All of them furnished us with new details and information about the Borley case. We wish to thank also the Hon Rebecca Poynter and the late Rosemary Risk for many hours of typing and word-processing. If we have forgotten to mention anyone who has assisted us, we hasten to assure them that this was inadvertent and we offer to them our most sincere apologies.

We would also like to acknowledge those who have contributed illustrations as follows:

Authors, Figs 16, 19, 28, 43, 46, 54, 70, 83, 85, 87.
Philip Babbs, Figs 38, 39, 40, 41, 42, 98, 99.
Edward Carter, Fig 68.
Colchester Royal Grammar School, Fig 22.
Margaret Ebeling, Fig 72.
Essex County Archives, Fig 71.
Stewart P Evans, Figs 1, 23, 35, 36, 37, 100.
Keld Fenwick, Figs 12, 13, 14, 15, 31, 32, 50, 55, 57, 58, 60, 69, 73, 74, 75, 76, 78, 79, 82, 90, 94.
Mr and Mrs W J Honeyball, Fig 44.
Kathleen King, Figs 4, 8, 9, 17, 18, 30, 91.
Paul Mathews, Figs 2, 3, 5, 6, 7, 10, 11, 20, 21, 27, 29, 33, 34, 45, 59, 64, 65, 66, 67, 77, 80, 81, 84, 86, 88.
Family of Mary Pearson, Fig 25.
Registrar General, Northern Ireland, Fig 95.
Registrar General, New Brunswick, Fig 96.
José Simmonds, Figs 24, 47, 48, 49, 51, 52, 53, 61, 62, 63.
Suffolk County Archives, Fig 89.
Alan Wesencraft, Fig 97.

Jacket images were provided by Edward Carter, Paul Kemp and Kathleen King; frontispiece images provided by Edward Carter and Alan Wesencraft.

INTRODUCTION

*By Alan Wesencraft, former curator of the Harry Price Library
at the University of London.*

A s a small boy in the 1920s, I was an avid follower of the adventures of the Noah Family, a children's feature written and illustrated by J F Horrabin, which appeared in my father's newspaper *The Daily News*. Under parental guidance I was soon exploring the more advanced portions of the newspaper and thus became aware of the existence of Harry Price, whose activities were always reported with fairness and accuracy. In the 1930s I enjoyed reading two of his most popular books, *Confessions of a Ghost-hunter* and *Leaves from a Psychist's Case-book*, both of which deserve to be re-issued.

At the end of 1937 I had the pleasure of meeting the man himself, though my encounters were few and very brief. The University of London library was then situated in the Imperial Institute at South Kensington and Price would sometimes visit the librarian to discuss various details concerning the bequest of his library to the University. He used to talk to me while waiting for the librarian to be available. Looking back on these few meetings my impression is that he certainly had no interest in discussing the weather but would plunge immediately, with a kind of boyish enthusiasm, into an account of his latest venture. I was always sorry when he was interrupted by the bell summoning him to the librarian's office. In view of the many vicious attacks which have been made on his character since his death in 1948, it is well to bring to notice the opinion of Richard S Lambert, author and administrator. Lambert was editor of the BBC publication *The Listener* for ten years and during that period enjoyed a close friendship with Price. He wrote in his introduction to a book by David Cohen:

> 'From my personal acquaintance I can say that Mr Price was generous, straightforward, loyal and honest. He possessed a cautious scepticism, a highly developed sense of publicity and a skilful pen.'

In 1956 I became involved in the maintenance of the Harry Price Library now safely established in the University of London library. I had known for some time about Price's two books on Borley and was well aware of the enthusiasm with which they had been received by readers and reviewers alike. I now began to examine with great interest Price's Borley material. One day in 1956 Dr Pafford, the University librarian, asked for my views on a disturbing incident concerning Borley. It seemed that a certain Trevor Hall, a member of the trio of Borley detractors appointed by the Society for Psychical Research, had borrowed a book from the Harry Price Library to assist him in his work. To Pafford's astonishment and annoyance Hall refused point-blank to return the book on the grounds, for which there was not a shred of evidence, that it did not belong to the library. Although incensed by Hall's effrontery, Pafford, on the advice of the University solicitor, agreed to let the matter drop. The book was in fact the so called *Locked Book* of Borley miscellanea compiled by Sidney Glanville, Price's friend and assistant. It was subsequently sold by Hall to an American collector for £1200. By a similar devious ruse Hall also obtained possession of the typescript of the Rev Lionel Foyster's *Fifteen Months in a Haunted House*, and this he later sold to America for £700. These two facts, coupled with Hall's false claim to have been awarded the degree of MA Cantab, must throw considerable doubt on his reliability as a genuine and trustworthy research worker.

Having read Price's two books on Borley and glanced through his accompanying material, I soon succumbed to its spell. The expression is not inappropriate because many who read about Borley do become fascinated and absorbed not only by its paranormal complexities but also by its human interest and they thirst for further information.

The authors of *Borley Rectory: The Final Analysis* have done much to satisfy this widely felt and insatiable curiosity concerning every detail of the haunt. By dint of accurate and painstaking research and with the help of many hitherto unpublished photographs they present us with a very clear picture of the rectory, its surroundings and entourage, from its heyday as an attractive building in the years before 1914, through its declining years to its destruction by fire in 1939. Many hitherto unreported paranormal experiences in the district have been scrutinised with great care and the authors have never refused to allow, in borderline cases, the possibility of a natural explanation. The first chapters of the book contain an excellent history of the salient features of the haunt and will be of value to readers with little or no knowledge of Borley. The final chapter, which gives the authors' thoughtful conclusions, contains a lucid explanation of ley lines and the part they may have played (and may still be playing) in the production of the Borley phenomena.

I have no hesitation in warmly recommending the book as a valuable and indeed indispensable guide for all persons anxious to learn more about the enigma of Borley Rectory and the effect it had on those who came under its influence.

Alan Wesencraft

We wish to record our great appreciation to Alan Wesencraft for writing this introduction. It makes fascinating reading and includes some astonishing information.

Edward Babbs
Claudine Mathias

CHAPTER ONE

The geography and the history

Borley is located in north Essex and part of the parish boundary adjoins the river Stour, which also defines the county border (between Essex and Suffolk) at this point. Borley is not really a village at all, rather it is a scattered and sprawling rural parish within the area of the Braintree District Council. It is not mysterious, remote and isolated as some authors would have us believe; if local residents will forgive the expression, 'dreary rather than eerie' would seem to be an appropriate description. Borley is situated about two miles from the bustling market town of Sudbury and the same distance from the large village of Long Melford. The main road between these two communities is the A134 which links Colchester to Bury St Edmunds.

Borley parish may be divided into three parts. The first of these (the eastern end) is very near to the A134 and the river. The largest and most historical building here is Borley Mill, thought by some to have been the original manor house. Other properties include some modern bungalows, some semi-detached houses and the old Victorian school which is now partly a private residence, the school room itself being used for village meetings.

The second part of the village may be reached by proceeding westwards along a gentle hill known as Hall Lane. At the top of the hill is located the church (of unknown dedication) and immediately next to it is Borley Place, which is another historical building and a much more likely candidate for the original manor house in view of its proximity to the church. There are many examples of this type of arrangement both locally and elsewhere, which would seem to indicate that the lords of the manor did not reckon to travel too far in order to take out insurance against any difficulties which may be in store for them in this world and/or the next. Immediately across the road from the church is the site of the former rectory and its large sprawling garden of nearly three acres. This is a long thin triangular plot stretching down Hall Lane towards the Stour and accommodates now four detached bungalows. The rectory was destroyed by fire in 1939, but the so-called

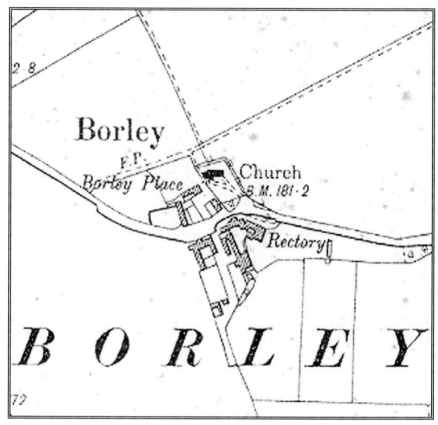

Fig 1. A 1905 map showing Borley Rectory and the buildings clustered round it

rectory cottage remains. It is a red-brick Victorian building and is by the standards of today a sizeable detached house. Other properties in this part of the parish consist of some relatively new houses and bungalows, some old cottages and farm buildings. From the churchyard there is a splendid panorama across the Stour valley and on a clear day it is possible to see on the skyline the huge church tower of Lavenham, which is about eight miles away by road.

Proceeding westward again, one comes to the third section of the parish which is known as Borley Green. Properties here are a mixture of farmhouses, thatched cottages and some more modern houses and bungalows. Leaving Borley Green there are two steep hills which drop down to the lane which leads to Sudbury in one direction and various small villages in the other.

The population of the parish is approximately 130, most of whom are either to do with agriculture or are retired. We have referred to a gazetteer of 1874[1], which indicates that there has been little change with regard to the number of residents. There is no village shop, but over the years there have been various attempts to bring private

Fig 2. The River Stour at Borley. The parish of Borley is to the right

enterprise to Borley. One of us (CM) remembers a sweet shop, an off-licence and a post office. The latter was run by the late Mrs Margaret Finch who features with her late husband, Alfred, later in this book. All these enterprises were run from private houses and there has never been any shop property as such at Borley.

The 'famous' Borley Rectory was built in 1863, on the instructions of the Rev Henry Dawson Ellis Bull, who had become the rector in the previous year[2]. The much-excavated cellars beneath the rectory were not in alignment with it, which would indicate that it was built on the site of an earlier house. Almost certainly this was the residence of the Herringham family, who had provided the two previous rectors. There

Fig 3. A view of the Stour Valley taken from Borley churchyard. The rebuilt vents of the maltings at Long Melford can be seen in the centre

Fig 4. Borley village school. The pursuit of knowledge at the beginning of the 20th century

is no evidence to support the legend that this was the site of a monastery or priory, although such buildings did exist at Sudbury, two miles away. The Rev Henry Dawson Ellis Bull died in 1892 and it is virtually certain that there is no one alive today who can remember him. He was said to be a typical wealthy 'squarson' and an athlete who enjoyed boxing and fox-hunting. Another manifestation of his physical prowess may have been the fact that he fathered at least 14 children - estimates vary! The increasing size of his family necessitated the building of another wing to the rectory in 1875. This large extension created an almost totally enclosed courtyard.

It seems clear that the alleged haunting of the rectory grounds by the spectre of a nun was well established during the lifetime of the Rev

Fig 5. Borley Green. The semi-detached cottages behind the telephone box at the extreme left of the picture were home to the late Alfred and Margaret Finch and Miss Marion Pitt, the village schoolmistress

Fig 6. The Rev Henry Dawson Ellis Bull's grave in Borley churchyard; regrettably it has been damaged by vandals. The inscription reads: IN EVER LOVING MEMORY OF HENRY DAWSON ELLIS BULL / MA PRIEST / 30 YEARS RECTOR OF THIS PARISH / WHO ENTERED INTO REST MAY 2ND 1892

Henry Dawson Ellis Bull. It was he who had built the large circular summer-house, so that he could keep watch over the long garden path adjoining the farmland and known as the Nun's Walk. After his death one of his sons, the Rev Harry Foyster Bull, became the rector having previously been the curate at Borley.

The Rev Harry Foyster Bull remained the rector until his death in 1927. For an Anglican clergyman, he seems to have had strong leanings towards the spiritualist approach. He was convinced that his garden and rectory were haunted and he would sit for hours at night in the summer-house, watching for the ghost of the nun. Then he would spend half of the day in the same place catching up on his sleep!

A number of important events are alleged to have occurred during his incumbency. One of these was the sighting of the nun in the rectory garden at close quarters by four of his sisters on 28 July 1900. This is said to have taken place in the evening and in reasonable light[3].

During the period commencing April 1916 until March 1920, the rectory cottage was occupied by Mr and Mrs Edward Cooper, Mr Cooper being employed by the Bull family as a gardener and coachman. The Coopers claimed to have seen the ghost of the nun on several occasions and reported many inexplicable disturbances in the cottage. Mr Cooper claimed also to have seen a phantom coach and horses driving through the rectory garden. Presumably he was familiar enough with the family phaeton in view of his duties and would have recognised this vehicle had it been the one he claimed to have seen. The Coopers were remembered by Alfred and Margaret Finch as being 'sensible and rather religious' people and at this distance in time one

Fig 7. The Rev Harry Bull's grave in Borley churchyard; it too has been damaged by vandals. The inscription reads: TO THE DEAR MEMORY / OF / HENRY [HARRY] FOYSTER BULL MA / PRIEST / 35 YEARS RECTOR OF THIS PARISH. / BORN 4TH JANUARY 1863 / ENTERED INTO ETERNITY / 9TH JUNE 1927

can only decide for one's self as to whether or not they are to be believed.

Following the death of the Rev Harry Bull, Borley was without a rector until the arrival of the Rev Guy Eric Smith and his wife in October 1928. In the period between these two events the condition of the once beautifully maintained rectory had deteriorated and the Smiths used only a limited number of the many rooms there. They were mystified by the alleged strange happenings and unaccountable sounds (although Mrs Smith denied this vigorously many years later) and Mr Smith wrote to the editor of *The Daily Mirror* asking for the name and address of a psychical research society which might be able to provide assistance[4]. This seems to have been a strange step to have taken, but the Rev Smith (an Anglo-Indian) was very bewildered and it must be remembered that 70 years ago people in general were far more naive than they are today. What the Smiths got, unfortunately, was a reporter from *The Daily Mirror*, Mr V C Wall, who wrote a number of sensational articles about the alleged haunting. This national publicity led in time to the village being invaded by hordes of rowdy visitors, many of whom were conveyed there by enterprising local coach firms who had hastily organised 'Ghost Tours'. Today, over 70 years later, Borley residents still receive the unwelcome attention of badly behaved people, especially on 28 July (presumably the hope is that the phantom nun will take another curtain call), at Hallowe'en and on New Year's Eve. Regrettably, there has been considerable damage done in the churchyard and on these dates there are now police officers on duty in the village.

The Smiths received also the first of many visits from Harry Price, who had been contacted by the editor of *The Daily Mirror*[5]. One should not be too cynical about the editor's action. Although there were those who did not trust Harry Price, to many he was, in the inter-war period, the ghost hunter *par excellence*. Further, it has been alleged that the matter had been referred previously to the London-based Society for Psychical Research, who had not pursued it. During the early hours of 13 July 1929, Harry Price organised a seance at the rectory which produced some surprising results, perhaps of dubious accuracy, but it has never been suggested that there was any element of fraud. About a month later the Smiths moved out of the rectory and organised the parish from rented accommodation in nearby Long Melford. They left the district altogether in April 1930.

Six months later, a new rector and his 'wife' came to live at Borley. They were the Rev Lionel Algernon Foyster and Mrs Marianne Foyster. They brought with them a small child whom they had adopted. The Rev Foyster was related to the Bull family and he and his 'wife' had returned recently from New Brunswick, Canada, where he had been engaged in missionary work[6].

The Foysters were an extraordinary couple by any stretch of the imagination. The Rev Foyster was a prematurely elderly man in poor health. He suffered from arthritis and was confined at times to a wheelchair; he was known to be a very forgetful, although intelligent man. His 'wife' was about 20 years younger and she lost no opportunity to be elsewhere other than at Borley, which she regarded as a totally boring place. By the time she reached the end of her life (in 1992) she had been 'married' four times, the Rev Foyster being her second 'husband'. In fact three of her four marriages were illegal[7].

We may have created the impression that most of the alleged phenomena took place in the area of the rectory rather than in the building itself. This is not the case and over the years there were many reports of inexplicable events within the house. During the Foyster incumbency these poltergeist associated phenomena appear to have reached a level of intensity never experienced previously. For example, there was a system of bells linking the various rooms to the kitchen passage. The bells are said to have rung frequently of their own volition, despite the fact that some of the wiring (non-electrical) incorporated in the system had been cut. Mysterious writings appeared on the walls and furniture and utensils were flung about. The spectre of the late Rev Harry Foyster Bull was said to have been seen, usually on the main staircase and attired in a favourite dressing gown, or so we are told.

In September 1931, two of the Bull sisters called upon Harry Price at his London office and reported to him this dramatic increase in the alleged psychic activity. A fortnight later, he and some colleagues went to the rectory to witness these wonders for themselves. It was Harry Price's last visit to Borley for a long time. After discussing the matter with his friends, he told the Rev Foyster that the phenomena could have been caused fraudulently by his 'wife', who was not present or not under control when events occurred. The rector was extremely upset and when Harry Price and his party left for London, the two men were on bad terms. Much later in her life, Mrs Foyster admitted that she had faked 'phenomena', which was of course just what the sceptics wanted to hear. However, we do not think that the position is as simple as it would seem, because critical authors have failed invariably to draw sufficient attention to the fact that the Foysters lived at Borley rectory for five years only. The legend of the haunting was established decades before their arrival and phenomena continued to be reported after their departure in October, 1935.

In March 1936, the Rev Alfred Clifford Henning was inducted to the combined living of Borley and Liston and he and his family lived at Liston Rectory[8]. The two parishes are almost adjacent to each other and Liston is even smaller than Borley. It is not an isolated place, being only a short walk from the large village of Long Melford, which had a railway station at that time.

The Rev Henning was deeply interested in the alleged haunting of Borley Rectory and its environs and, some people felt, to the extent that he tended to neglect his official duties. It is certainly true that during his incumbency a great deal happened at and to the rectory, including of course its eventual destruction by fire.

The condition of the empty house continued to deteriorate and the church authorities were trying to sell it and cheaply. They offered it to Harry Price, but he declined to purchase it. Instead, he rented it for a year commencing in May 1937 and set up teams of observers there[9]. He was criticised later for seeking volunteers with no previous experience of psychical investigation and for issuing to them a booklet which suggested strongly what they may encounter. A likely explanation of this procedure is that Harry Price wished to distance himself somewhat from the operation but at the same time control it closely and prevent interference by other psychical researchers.

Opinion varies considerably over the worth of the evidence collected by the teams of observers. Some say that it was impressive. Others claim that it did not amount to very much. Two of the observers, Dr H F Bellamy and his son, set up a 'Harry Price type' electrical control apparatus attached to some books placed on the dining room mantelpiece. The arrangement was such that if the books should be moved then an electric bell would ring. Some hours after the gadget was put in place the bell rang and when Dr Bellamy and his son went to investigate, they discovered that the books had been disturbed. Critics have suggested that this may have been due to a cat which may have strayed into the building. One of us (EB) and the Bellamys have mutual friends who lived in the Bromley area who report only that the doctor and his son rejected totally this explanation. The dining room was sealed and the house was patrolled regularly.

One of the most enthusiastic of the observers, the late Sidney H Glanville, made meticulous plans of the rectory, conducted many inquiries of his own and became in effect Harry Price's right hand man. He and members of his family carried out some experiments with a planchette board which they owned already[10]. One has to have reservations about 'information' gleaned in this manner: some of it is nonsense, some of it is said to emanate from the subconscious mind(s) of the sitter(s), but some of it cannot be explained away so easily and has to be taken much more seriously. Whatever one's views on the subject, we have to report briefly on two of the planchette sessions because of their relevance to the alleged haunting of Borley Rectory.

On 31 October 1937, information 'came through' via the planchette and appeared to identify the phantom nun. It was stated that her name was Marie Lairre, that she was a novice from a convent in France, that she was brought to Borley under false pretences by a member of the Waldegrave family and then murdered by him in 1667.

The ancient Waldegrave family were the lords of the manor and patrons of the living there for about 300 years, although the family seat proper was, and is still, near Bath. There are two memorials to members of this family in Borley church. One is a wall tablet and the other appears to be a huge canopied tomb dedicated to the memory of Sir Edward Waldegrave, his wife and their six children. Sir Edward was a Member of Parliament and Chancellor of the Duchy of Lancaster during the reign of Queen Mary, but during the reign of Elizabeth the First he was imprisoned in the Tower of London and then he died there. The family was Roman Catholic and it seems that Sir Edward paid the ultimate price for being unable or unwilling to adjust his religious opinions. It is possible that at a later date, a member of this family enticed a young lady to Borley (which was isolated and lonely then) and then ended her life when she became inconvenient. One cannot go further than that and the matter cannot be proved one way or the other.

On 27 March 1938, another remarkable message came through at a session with the planchette. The wording was:

'Sunex Amures[11] and one of his men mean to burn the rectory tonight at nine o'clock end of the haunting go to the rectory and you will be able to see us enter into our own and under the ruins you will find bone of murdered (indistinct) wardens (indistinct) under the ruins mean you to have proof of haunting of the rectory at Borley (indistinct) the understanding of which (indistinct) tells the story of murder there.'

There was a brief addition to the message, in which it was stated that the fire would start 'over the hall.' It is a matter of history that the rectory was destroyed by fire, that the fire did commence in the hallway and that human remains were discovered under the cellar floor. Critics of the case have made the most of the fact that the planchette communicator got the date wrong (by 11 months) and have implied that human bones were planted under the cellar by tricky old

Harry Price in order that they could be 'discovered' at a later date. With regard to the first point, we have commented already about the reliability and precision of such information. With regard to the second point, we feel that this allegation is quite unsustainable and will deal with it in detail later.

In November 1938, the rectory and cottage were sold at last, the new owner being one Capt William Hart Gregson[12]. He and his sons moved into the cottage in December, as a temporary measure. The family did not enjoy the facilities at the rectory, such as they were, for very long. On 27 February 1939, the predicted fire occurred. Capt Gregson stated that he was in the hall of the rectory sorting out his books when he knocked over an oil lamp (there never was any electricity in the house). By the time that local fire engines arrived the blaze was out of control and by morning the once large and solid rectory had been reduced to blackened ruins. Capt Gregson had problems with his insurers, who refused to pay out, claiming that he had started the fire deliberately. Eventually, a compromise was reached and the captain did not have to face a charge of arson. Predictably, sceptical authors have seized upon this issue in their interminable quest to discredit everyone involved in the Borley saga. However, there seems sometimes to be a considerable gulf between the facile promises that are given when policies are taken out and the hardening of attitudes when claims are made under the terms of those same policies. With reference to this particular case, it may be advisable to keep an open mind.

After the place was ruined, Harry Price was urged by Canon W J Phythian-Adams, of Carlisle, that it might be pertinent to excavate the cellars in the search for an explanation of the alleged haunting[13]. It is important to note that this suggestion was based primarily upon the canon's interpretation and analysis of the very confused wall-writings that appeared in the rectory and not merely upon the planchette communication of 31 October 1937. Canon Phythian-Adams did not visit the rectory; he had read Harry Price's first book about Borley which contained reproductions of the wall-writings. The canon seems to have been somewhat impatient with Harry Price for not following up his suggestion at an early date. However, there were problems. Although the former rectory was in ruins Capt Gregson's permission had to be obtained (and he was trying to sell the site and the cottage), the cellars were full of rubble and debris and Harry Price had to rely on others to do the manual work because he suffered from a serious heart condition.

The excavations commenced eventually on 17 August 1943 and there was also an unsuccessful attempt to locate a crypt under Borley church. A jaw-bone and part of a skull were found under the cellar floors and were identified immediately by a pathologist as being human, belonging probably to a woman. Further digging carried out during the following days did not reveal any more human remains. The only other item of interest was the discovery of a Sheffield plate cream jug in one of the rather dangerous wells in the cellar. It was examined in due course by experts who expressed the opinion that it was about 80 years old. The jaw-bone was subjected to tests by a dental surgeon who confirmed that it had belonged to a woman and probably a young one, the age at death being not more than 30. The bones were placed in a casket and then interred at Liston churchyard in 1945. In his second book about Borley, Harry Price suggested strongly that the bones could link up with the 'Marie Lairre' theory, but other authors have been very cynical about this. Other people continued to excavate under the cellars for several years, but no further human remains, nor anything else of importance were found.

In 1947, the cottage and rectory site were purchased by the author James Turner. He and his family lived in the cottage for many years. He built a brick wall indicating the outline of the old rectory and created a rose garden in the enclosed area; it and the wall have been removed now. The main rectory garden was sold off in plots and bungalows were built on them.

Over the years, reports of various alleged phenomena, including sightings of the spectral nun have continued to be made. We feel that it is unacceptable to label all of the people who have claimed such experiences as being either simpletons or liars.

The players were beginning to leave the stage. The Rev Guy Eric Smith died in 1940, the Rev Lionel Algernon Foyster in 1945, Harry Price in 1948 and the Rev Alfred Clifford Henning on 14 January 1955. On 28 July 1955, (a significant date in this saga) the Rev Edward Lanfranc Morgan Mathias was inducted to the living of Borley and Liston and he was the last rector to look after these two small parishes on their own.

CHAPTER TWO

The trees for the wood

Harry Price wrote two books about Borley Rectory and was preparing a third work when he died. Two books highly critical of the alleged haunting have been published since Price's death. The first of these was originally a report and appeared also in book form in 1956, entitled *The Haunting of Borley Rectory*. It was written by three members of the Society for Psychical Research, the result of five years of investigation by the authors. They were Dr Eric Dingwall, Mrs Kathleen Goldney and Trevor Hall and their work was carried out at the instigation of the Society. The first two authors were former colleagues of Harry Price and the third one claimed never to have met him. Price was a member of the Society for Psychical Research during the early 1920s and it seems not to have been an easy relationship. Despite a serious heart condition, he was a man of considerable energy and enthusiasm and felt that the Society was over-cautious and over-conservative in its approach to the various aspects of the subject. He was the owner of a huge library to do with magic and the occult; for a time it was housed at the Society's headquarters and made available to its members, but even this apparently useful arrangement foundered in the end, causing bitterness on Harry Price's part. It is hardly surprising that he set up a rival organisation in 1926, financing it out of his own considerable wealth[1]. *The Haunting of Borley Rectory* is still fairly easy to obtain and we feel that it is an anti-Harry Price book rather than an anti-Borley book. We shall refer to this book again.

In 1992 a book called *The Widow of Borley* was published, the author being one Robert Wood and the widow being the late Marianne Foyster. *The Widow of Borley* is sub-titled *A Psychical Investigation*. This work seems to go in more than one direction; primarily it is the biography of an extraordinary and untruthful character, but the early chapters are devoted to the alleged haunting of Borley before Marianne Foyster went there and also to the career of Harry Price prior to his arrival on the scene. With regard to the biographical part of the book, very few chances are missed in the first 163 pages to denigrate Marianne's behaviour and then on the final page the author appears to express the opinion that perhaps she was not too bad a girl after all.

In the introduction to the book, we are told that it is not about psychical research, which seems to be in conflict with its sub-title. Robert Wood goes on to say that authors of other Borley books and articles describe themselves as trained and serious investigators; he wonders where they received their training and who the less than serious investigators are. There are only a few establishments which offer courses in the subject, but there are many people who take the view that experience is the best of all universities. The word 'serious' means earnest and non-flippant and Wood's 'serious' research seems to be based on three points: First, he tells us that he spent his boyhood in Acton, Suffolk, which is a village fairly near to Borley; second, he states that he has never seen a ghost at Borley and feels clearly, therefore, that no one else ought to have done so either; third, with regard to the biographical part of his book, he acknowledges that it relies to a large extent upon the enquiries carried out and set in motion by the late Trevor Hall, one of the authors of the Society for Psychical Research book about the alleged Borley haunting.

The introduction to *The Widow of Borley* includes a lecture on the subject of what constitutes evidence and the difference between the observation of something and the interpretation of what has been seen. This is in direct reference to and is an attempt to diminish the authenticity of one of the most famous alleged sightings of the phantom of the nun in the rectory garden. It took place on 28 July 1900, during the evening. Three of the Bull sisters, the Misses Ethel, Freda and Elsie were returning from a garden party and had entered their own garden, when they saw (so they claimed) the figure of a nun gliding rather than walking along the path known as the Nun's Walk. They said that she was moving away from the rectory and towards the stream which flowed across the garden, more or less cutting it in half. The sisters were very frightened and one of them went to fetch another sister, Dodie. She was the eldest of the many girls in the family and bringing her to the scene seems to have been a perfectly sensible and a natural thing to do. Dodie claimed also to have seen the spectral nun on this occasion. There are many instances when cautioning on the difference between observation and interpretation will be appropriate, but this is not one of them. In this case the issue is simple and clear-cut: The four sisters claimed to have seen a figure dressed as a nun in reasonable light and at close quarters and then she vanished. Either they did see such a figure, or to put it bluntly, all four of them were lying. There is no proof one way or the other, but one of us (CM) knew Ethel Bull (and her brother Alfred) and did not regard her as being dishonest nor as the possessor of a hyperactive imagination.

Two further matters are raised in the first chapter of *The Widow of Borley*. The first is to do with the Rev Harry Foyster Bull's wedding, which took place at St Alban's Church, Holborn, London, on 12 September 1911. His marriage caused a family feud. Robert Wood feels

Fig 8. The Rev Harry Bull and Borley church choir photographed after his wedding in 1911. The small boy in front is Alfred Finch, aged 11

that this may be the reason why the service was held not at Borley, but in what he describes as an unfashionable London church. This may be a correct assumption, but there is an equally strong alternative reason and it is quite incorrect to dismiss St Alban's church as unfashionable. Thirty years before Harry Bull's wedding it was the scene of great controversy and excitement.

This argument had its roots in the Oxford Movement, which became a force to be reckoned with during the middle part of the 19th century. It advocated a highly ceremonial and flamboyant type of church service, laying heavy emphasis on the importance of the communion. There was considerable use of incense and lots of lighted candles at the altar; the priests would conduct much of the service facing east and would loosen up their joints by means of frequent genuflection. However, many influential people within the Church of England deplored this 'Anglo-Catholic' approach and felt that it was far too near to the procedures of the Church of Rome. An organisation known as the Church Association came into being in order to oppose such practices and it proceeded to take legal action against some of the clergy who indulged in them. One unfortunate priest finished up in prison. Another one was Father Alexander Heriot Machonochie, the incumbent at St Alban's, Holborn, from 1863 (when the then new building was complete) until the time of his virtually forced resignation in 1882[2]. He favoured and enacted a very Catholic type of service including all of the features mentioned earlier and he erected a confessional within the church. Father Machonochie was regarded by the Church Association as being the worst of all of the offending clergymen and they took legal action against him on many occasions on the grounds that he was acting unlawfully with regard to the conduct of his services. Apparently no allowance was made for the fact that Father Machonochie (and/or his style of service) was 'packing them in'. It may seem strange to us, more than a century later, that people felt so strongly about such matters but clearly at the time passions were much aroused. The extraordinary point about all this was that when this particular troublesome priest resigned eventually, the church authorities allowed the Anglo-Catholic style of service to continue at St Alban's and the church became noted for such services.

To return to the matter of the controversial wedding of the Rev Harry Foyster Bull, an ordained priest and a wealthy man. Apart from the risk of unpleasantness from his disapproving relatives, he may have had Anglo-Catholic beliefs himself and wished to be married in a church associated with that tradition, rather than in a simple little country place of worship such as the one at Borley. Unhappily, the St Alban's church that Father Machonochie and the Rev Harry Bull knew was destroyed almost totally during the air raids in 1941 and had to be rebuilt after the war.

The other matter in chapter one of *The Widow of Borley* is the letter which Mrs Mabel Smith wrote to *The Church Times* in 1945. She was the widow of the Rev Guy Eric Smith, who was the rector at Borley for about 18 months after the Rev Harry Bull died. The wording of Mrs Smith's letter has been reproduced in several books and reads as follows:

'Sir, I have read with interest your articles and letters on "Thump Ghosts" and as I was in residence for some time at Borley rectory, Sussex ("the most haunted house in England") I would like to state definitely that neither my husband nor myself believed the house haunted by anything else but rats and local superstition. We left the rectory because of its broken-down condition, but certainly found nothing to fear there.

G Eric-Smith.'

This communication brought joy to those people who were sceptical about the alleged haunting at Borley and Robert Wood claimed that it annoyed two members of the pro-Borley lobby so much that they implied that Mrs Smith's mental powers were in decline. He was referring to Peter Underwood and the late Dr Paul Tabori who wrote a book called *The Ghosts of Borley*, which was published in 1973. It is a detailed book and a balanced assessment of this case. There is a somewhat saccharine dedication to the memory of Harry Price, but the authors did not flinch from discussing in depth those events which did not show the famous ghost hunter in too favourable a light. To return to the question of Mrs Smith's letter, we feel that Underwood and Tabori were probably right about her state of mind, unfortunately. With regard to the actual wording, first of all she appeared to have forgotten where Borley is and to have moved it a couple of counties away from its true location. Then she signed the letter in her husband's name, spelling it incorrectly and overlooking the fact that he had died five years previously. There are other factors which indicate that Mrs Smith had become somewhat confused. Ethel Bull stated that Mrs Smith was very frightened whilst she was at Borley. Also, Sidney Glanville interviewed the Smiths on 6 October 1937, at Sevington. At this time, the Rev Guy Eric Smith was the rector there, a small parish near Ashford in Kent. It is quite clear from Sidney Glanville's notes that the rector felt the alleged phenomena which were said to have occurred in and near to Borley Rectory defied a normal and rational explanation and he viewed them much more seriously than his widow appeared to do eight years later. Viewed with the perspective of time, it seems at least possible that the letter was sent by an imposter and that the letters editor of *The Church Times* had not checked that the sender was indeed Mrs Smith[3].

The second chapter of *The Widow of Borley* concerns itself with the early career of Harry Price and then his first visit to Borley Rectory on 12 June 1929. There are two points in this chapter which should be discussed.

The first matter is not so much to do with Borley, but with a sweeping generalisation about psychical research as a whole. Harry Price tested many mediums in his laboratory and found some of them to be fraudulent[4]. According to Robert Wood, however, every psychical researcher has the dream of discovering genuine mediums, be they clairvoyant, the centre of telekinetic phenomena or whatever. This is perfectly fair, but then comes the claim that psychical researchers are disappointed invariably because all mediums are found to be fraudulent, sooner or later. This is quite incorrect and we can conclude only that Robert Wood is not merely sceptical about the alleged paranormal phenomena at Borley, but about such occurrences in general. He claimed that Harry Price became disappointed in his investigations for this reason and also because he failed to persuade orthodox science to take seriously the subject of psychical research. The reality is that many scientists did accept and continue to accept that this difficult subject cannot be slotted conveniently into the grooves of the laws of orthodox science; furthermore, some universities in this country and abroad have established departments and studentships devoted to the study of what is known now as parapsychology[5].

The other matter concerns the events of the day and the seance which was held in an upstairs room, known as the Blue Room, at Borley Rectory during the course of Harry Price's original visit to the house. He stated that after he arrived there and was met by the Smiths, who gave an account of their experiences in the place, he and his secretary searched the building thoroughly from the attics to the cellars. He said also that later in the day there was an outbreak of poltergeist activity witnessed by himself, his secretary, the Smiths and V C Wall, the reporter from *The Daily Mirror*. Harry Price claimed that after they had descended the stairs a glass candlestick, which they had seen on the mantelpiece in the Blue Room, was hurled down the stairs and smashed into pieces. It was followed shortly afterwards by other objects including stones and a mothball. He said that when these objects came down the stairs the light was good and the entire party was assembled in the hallway. Of course, we are aware of the fact that there are those who are determined not to believe a word that Price spoke or wrote. However, it seems to us that he cannot be accused of producing fraudulently these phenomena because even an expert amateur conjuror (which he was) could not be upstairs and in the hallway at one and the same time. The only alternative explanations are that he had an accomplice hiding in the rectory whose presence was unknown to the others, or that he was lying about this incident which means in effect that the rest of the party were involved in such falsehoods. Such alternative explanations are neither likely nor convincing.

Later on, in the early hours of the next day (13 June 1929) Harry Price organised a seance in the so-called Blue Room at the rectory. In addition to himself there were six other people present. They were his secretary, Lucie Kaye, the Smiths, V C Wall and two of the Bull sisters, who had come to the rectory during the course of the evening. They lived now, together with several siblings, in another large house called Chilton Lodge at Great Cornard, which is near to Sudbury. Harry Price opened the proceedings by asking out aloud that if there was an entity present, then perhaps there could be an indication that this was the case. After a short interval, a tap was heard clearly and it appeared to come from a dressing table mirror. Then the sisters tried to obtain information from the entity by asking questions, hoping that a much used system (three taps for 'yes', two taps for 'no' and one for 'uncertain') would be effective. Of course, all of the questions were of the leading variety and we feel that 'information' gleaned by this method must be viewed in the same light as 'information' obtained from a planchette board.

This seance has been discussed in many of the books about Borley. The communicating entity identified itself as being 'Harry Bull', who indicated that he was not happy in the 'after life' and that he had been murdered. Robert Wood described the whole proceedings as being rather like a game-show and maintained that the reference to murder was in answer to a question put by the Misses Bull, whom he described on several occasions in his book as being malicious and vindictive old women. They were not, although they disliked their widowed sister-in-law for many reasons as discussed in the next chapter. Robert Wood misses the point here. The accuracy of the 'information' is suspect, as always, but it is not at all normal for a piece of furniture to make tapping noises upon request. It is paranormal and there has never been any suggestion to the effect that these sounds were produced fraudulently. Seven people, some of whom had met for the first time, were in the room which could not have been prepared in advance. The only conclusion is that either the phenomena were genuine, or that all of those present were party to a completely false report of alleged events which never took place. We believe that the former alternative is correct and note that even the sceptics have not subscribed openly to the latter. The mirror belonged to the Smiths and according to Peter Underwood and the late Dr Paul Tabori in their book *The Ghosts of Borley*, it produced similar effects subsequently at other addresses. It is almost as if the piece of furniture had its own source of energy, or was a focus for energy supplied by the sitters.

The fourth chapter of *The Widow of Borley* concerns itself with Harry Price's tenancy of the now empty rectory in 1937. One of his most enthusiastic helpers was Sidney Glanville and he, his son Roger and some of their friends became part of the team of voluntary observers during the year-long tenancy. He was not, as Robert Wood tells us, at one and the same time careful and cautious and also naïve and too trusting. Sidney Glanville was an extremely intelligent man and a highly qualified civil engineer; his integrity was never questioned and he kept an open and enquiring mind about the alleged haunting at the rectory.

In order to help to pass the time during the long hours whilst 'on duty' at Borley, Sidney Glanville constructed a lightweight table, which stood about two feet high and took it to the rectory with a view to carrying out some experiments in table tipping. Several sessions were held, the sitters consisting usually of Glanville himself, his son and their friends in the team of observers. The same technique was used as in the case of the tapping mirror for the most part and the communicating entities identified themselves as the Rev Henry Dawson Ellis Bull and his son, the Rev Harry. We repeat our cautioning about the value and accuracy of such 'information' and as is so often the case, the answers to some of the questions were gibberish. According to Robert Wood, one has to have doubts about the mental condition of those who take part in such sessions, sitting in semi-darkness and suffering the inconvenience of cold draughts behind the ears! It is fairly easy to be flippant, but our purpose in writing this book is to present as balanced and detailed a view as possible of the alleged haunting. As in the case of the tapping mirror, Robert Wood has missed the point, or perhaps has masked the point in order to draw the attention of his readers away from it. It is not normal for a small table to start rocking of its own volition and to order. It is paranormal, unless of course the sitters were cheating. We consider this unlikely. The technique consists of those present resting their hands very lightly on the table and hoping for some results. If one of the sitters pushed the table deliberately, then the others would know, apart from the difficulty of controlling with any degree of accuracy the movement of what ought to be an inanimate object. The alternative explanation is, once again, that all of the sitters were lying and acting in collusion. This theory also is most unlikely. If they were going to cheat, then the likelihood is that they would have reported far more lucid and spectacular communications than they did. And we must make the point again that all of the people who knew Sidney Glanville found him to be a man of complete integrity. With regard to the reported cold draughts behind the ears, one of the instances where the difficult subject of psychical research does slot into the grooves of the laws of orthodox science is the question of temperature variations at seances. These variations can be and have been, measured scientifically and accurately and on many occasions drops in temperature have been recorded. Rarely, if ever, does the temperature rise on such occasions.

Chapter six of *The Widow of Borley* is entitled 'Marianne's early life', but about half of it is devoted to the early career of the Rev Lionel Algernon Foyster, who became Marianne's second 'husband'.

Foyster was born in Hastings in 1878 and his father and uncle were both clergymen and patrons of their own livings in that town. The family were in a good financial position and it seems that life for them must have been comfortable and genteel in that particular part of Sussex by the sea. The Rev Foyster was ordained as a priest in 1904 and was a curate in Yorkshire from the previous year until 1905, that is for two years only. His father resigned from his living in Hastings in the same year that Lionel Algernon became a fully qualified priest. Robert Wood wonders why the very recently ordained Rev Foyster did not take up the living at Hastings of which his father was the patron. Instead, he took another curacy in Cheshire until he emigrated to Canada in 1910. The clergyman at the parish in Cheshire was his brother-in-law and it was whilst he was here that Foyster met his future 'wife,' who was still a child in 1905. Robert Wood proceeds to insinuate that Lionel Algernon did not accept, or was not offered the living at Hastings in 1904, or very soon afterwards, because the young reverend gentleman had in some way 'blotted his copybook'. Then the author goes on to say that this could account also for Lionel's decision to take up missionary work in a remote part of Canada about six years later. In the following pages of his book, Robert Wood surmises that there must have been some sort of scandal, probably of a sexual nature.

There is no justification at all for coming to this conclusion. The facts are that in the earlier part of the 20th century many more people were regular churchgoers than is the case today. There were many more clergymen and there was a lot more for them to do. Apart from their religious duties, they did a great deal of social work in those years before the gradual establishment of the welfare state. It was not merely common, but normal procedure, for priests to serve at least two and sometimes three curacies before applying for their first living. The Rev Lanfranc Mathias (CM's late husband) was a highly qualified priest. He came down from Cambridge with two degrees, but proceeded then to take up three curacies, totalling 15 years service, before accepting his first living. It would have been very unusual and would have been an open invitation for accusations of nepotism, for the Rev Lionel Foyster to have accepted the living of which his father was the patron, without having served for at least a reasonable time as a curate. We see nothing untoward in the fact that his second curacy was in the same parish where his brother-in-law was the incumbent, although Robert Wood implies that this was an arrangement which allowed the brother-in-law to keep an eye on Foyster. A much more likely and natural explanation of the situation is that the clergyman advised the young Lionel Algernon of a forthcoming vacancy and that both of them liked the idea of working together. Perhaps there was a touch of discreet nepotism after all.

During the course of his book, Robert Wood seems to be inconsistent in his attitude when he discusses at various stages the relationship between the Rev Lionel Foyster and his young 'wife'. Let us look first at the situation whilst the couple were at Borley Rectory — not that Marianne was at the rectory for any great length of time due to the fact that her other activities appeared to have been quite time-consuming. And we make the point again that the Rev Foyster was the incumbent for five years only. With regard to the alleged violent poltergeist activities which were said to have taken place during this period, Robert Wood implies that they were all fraudulent and organised by Marianne and/or one François d'Arles, who was the tenant in the rectory cottage and one of her lovers. The author states that it was fairly easy to convince the rector that the 'phenomena' were genuine because his mental powers were in decline. If this is correct, it would seem to indicate premature senility because Foyster was only in his early 50s when he took up residence at Borley Rectory. He appeared to be older than he was, partly because of a chronic and serious arthritic condition and partly because of the considerable difference in ages between himself and Marianne. On the other hand, Robert Wood tells us that the Rev Foyster was mentally alert enough to be aware of his 'wife's' sexual adventures and condoned them. Indeed, the theory is that he gained perverted pleasure from them, may have been a paedophile and a voyeur and eventually his departure to the next world was expedited by Marianne. Poor old Lionel Algernon! He does not seem to have had a lot going for him. We feel that the balance of probability is that some of the phenomena were genuine and that the rector was becoming mentally ill and therefore was not really aware of Marianne's extraordinary activities.

Finally, we wish to comment on the alleged paranormal ringing of the house bells. When Harry Price and his team visited the rectory in October 1931, they suspected that Marianne was responsible for the 'phenomena' and told the Rev Foyster so[6]. This caused considerable bad feeling between the two men and Marianne denied such responsibility. She prayed there and then that a poltergeist effect would happen and right on cue one of the bells rang. In view of the ill-feeling between the two groups, we believe that false reporting can be ruled out. The other possibilities are that Marianne had a hidden accomplice blessed with wonderful hearing, or that the phenomenon was genuine.

There is another interesting point in *The Widow of Borley* to do with the house bells. In chapter ten the claim is made that a piece of string was found in the ivy on the outside of the rectory, that it was attached to some wiring and that when pulled the bells rang miraculously. This claim is possible but unlikely. During his 1929 visit to Borley, Harry Price reported that many of the bell wires had been cut in an attempt to eliminate this nuisance[7]. One of us (EB) lived as a boy in an old Georgian house which contained a similar system of house bells. With regard to the rectory, it is most unlikely that any of the mechanism would have been located on the outside of the building; furthermore, even in this peculiar household surely someone would have been suspicious sooner or later if 'paranormal' bell ringing was coincidental with someone else standing at the same point outside the place and fiddling about in the ivy.

Robert Wood is entitled to his views and his biography of Marianne Foyster is fascinating and almost incredible. However, we feel that his determination to pour scorn on the Borley saga as a whole has not resulted in a balanced assessment of it and has led him into making many assumptions that are not based on firm foundations.

CHAPTER THREE

The Bull family

'Harry (Bull) was the rector of Borley you know,
Who had a lot of sisters who sat all in a row
Freda was the eldest* and Ethel coming next,
She listened to the sermon and never knew the text,
Mabel was the third one who was not often at home,
She had her digs in London where often she would roam.
Then came the three youngest all stomping down the aisle,
The noise they all created made all our aunties smile,
Then there was Chinery the coachman who sat behind the boys,
Who frowned upon them hugely when 'ere they made a noise.
And in the pew beside them there lay a great long stick,
And when those boys were talking hard, the whacks came mighty thick.'

*She was not, Dodie was.

The above poem was composed in the early part of the century by Mildred and May Gardiner of Borley Lodge[1]. Apparently the Bull family occupied the pews under the pulpit and the Gardiners sat behind the Waldegrave tomb on the opposite side of the aisle. The Gardiners were and are still, a large farming family in the north Essex area.

The Bull family had its origins in the nearby village of Pentlow and in many senses of the expression they left their mark on the place. They were wealthy local landowners, squires and parsons, the so-called 'squarsons.' No less that four members of the family held the living consecutively and there was a Rev Bull leading the prayers at the tiny church with its very unusual round tower from 1756 until 1927. There were two Johns, then Edward and then Felix. The last named was the brother of Henry Dawson Ellis Bull, who had built Borley Rectory in 1863. Thus the two brothers were rectors concurrently in these two small and nearby rural parishes, although Felix outlived Henry by 35

Fig 9. The Rev Harry Bull (ringed) and Borley church choir photographed after his induction in 1892. Mr Chinery (middle row, fourth from left) was coachman to the Bull family

years. There is a wall tablet in Pentlow church dedicated to the memory of Capt Orlando Bull telling us that he was lost in the China seas in 1842. He was the Rev Edward Bull's brother.

Pentlow village is remarkable for a large structure known as Bull's Tower or by some people as Bull's Folly. It was built by Edward Bull in

Fig 10. Pentlow church, Essex, with its remarkable round tower

Fig 11. The Rev Edward Bull's grave in Pentlow churchyard. The inscription reads: IN MEMORY OF/EDWARD BULL MA/BORN JANUARY 21ST 1803/DIED FEBRUARY 4TH 1871/RECTOR OF THIS PARISH FOR 37 YEARS. *Four other members of his family are buried in the large grave*

1858 in the rectory garden as a memorial to his parents, although local legends suggest two other possible reasons for its existence. One is that Edward Bull wanted to see the sea from the top of his tower and the other is that he was able to watch the farm labourers in his fields and would take note of those who were not working hard. There may be some truth in the latter theory, as it seems that Edward Bull was something of a tyrant. Some years ago, a local publican told one of us (EB) that when 'Old Bull' was riding around the village in his trap if the locals failed to adopt a sufficiently grovelling posture when he passed by they were liable to feel his whip across their backs. There is another local legend which tells of an incident when the Rev Edward was one of the guns in a local shoot. The story has it that the reverend gentleman was waiting for the birds to come over when an innocent pig happened to amble by. Since there was nothing much happening, Bull shot it. Another version has it that the pig bit the rector first. We prefer this; there is an element of divine retribution in it. Happily, country parsons do not behave in this fashion today, but even so local residents must accept Edward Bull's highly individual and eccentric contribution to their landscape. When the tower is viewed from close quarters one can admire the fine brickwork and crenellated top, but at

Fig 12. An early photograph of the Rev Edward Bull's 90 feet high tower in the grounds of the old rectory at Pentlow. The building at the left of the photograph covers a well in excess of 100 feet deep from which water was drawn by bucket and windlass

Fig 13. Detail of the dedication above the door. It reads: ERECTED TO THE MEMORY / OF HIS HONOURED PARENTS / THE REV^D JOHN BULL MA / AND MARGARET HIS WIFE / ON A SPOT THEY LOVED SO WELL / BY EDW^D BULL MA 1859

a distance of a mile or so it looks rather like a chimney poking out of the middle of a wood. There is a stairway inside the tower but it is no longer safe to use it.

The Rev Henry Dawson Ellis Bull became the rector of Borley and whilst his eventually famous rectory was under construction he and his family lived across the road from the building site in Borley Place. The new rectory was a large L-shaped structure of red brick and was surrounded by tall, mature trees such as elms and cedars of Lebanon. The Bull family increased in numbers to such an extent that it became necessary to add a further wing to the already large house. This in turn created an almost totally enclosed

Fig 14. An early photograph of the former rectory at Pentlow, the other and surviving 'Bull' rectory

Fig 15. As at the time of writing

courtyard and sceptics have suggested that this arrangement could have caused peculiar acoustical effects which may have provided a normal explanation for some of the alleged phenomena. It is possible that the sceptics are correct, but we feel that it is most regrettable that there are so many 'could have' and 'may have' situations in this matter. Both the 'pro-Borley' and 'anti-Borley' lobbies will agree about this, if not much else.

Plans of the ground floor and first floor of Borley Rectory were drawn up carefully and accurately by Sidney Glanville and they have been reproduced in all of the books about the alleged haunting. It is clear from these plans that the front door (located under a small tower) was really on the side of the house and facing Hall Lane and that the main aspect of the building, which included the huge windows of the lounge and dining room, looked across the large lawns and down the length of the garden. In addition to the lounge and dining room, the ground floor rooms included a library, which was used later by Harry Price's team of observers as their base of operations. There was also a

Fig 16. Margaret Finch, Alfred Finch and Kathleen King, née Finch

large kitchen and ancillary rooms including a butler's pantry, a sewing room, a scullery, a larder, a dairy and several storerooms. The first floor consisted of eleven bedrooms, a bathroom, a lavatory and a chapel. One of the bedrooms which looked across the lawns became known as the Blue Room and was said to be the scene of much paranormal activity. The chapel was located in the small tower and readers will have to make up their own minds as to whether the room owed its existence to devotion or eccentricity.

The authors of the various books about the alleged haunting of Borley Rectory describe the place as being dark, gloomy, eerie, cold, neglected and anything but 'home, sweet home'. However, it was not always so. We are indebted to Alfred and Margaret Finch for a wealth of detailed information about life at the rectory during the time of the Bulls[2]. Margaret Finch was employed as a servant by the Rev Harry Bull during the 1920s and she and another young lady lived in. Margaret is very definite that when she lived there, the rectory was a lovely house and was kept in excellent condition. It was overfilled with furniture and pictures by the standards of today, but this was fairly typical of affluent Victorian and Edwardian residences. The point is that during the era of the Bulls the rectory was a lovely home and it was only later on and during the occupancy of subsequent incumbents that it acquired its dreary image. Clearly the Bull family was in the financial position to maintain a large country rectory in an appropriate manner and we believe that this more than made up for the lack of services which we take for granted today. There was no electricity supply in the village, there is not a gas supply even today and water had to be pumped by hand from a well in the courtyard. Their successors were not so fortunate. By the time that the Rev Guy Eric

Fig 17. Borley Rectory in 1926. The path to the left is the Nun's Walk. The Rev Harry Bull, his stepdaughter, Constance Brackenbury, and his wife, Ivy, are posing on the tennis lawn

Fig 18. The Misses Everett and Cook in service at Borley Rectory at the beginning of the 20th century. They are posing in the rectory courtyard

Smith and his wife came to Borley, the rectory was beginning to suffer from the effects of being unoccupied, except perhaps by rats and mice. The Smiths had no children, so they furnished and used only a limited number of the rooms in the large house. It does not take long for the fabric of a building to deteriorate and the process had continued further when the Rev Lionel Algernon Foyster and his 'family' arrived in 1930.

The very big garden contained a number of interesting features. We have mentioned[3] already the large round summerhouse in which the Rev Henry Bull, and later his son Harry, would sit for hours watching the Nun's Walk in the hope of catching sight of the elusive lady herself and also the little stream which cut the garden in half. There was another and smaller summerhouse at the eastern tip of the garden. It was situated at the farthest point from the rectory itself, located beyond the area used for growing fruit and vegetables. A further

Fig 19. A recent photograph of Hall Lane, Borley. The hedge to the left, now intersected with driveways to the bungalows, marked the length of the large rectory garden. Borley church is in the background

curious feature of the garden was the cats' cemetery, which contained many little graves all with their own headboards bearing names such as 'Sandy', 'Gem' and 'Rollo'. In all probability this was to do with the Rev Harry Bull who kept a large number of cats, about 20 or 30 at a time. It is said that he knew them all by name and that they used to follow him around in a group. This was before his controversial marriage in 1911, after which he had only a few cats at a time. Presumably his fastidious wife (an ex-nurse) put her foot down about his menagerie. Rather oddly, an intruder dug up the cats graves one night in 1937 and to date no logical explanation of this action has been put forward.

Finally, a gravel coachway (with large gates at each end) passed by the front door and it is clear from early photographs that the lawns were used for games of tennis and croquet. Margaret Finch tells us that the grounds were kept in immaculate condition by two full-time gardeners.

Now we shall turn to the Bull family who lived in the large rectory at the top of the hill. The Rev Henry Dawson Ellis Bull died in 1892, so there is no one alive now who would remember him. Unlike the other members of his family who became ordained, he attended Oxford University and not Cambridge. Life for him at Borley seems to have been fairly congenial and relaxed and in addition to his hunting activities, it is said that he used to lie on the floor of the dining room and take shots with his rifle at any rabbits bold enough to put in an appearance on his well manicured lawns. We reiterate that the legend of the spectral nun was well established in his time and that the path

Fig 20. Caroline Sarah Bull's grave in Borley churchyard; regrettably it has been damaged by vandals. She was Henry Dawson Ellis Bull's wife and Harry Bull's mother

down the side of the garden was known already as the Nun's Walk.

Mrs Bull outlived her husband by 22 years, dying eventually in 1914. Alfred Finch remembered her. As a boy he attended Sunday school at the rectory taken by Miss Freda Bull. Alfred and the other children had to use the servants' entrance and the Sunday school services were held in the sewing room next to the kitchen. On Easter Sundays, old Mrs Bull would sit at the hall doorway, with the green baize door kept shut and dispense hot cross buns to the children. Alfred Finch recalls that she appeared to be very aged and frail and very small in stature. To be precise, she was so old that she had to be assisted into and out of the chair in which she sat and the children had to help themselves to the buns which were in a basket which she held.

The Rev Henry Dawson Ellis Bull and his wife had a very large family. Estimates as to the exact numbers vary in the other books about the alleged haunting of Borley Rectory and it may well be that these variations could be accounted for by the very high rate of infant mortality in Victorian times. Alfred and Margaret Finch say that 14 survived: Constance, Dodie, Elsie, Ethel, Freda, Kathleen, Mabel, Milly, Alfred, Basil, Gerald, Harry, Hubert and Walter. Nevertheless, the Bulls achieved the remarkable accomplishment of increasing the population of their parish by approximately ten per cent, which may be one method of dealing with the problem of dwindling congregations. Eventually, Alfred Bull became a schoolmaster (but he did not teach at the local school) and Harry succeeded his father as the rector of the parish, having served first two curacies, one in Durham and the other at Borley itself.

The Bull family looked after the parishioners, perhaps in a slightly patronising way by the standards of today. The family was regarded generally by the parishioners as being benevolent and kindly, genteel and somewhat eccentric. Alfred and Margaret Finch remember that a big treat for the villagers was a Christmas party each year at the rectory and there would be gifts of tobacco for the men and sweets for the children. Alfred recalled an illuminating incident from his early childhood. One day, he and his mother were walking back home from Sudbury and his mother was pushing along a pram with the baby of the family in it. As they were ascending the hill leading to the church and the rectory (Hall Lane), they were overtaken by Hubert Bull who proceeded to push the pram the rest of the way for them.

Apparently there were many tennis parties held at the rectory during the summer and members of the Bull family would be invited in turn to similar parties at the neighbouring rectories. In the winter there would be dinner parties at Borley and once again there would be reciprocal arrangements. All in all, life at Borley Rectory (and the house itself) seems to have been anything but gloomy in those early days.

The legend of the ghostly nun, and other alleged phenomena, were well established during the lifetime of the Rev Henry Dawson Ellis Bull. That legend was reinforced strongly when his son, the Rev Harry Foyster Bull became the rector of Borley. The two clergymen, father and son, held the living and were also patrons of the living for 65 years continuously. Harry Bull was convinced that his rectory and garden were much haunted and we will discuss his life and times before going on to consider the phenomena which were said to have occurred during his incumbency.

Harry Bull became the rector of Borley in 1892 and remained in the post until his death in 1927. Alfred and Margaret Finch remember him well. He was a tall and athletic man, but suffered much from bronchitis. He liked walking and playing tennis, but his wheezy breathing was very obvious and was audible from a considerable distance. He was only 64 when he died in the so-called Blue Room in the rectory, the cause of death being certified as chronic bronchitis. Harry Bull liked to sleep a lot and often, after being absent for many hours he would be discovered catching up on his rest in the large summerhouse in the rectory garden[4]. It has been suggested that he suffered from narcolepsy, a condition associated with syphilis and a symptom of which is the need for an excessive amount of sleep. This is a most unlikely theory; if he was a victim of these unfortunate conditions, they did not affect his wife who outlived him by nearly 30 years. In all probability he was catching up on his sleep. He would spend hours during summer nights in the summerhouse watching for the spectral nun and claimed to have seen her, or at least to have been aware of her presence on many occasions.

Harry Bull was a popular priest. He visited his parishioners regularly and his services attracted good congregations. During the early part of the century his little church boasted a large choir and was always full on Sunday mornings. We think it likely that he was a frustrated Anglo-Catholic but that he had to be content with relatively simple services for the benefit of his flock, most of whom would have been agricultural workers and would have received only a basic education. Alfred Finch told us that he left school at the age of 12 because he 'had a job to go to' (he was a herdsman) and those of his classmates who stayed on until they were 14 did so only because they did not have a job to go to. To return to Harry Bull and his religious views, whatever they may have been officially, it is clear that unofficially he was orientated very much towards spiritualism and the possibilities of making contact with those in the 'after-life'. He used to say frequently that if he found that he was dissatisfied with the after-life, then he would make his feelings and presence known to those who survived him.

In about 1910, the Rev Harry Bull commenced to make his feelings and presence known to someone whilst he was very much in this life. In addition to visiting his parishioners in their own homes, it was noticed with some amusement that he appeared to become rather more diligent with regard to visiting those members of his flock who were unfortunate enough to be patients in the local hospital, St Leonard's at Sudbury. One of the nurses who worked there was a young widow called Ivy Brackenbury and she had more than a little to do with the increasing frequency of the visits to the hospital. As one Borley resident put it to another who was a patient at St Leonard's: "I dooo believe that he comes here to see her and not you!" In his copious notes, Sidney Glanville commented at one point that Ivy Brackenbury kept a sweetshop in Sudbury and at another that she was indeed a hospital nurse. Alfred and Margaret Finch have no knowledge of the sweetshop and maintain that the good lady's only occupation was that of nurse. It may be that the sweetshop was a joint venture and that Ivy had two part-time jobs. Whatever the explanation of this minor mystery, on 12 September, 1911, she became Mrs Ivy Bull[5] and life was never quite the same again for the family into which she had married. The Rev Harry acquired a stepdaughter, Constance Brackenbury, who became known to the servants at the rectory as 'Miss Constance', which was slightly confusing as one of Harry's many sisters had the same name and was referred to also as 'Miss Constance.'

The Bull sisters did not approve of the marriage and did not like their new sister-in-law. There were a number of reasons for this unfortunate state of affairs. The family were affluent, genteel, Victorian people who lived in a time warp. In all probability they were hardly aware that the 20th century was well under way at the time when their brother Harry decided to get married. They were the sort of family who were in a rut, who liked to be in a rut and were suspicious of any change. It is highly significant that only a few of the 14 second-generation Bulls of Borley got married. It is certain that they were suspicious of Ivy Brackenbury's motives when she became the wife of a fairly wealthy man who was in late middle age (by the standards of the time) and who was nearly 20 years older than she was. She had appeared out of the blue, or so it must have seemed to the family and had become established immediately as the most important female member of the Bulls of Borley. Worst of all, they would have to move out of the house which had been home to them for so long. Although the Rev Harry and his new family lived for a time at Borley Place, it was obvious that sooner or later the rector would want to live in his own rectory. This happened and most of his siblings settled eventually at Chilton Lodge in Great Cornard, now virtually a suburb of Sudbury.

Margaret Finch was a servant who lived in at Borley Rectory during the 1920s and she has told us some interesting and amusing facts about the family whom she came to know very well[6]. She describes Harry Bull as a slightly strange man who seemed to live in his own dream world all the time. On the other hand, he may have been suffering from the effects of those long nocturnal vigils in the summerhouse. Apparently, Harry and his wife had separate bedrooms and in view of his lengthy night time expeditions into the garden we are not surprised. Gradually his squad of cats diminished in numbers and eventually he had only one left. He used to take this sole survivor to church with him. Margaret Finch remembers Ivy Bull mainly for the facts that she always wore clothes that rustled and that she was in the habit of coming down the stairs backwards in order to see that they had been dusted properly. It seems that it was a case of 'once a nurse, always a nurse' and no doubt in her own mind she had achieved the dizzy heights of 'matron'. One wonders if the marriage was really a happy one and it is certain that Harry and his stepdaughter did not like each other at all. 'Miss Constance' used to make faces at her stepfather when his back was turned and on one occasion when he was not present she amused the servants by picking up one of his waistcoats

Fig 21. A recent (2002) photograph of Eyston Hall, Belchamp Walter

with tongs, thus implying that she did not consider that it was fit to be touched with bare hands. Constance Brackenbury became a dressmaker and although she had her own rooms at the rectory she was not there very often. She used to go to see a Mrs Mansfield who lived at Eyston Hall and spent a lot of time with her. The Hall is still in existence and it is a large Georgian house just outside the Borley boundary at the west end of the parish. One other insight into life at the rectory recalled by Margaret Finch concerns the morning prayer service which Harry Bull would hold in the dining room, for the benefit of the servants. He would stand with his back to the windows whilst saying the prayers and frequently Mr Brown, the head gardener, would appear outside the windows and indulge in various antics in order to try to make the servants laugh. Mr Brown lived in the rectory cottage after Mr and Mrs Cooper (see chapter one) had left and moved to Sudbury.

Now we shall discuss the alleged phenomena. Harry Price's two books include many accounts of a variety of incidents referred to him, but some of them are concerned with relatively trivial occurrences which could have a normal explanation, or which are lacking in sufficient detail to warrant further examination. Indeed Harry Price's second book, *The End of Borley Rectory,* consists largely of reproductions of letters which he received following the publication of his first work and one gets the impression that it almost wrote itself, figuratively speaking. To be fair, it included details of events which took place after the first book was launched, the most important of which was the discovery of human remains beneath the cellar floors of the ruined building.

The spectral nun who is said to have patrolled the Nun's Walk and also the garden generally, was alleged to have been seen by many people and we have described already the famous sighting by four of the Bull sisters on the evening of 28 July, 1900. One of the four (Ethel) claimed that she saw the ghost of the nun again in November of the same year. This time the figure was leaning over one of the garden gates and Ethel was accompanied by one of the servants who said that she also saw the apparition.

Harry Bull claimed to have seen the ghostly nun on many occasions and he made no attempt to keep it a secret. He discussed the matter frequently with his relations and friends and would make such remarks as 'she was very active last night.' It seems that those long observational periods in the summerhouse were well rewarded. One of the close friends in whom the Rev Harry confided was a Mr P Shaw Jeffrey, MA, who became eventually the headmaster of Colchester Royal Grammar School[7]. He was a student at Oxford at the same time as Harry Bull was and he spent many of the long vacations with him at Borley Rectory. This was during 1885 and 1886. Jeffrey was one of the many correspondents who wrote to Harry Price after the publication of *The Most Haunted House in England* and he claimed that

Fig 22. P Shaw Jeffrey MA spent vacations at Borley Rectory in 1885 and 1886 and claimed to have witnessed paranormal phenomena whilst there. He was the headmaster of Colchester Royal Grammar School from 1899 to 1916

he saw the phantom nun on many occasions. He reported also many other incidents; he stated that he heard the sounds of a coach rumbling down the lane past the rectory when no vehicle was present and that he witnessed several poltergeist effects within the building itself. He felt that the most spectacular of these concerned a large French dictionary which he had been using in connection with his studies. The book was missing for several days despite much searching, until he was awoken one night by a bump on his bedroom floor. When he lit a candle he saw his dictionary, which was now in a battered condition, lying on the floor. He claimed that the door of his room was locked at the time. Jeffrey wrote to Price many years after the alleged events and when he was in retirement. One can only make up one's own mind as to whether or not the various witnesses are or were simpletons or liars, or people who told the truth. We feel that the late Mr Jeffrey would belong to the latter category.

The phantom nun was said to have been seen on four separate occasions by one Fred Cartwright, a carpenter who lodged in Sudbury[8]. He told Harry Price that during the early autumn of 1927 he

Fig 23. A photograph taken in the early 1920s showing the location where Fred Cartwright claimed to have seen the 'nun' on four occasions. Borley Rectory is at the extreme right of the picture

was working on some farm buildings at Clare and that his daily journey took him past Borley Rectory. The building was unoccupied at the time, as it was during the period between the death of Harry Bull and the arrival of the Rev Guy Eric Smith. Cartwright walked to his work and although this involved a journey of several miles this was not at all an unusual practice in those days. He claimed that he saw the 'nun' on four different mornings and that she was in the lane outside the rectory grounds. He is alleged to have said that she stood perfectly still and looked rather ill. On the fourth occasion Cartwright asked her if she needed any help and the figure vanished. He opened the gate by which 'she' had been standing and looked around the garden of the empty house, but he could not see anyone about. Apparently this narrative cost Price a pint of beer at The White Horse in North Street, Sudbury, and the sceptics have wondered how many more free pints Cartwright consumed on the strength of his story. Several years after these alleged events efforts were made to trace him, but they were unsuccessful. Utterly predictably, even more cynical people claimed that this failure was due to the fact that he had never existed except in Price's fertile imagination. On the other hand, if Cartwright was a real person and was telling the truth, then his claim to have seen the spectral nun in Hall Lane is of some significance, as will become clear.

Another alleged apparition which was said to have been seen and/or heard by many people in the environs of the rectory is the phantom coach. We must reserve judgement in this matter, the problem being that as is so often in such cases, there seems to be almost a compulsion to include a phantom coach on the grounds that all good haunts should have one. At the same time, it must be said that three of the many witnesses who claimed to have seen or heard a coach were the type of people who should be taken seriously. Edward Cooper told Harry Price that he saw the coach sweep through the rectory grounds on a clear moonlit night[9]. It is the opinion of those who remember Cooper that he was a sensible and rather religious sort of man. He was neither a drinker nor the type to make up things. On further

Fig 24. Mr and Mrs Edward Cooper, photographed between 1916 and 1920

interrogation at a much later date, his testimony was consistent with his earlier description of events and he maintained even that he had been reported incorrectly by Price. As we have seen, P Shaw Jeffrey claimed that he had heard on a number of occasions the sounds of a coach rumbling down Hall Lane when no vehicle was present. The Rev Harry Bull told many people that he had seen and heard the coach on several occasions. A possibly less reliable witness was Mary Pearson, one of the maids employed at the rectory, who was said to have been laughing when she gave her account of seeing the ghostly coach on two occasions in the garden. We shall discuss this later.

There have been many attempts to link together the ghostly nun and the 'ghastly' coach, as Harry Price referred to it on one occasion. This was a slip of the tongue during the course of a live radio broadcast and he is said to have been very annoyed with himself about this incident. (Sidney Glanville was present at the recording, during which

Price interviewed someone who claimed to have seen the phantom coach.) The general thrust of such legends is that a nun eloped with a monk and that they fled away in a coach. They were said to have been pursued by their superiors, caught and put to death. This is the very essence of fantasy and folklore and it is outside the area of serious psychical research. We reiterate that there is no evidence to indicate the existence of monastic or conventual premises at Borley, although they did exist at Sudbury and do still at Clare, which is just over the county boundary in Suffolk. There are many variations of this tale of illicit love and elopement, but in our opinion it remains a tale and nothing more.

Finally, we note that whilst we have commented on alleged phenomena in the rectory grounds, there were reports of occurrences which defied a rational explanation in the house itself[10]. Members of the Bull family and their guests said that on many occasions apparitions had been seen. There were disturbances such as the spontaneous ringing of the house bells. This was a cause of great concern to the Rev Harry Bull, who believed that it was an indication that there was misfortune in store for himself or members of his family. Also, unaccountable footsteps were heard and doors were said to close, open and even lock themselves of their own accord. We are not dismissing by any means these alleged phenomena as being fraudulent or unimportant. However, for the time being we propose to put them in the 'miscellaneous' category and we shall deal with them more fully in the next chapter.

The Rev Harry Bull died in the so-called Blue Room at Borley Rectory on 9 June 1927. His parents had passed away in the same room and it was the end of an era. Never again was the rectory occupied by a large family nor one who could afford to maintain it properly. The house remained empty for some months and it was at this juncture that it acquired its gloomy and sinister reputation and its neglected appearance.

CHAPTER FOUR

The Smiths and the Foysters.

After the Rev Harry Bull died, the parish of Borley was without a rector for over a year. The huge rectory and the large rambling garden were beginning to look decidedly uncared for and rightly or wrongly the place had acquired a reputation. Harry's strongly held views on the subject of the haunting had been disseminated among the local population, some of whom were said to be too frightened to be in the vicinity of the rectory after dark. It is quite likely that this was really the case, as most of them were agricultural workers who would not have had the benefit of a full education. Also people in general were more naïve in the early part of the 20th century than they are in the 21st century and there would have been at least an element of superstition in their thinking. Be that as it may, 12 clergymen applied for the living at Borley, came, saw and departed with alacrity.

Eventually a new priest did take the plunge. He was the Rev Guy Eric Smith and he commenced his duties in October 1928[1]. He did not view the rectory in advance and the size and condition of the place must have been a terrible shock to him and his wife. The couple were childless and they used only a limited number of the many rooms in the building. They spent a considerable amount of their own money on refurbishment, but apparently this did not make very much difference. Alfred and Margaret Finch remember the Smiths well. The new rector was a huge man who wore spectacles all the time and he was of dark complexion. He was an Anglo-Indian and had worked in the Indian Civil Service. Subsequently, he and his wife, who was English, came to this country and he trained as a clergyman. After ordination and service as a curate, he arrived at Borley. He was a gentle and likeable man, but according to Alfred Finch he did not visit the parishioners very much. Mrs Smith was not seen about the village and was said to be 'nervy'. It is a matter of conjecture as to whether the rectory made her so, or whether she was like it already.

The alleged phenomena did not die with Harry Bull. It was not long before the Smiths became aware of the same manifestations which had been reported for years. It was said that the spectral nun was seen gliding along her famous 'Walk' and also in other parts of the garden. There were familiar disturbances inside the house. The bells rang spontaneously, heavy footsteps were heard when no one was about, doors locked themselves and sometimes the keys would be shot out of the locks. The Smiths said also that they heard voices whispering and Mr Smith claimed that on one occasion he was able to make out the words: "Don't, Carlos, don't". It has been said that Carlos was the nickname of the Rev Henry Dawson Ellis Bull and that he was inclined to be over-familiar with the maidservants. Of course this cannot be proved and it may be grossly unfair to the man who had the rectory built.

There were reports of another phenomenon. Observers outside the rectory would see lights in upstairs rooms when those rooms were in fact unoccupied[2]. At the time there was a railway line at the bottom of the hill, just beside the river Stour. Sceptics have suggested that the apparent lighting up of the windows were reflections of lights from passing trains. It is difficult to justify this theory. The railway line was about half a mile away, the rectory grounds were surrounded by tall, mature trees and the lights observed at the windows appeared at times other than when trains were travelling along the line. It was Mrs Smith who drew the attention of other people to this manifestation and this seems strange in view of the opinions which she expressed about the alleged phenomena many years later.

The Rev Guy Eric Smith was genuinely puzzled by these occurrences and complained that the rectory had an evil atmosphere; he believed that the place was haunted and he never changed his mind about this. According to Ethel Bull, Mrs Smith used to shriek with fright when at Borley, but eventually the rector's wife did change her mind about the place after she had been away from it for several years. For better or for worse, the Smiths decided to write to the editor of *The Daily Mirror*, asking that they be put in contact with a psychical research society who might be able to help with their problems. As we have seen, what they got were Messrs V C Wall and H Price (accompanied by his secretary, Lucie Kaye). The former wrote some sensational articles in *The Daily Mirror* on the 10th, 11th, 12th, 14th, 15th and 17th June 1929. The latter claimed eventually that he had devoted ten years to investigating the case. Both gentlemen were very publicity conscious and the rest, as they say, is history.

Contacting the editor of a newspaper not noted for its intellectual qualities about such inexplicable occurrences, seems to have been a very strange step to have taken. However, the case had been referred already to the Society for Psychical Research who had failed to take any official action in the matter, although individual members (including Lord Charles Hope) did visit the rectory. Furthermore, Harry Price was regarded as an expert in such affairs and he had established already a formidable and well-equipped rival organisation known as the National Laboratory of Psychical Research. The newspaper editor's action in contacting Price was a perfectly reasonable one and it was most definitely not merely a question of inviting him to 'jump on the bandwagon'.

It has been suggested that the Smiths contacted the media because they wanted publicity, the reason being that Mrs Smith was in the process of writing a novel called *Murder at the Parsonage* and she felt that the reports and excitement would make it easy to attract the attention of the various publishing companies when she had completed her book[3]. It has been suggested also that Mrs Smith became hostile in her attitude towards Harry Price later on because she had hoped that he might use his influence in order to get her book published, but the fact is that he did not do so. With regard to the first suggestion, there may be some truth in it from the point of view of motivation, but the experiment was not at all successful and it backfired horribly on the Smiths. The rectory grounds were invaded by hordes of sightseers, many of whom were rowdy and badly behaved and a police presence was frequently necessary. With regard to the second suggestion, there was no reason why Harry Price should have assisted in trying to place the manuscript with a publisher. He may have read it and if its title was any indication then the balance of probability is that it was an amateurish effort. As a serious investigator he was not interested in fiction, although his detractors may disagree with this statement. At least he gave the novel a mention at the end of chapter three in his *The Most Haunted House in England* and that, we feel, was quite enough.

After about nine months at Borley Rectory, the Smiths moved out. Apart from the inexplicable disturbances, the place was depressing and difficult to heat and Mrs Smith became ill. They went to nearby Long Melford where they lived in rented accommodation and they looked after the parish of Borley for a further nine months. In April 1930, the short-term rector preached his last sermon there and the couple left the district altogether, Mr Smith having accepted another post as a curate at Sheringham in Norfolk.

We must now discuss Mrs Smith's later and extraordinary change of attitude towards the alleged haunting of Borley Rectory. In chapter two we commented on her rather strange letter to *The Church Times* in 1945. Four years later she was interviewed about her experiences at Borley by Kathleen Goldney. We have met this lady already; she was one of the three authors of *The Haunting of Borley Rectory* (the book which was published in 1956 and was in fact a report associated with the Society for Psychical Research). Also, she was a member of the group which Harry Price took to Borley Rectory in 1931, when he upset the Rev Lionel Foyster by suggesting that his 'wife' could have been responsible for at least some of the phenomena. Mrs Goldney described Mrs Smith as being a sensible, practical woman in middle age. Perhaps the latter's nerves had improved. In any event, she told

Mrs Goldney that she did not think that Borley was haunted and that nearly all of the mysterious happenings could be explained normally. She went on to say that she believed strongly in the after life, that the probability was that her late husband had met Harry Price (who would have been a fairly recent arrival in the next world) and that the latter regretted all of the trouble that he had caused by his exaggerations and his desire for publicity in connection with the case[4].

It is difficult to know what to make of this complete reversal of opinion. However, we have to draw attention to the wording of Mrs Smith's letter to *The Church Times* (see chapter two), which seems to be not in the least consistent with what one would expect from a sensible, practical woman in middle age. Furthermore, one of us (EB) met Mrs Goldney and feels that she was a forceful personality. It is possible that she tended to dominate the interview with Mrs Smith and that it may have consisted to some extent of leading questions being put to the latter. There is also the matter of Mrs Smith's unpublished novel. She was disappointed at Harry Price's failure to act as an intermediary between herself and one of the publishing companies and perhaps this caused her to be very annoyed and upset for a long time. Whatever the reasons for Mrs Smith's change of heart, her later statements were in direct contrast with those of her husband, who had maintained to the end of his life that Borley Rectory was haunted and possessed a most unpleasant atmosphere.

Before turning to the next occupant of the rectory we should discuss the involvement of the Smith's maid, Mary Pearson, about whom we have discovered a great deal. She married and had ten children, all of whom were still alive at the time of writing (2002). One of us (EB) has met the eldest daughter and one of the sons, both of whom have been very helpful. As stated earlier, Mary was said to have been laughing when she reported seeing, on two occasions, an old-fashioned coach in the rectory grounds. But this was according to Mrs Smith whose attitude to the haunting was ambivalent, to put it mildly. What Mary told her children was very different.

The first interesting point to emerge was that other authors have been mistaken about Mary's age. Some of them have described her as 'a young girl' and in the Society for Psychical Research report (published as *The Haunting of Borley Rectory*) it was stated flatly that she was only 15 years old when she worked for the Smiths. Mary Katherine Pearson was born in the neighbouring village of Belchamp Walter on Christmas Day 1911. She was therefore 17/18 whilst in the employ of the Smiths. Her surname appears to have been Pearsons. She was baptised at Belchamp Walter on 20 November 1912 and her birth and baptismal certificates[5] show this spelling although later documents give her name as Pearson.

Mary described her experiences at Borley to her children. She claimed to have seen the apparition of the nun, always moving away from the rectory and along the Nun's Walk, and to have seen the coach

Fig 25. Mary Pearson in the early 1960s, a few years before her death

'like a big cab;' this time she was not laughing. Inside the house, she claimed to have heard the mysterious bell-ringing and footsteps on many occasions and to have witnessed keys shooting out of their locks without human assistance. Questioning ascertained that her mood was serious and not flippant when giving these accounts. Mary's opinions of some of the other characters involved are interesting; according to her eldest daughter, she 'adored' the Smiths despite the long working hours. In direct conflict with statements made in chapter four of *The Haunting of Borley Rectory*, she neither criticised Harry Price nor accused him of trickery. Mary's life came to an early and tragic end; when only 55 she fell down the stairs at her home and died shortly afterwards from her injuries.

Once again the devout parishioners of Borley found themselves without a captain at the helm, but it was not long before there was a new incumbent. This may seem surprising in view of the difficulties encountered after the death of the Rev Harry Bull, but perhaps there was a touch of nepotism in the air. The new incumbent was the Rev Lionel Algernon Foyster and he was Harry's cousin. He had returned recently from New Brunswick, Canada, where he had been engaged in missionary work for many years. He and his 'family' moved into Borley Rectory in October 1930 and lived there for exactly five years, with frequent absences on the part of Marianne Foyster. Although the family lived at the rectory for a relatively short time compared with the long incumbencies of the two Bulls, we enter now into the most controversial part of the entire alleged haunting.

The Rev Lionel Algernon Foyster was born in Hastings in 1878, came from a family of wealthy clergymen, was ordained in 1904, served two curacies and then went to Canada for 20 years. As a young man he had stayed often with his cousins at Borley Rectory and may have been familiar with the legend of the haunting. Whilst in Canada, he had kept in touch with Marianne's family and we remember that he had baptised her whilst he was a curate in Cheshire. The family had moved to Northern Ireland and we are told that Lionel came back from Canada several times whilst on leave from his ecclesiastical duties and that he visited them. The sea journeys must have been hazardous during the period of the first world war. Clearly, he was aware of the fact that the small child he had baptised had grown up into an attractive woman. What he may not have been aware of was the far less agreeable fact that she had been involved already in her first marriage. At the time, she was only 15[6] and when she was 16 she had a child. He was passed off always as her younger brother and was known as Ian Shaw. Marianne's husband left her soon after the birth of the baby and was not seen again. This marriage was never terminated officially by means of divorce proceedings. In 1922, Lionel Algernon wrote to Marianne proposing marriage; she accepted and joined him in Canada. The subsequent marriage was, of course, bigamous and there has been considerable argument as to whether or not the clergyman was duped by Marianne, or was aware of the true position. We are inclined to the former view and to give him the benefit of the doubt[7].

What kind of man was Foyster? According to those who can remember him, the outstanding feature about him was his very poor health. He was only 52 when he took the living at Borley, yet he seemed to be much older. Alfred and Margaret Finch described him as a very tall man who was bent over due to arthritis and his hands were swollen because of the same condition. He walked with a limp and with the aid of a stick; later on he was confined occasionally to a wheelchair. He was extremely thin and gaunt. Apparently, whilst he was in Canada he used to swim a lot, which may not have been wise in view of his developing arthritis and he was said to have suffered a heart attack whilst doing so. He was kindly in manner and quite well liked in Borley, although he upset Margaret Finch on one occasion by remonstrating with her for not attending church. She replied that she had a small baby who could neither be left alone, nor taken into church where she may have started crying and disturbing the service. It seems that this explanation was brushed aside as being an excuse and the rector said that it would not matter if the baby did become noisy.

Margaret Finch was not prepared to take the risk and remained firm about the matter. Other points remembered about the Rev Lionel Foyster are that he was an Anglo-Catholic (which fact may increase the likelihood that his cousin the late Harry Bull was of the same persuasion) and that his visiting activities were hampered frequently by the presence of two small children whom he had to look after.

Now we have to consider that extraordinary and controversial character, Marianne Foyster[8]. The story of her early life is that she was born in 1899 near Stockport, Cheshire and her real name was Marianne Emily Rebecca Shaw, not, be it noted Mary Anne as indicated in *The Widow of Borley*. Her parents were poor and moved frequently and this state of affairs seems to have been connected with the fact that her father was spectacularly unsuccessful at the various occupations which he attempted to follow. They ranged from teaching and coaching to running a public house.

When Marianne was two years old her family was living near Warrington and it was whilst they were at this address that they became acquainted with the local young curate who was none other than Lionel Algernon Foyster. The curate and the family remained friends for many years and Lionel baptised Marianne when she was seven years old. Apparently he was fascinated by the pretty child and the author Robert Wood has implied that there may have been a somewhat unhealthy aspect to the relationship between them. There is no evidence at all to support this suggestion. In 1907 the Shaw family moved to Northern Ireland and three years later the Rev Lionel Foyster emigrated to Canada. The family and the clergyman kept in touch and as we have seen, the latter returned occasionally to the United Kingdom during his periods of leave.

In 1914, Marianne married one Harold Greenwood and in the following year a son was born. A few weeks after the happy event, Harold left his family and was never seen again. The child was raised by Marianne's parents, was known as Ian Shaw and was passed off as Marianne's young brother. In due course, there came the proposal of marriage from Foyster and Marianne spent eight years in Canada with him. Her 'brother' Ian joined them there in 1925 as it was felt that the climate would be good for his health. It may have done something for his imagination as well. Much later on, he claimed that his mother was involved in many amorous adventures whilst she was living in Northern Ireland and that there were many more such episodes during the eight years which she spent in Canada. There is the need to be very careful about these claims. On the one hand such behaviour was not inconsistent with the events of Marianne's later life, but on the other there is no documentation at all in support of any of Ian's allegations and according to Robert Wood he disliked his mother intensely. Perhaps the extent of her extra-marital affairs was somewhat exaggerated and the old adage that 'there is no smoke without fire' may be appropriate. For his part, Lionel Foyster seems to have been

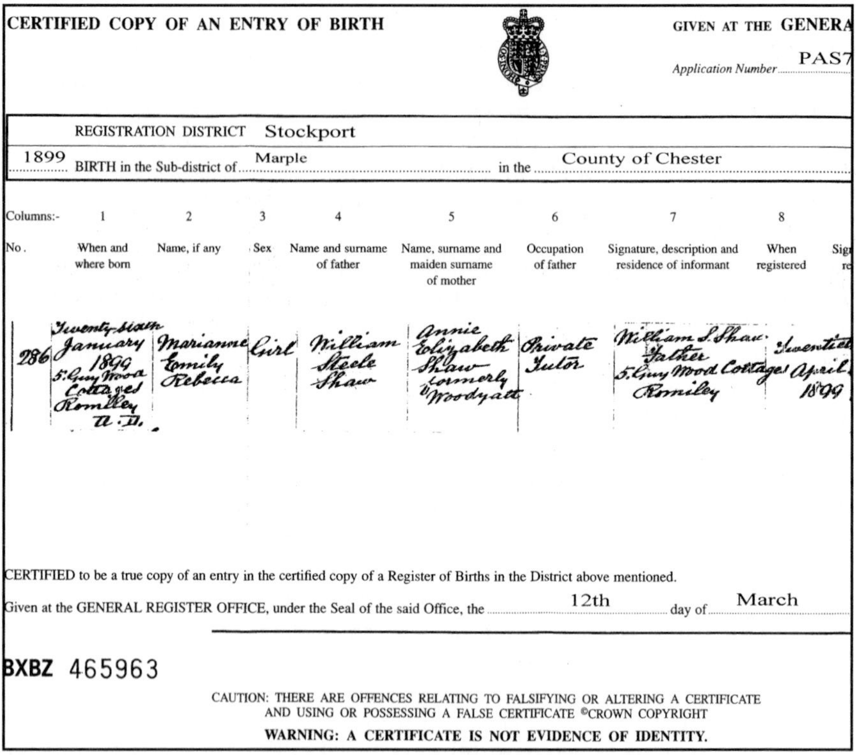

CERTIFIED COPY OF AN ENTRY OF BIRTH   GIVEN AT THE GENERA

Application Number........... PAS7

REGISTRATION DISTRICT   Stockport

1899   BIRTH in the Sub-district of.....Marple..................... in the .....County of Chester.........

Columns:-	1	2	3	4	5	6	7	8	
No.	When and where born	Name, if any	Sex	Name and surname of father	Name, surname and maiden surname of mother	Occupation of father	Signature, description and residence of informant	When registered	Sig re
286	Twenty-sixth January 1899 5: Guy Wood Cottages Romiley U.D.	Marianne Emily Rebecca	Girl	William Steele Shaw	Annie Elizabeth Shaw formerly Woodyatt	Private Tutor	William S. Shaw. Father 5: Guy Wood Cottages Romiley	Twentieth April 1899	

CERTIFIED to be a true copy of an entry in the certified copy of a Register of Births in the District above mentioned.

Given at the GENERAL REGISTER OFFICE, under the Seal of the said Office, the ....12th........... day of.......March

BXBZ 465963

CAUTION: THERE ARE OFFENCES RELATING TO FALSIFYING OR ALTERING A CERTIFICATE AND USING OR POSSESSING A FALSE CERTIFICATE ©CROWN COPYRIGHT

WARNING: A CERTIFICATE IS NOT EVIDENCE OF IDENTITY.

Fig 26. Part of Marianne Shaw's birth certificate showing her correct name. Reproduced with the permission of the General Register Office

unaware of the alleged goings-on and to the end of his life he refused to accept any criticism of his 'wife's' behaviour.

We wonder what the residents of sleepy little Borley made of their new rector's wife. Many of them felt that she appeared to be more like his daughter than his wife and it was remarked upon that this seemed to be the relationship between them. Certainly, Foyster became very anxious and agitated when she was not with him, which was frequently the case. Marianne was dark-haired and attractive and very much one of the 'bright young things' of the inter-war years. She found the male of the species to be of interest and the pursuit of this particular interest took her away frequently from Borley, as did her part ownership of a flower shop in outer London. Quite apart from her basic urges, she found Borley utterly dull and made no secret of the fact. Alfred and Margaret Finch remember her well[9]. For most of their long lives, home was a semi-detached cottage at Borley Green and the adjoining cottage was occupied during the early 1930s by a Miss Marion Pitt, who was the village schoolmistress. Marianne used to visit her frequently and the two women could be heard shrieking with laughter. Apparently, Marianne had designs on a local resident, Herbert Mayes, and we wonder if he was the subject of these hilarious conversations. He has been mentioned in other books about the alleged haunting of Borley and for many years he was the chauffeur-gardener to the next rector, the Rev Alfred Clifford Henning. During the incumbency of the Foysters, Herbert Mayes did casual gardening work at Borley Rectory. Alfred Finch remembered him as being a very delicate man and it can only be a matter of conjecture as to how he dealt with the overtures of the rector's vivacious young 'wife'.

When the Foysters returned from Canada, they brought with them a small girl called Adelaide, whom they had adopted[10]. It is not clear if this was an unofficial arrangement, or whether adoption procedures had been followed, or indeed if any procedures were required in Canada nearly 70 years ago. However, the fact is that Adelaide's parents were dead and the Foysters took her under their wing, which some would regard as an extremely mixed blessing. She was said to be withdrawn and backward and Lionel Foyster called her 'baby,' although she was two and a half years old. It was not long before another child joined the family, a small boy called François d'Arles. His father, who affected the same name, was said to have advertised in *The Times* seeking a home for his small boy and the Foysters replied. The consequence of this was that François junior came to live at the rectory with the Foysters and as company for Adelaide and François senior became the tenant of the rectory cottage. It has been alleged that he became a lot more besides and his role in the drama must be examined.

François d'Arles' real name was Frank Charles Pearless[11]. He was a cockney and a divorcee and it remains a mystery as to why he pretended to be a French-Canadian, used a French name and inflicted it on his son as well. Although nominally the tenant of the cottage, he slept frequently at the rectory and nearly always took his meals there. He was said to have been a rough, tough type of character and to have been a dominant force in the household. If we add to this Marianne's personality — also forceful, if unstable — it becomes clear that the frail rector, who may well have been in mental as well as physical decline, was anything but the master of the house.

D'Arles was the other partner in Marianne's flower shop venture. This was called *Jonquil et Cie* and was located at 20a, Worple Road, Wimbledon[12]. During the week Marianne and d'Arles would be at the shop and returned to Borley only at the weekends. According to Robert Wood, they were lovers; they lived in the flat over the shop and they informed their neighbours in Worple Road that they were a married couple. The business failed in 1934 after 18 months and François d'Arles left the scene taking his son with him. Apparently the parting of the ways created an atmosphere of considerable bitterness. It was during the flower shop period that Lionel Algernon endeavoured to combine his parochial duties with keeping an eye on the two small children. Sometimes he would have to take them with him when he went out on his visits.

Reverting to the manner in which François d'Arles and the Foysters made contact, Robert Wood has argued that the former was hardly the type who would have read *The Times* or used its advertisement columns. Wood's opinion is that the supposed advertisement was another of Marianne Foyster's inventions and that it is far more likely that she met d'Arles casually during one of her visits to London. In an attempt to clear up this matter one of us (EB) looked through the personal columns of dozens of editions of *The Times* for the appropriate period, ie, late 1930 and early 1931, without success. There were a few possibilities but not surprisingly they were listed under box numbers.

However, this research did produce what we believe is a possible explanation of this minor mystery. In those days adoptions were not arranged through local government services. Some were arranged informally and others through adoption societies. Two of these societies, The National Adoption Society and the National Children's Adoption Association, advertised two or three times each week in the newspaper's personal columns during the period in question. François d'Arles may not have been a likely reader of *The Times* but we remember that he was a working man and a divorcee and the adequate care of his small son may have been a problem. It is possible that he was advised to contact one of these adoption societies as a solution.

On the other hand the Rev Lionel Foyster was an educated clergyman who could have been a likely reader of *The Times* and he and Marianne had already adopted the small girl Adelaide (later on Marianne adopted other children). A very likely explanation of how these two families came together is that the Foysters approached one of the adoption societies who advertised in *The Times* and consequently d'Arles and his son arrived in due course at Borley.

Two other members of the 'family' have to be mentioned because they lived at Borley Rectory at least for a time. In 1933, Marianne's young 'brother,' Ian Shaw, returned from Canada and took up residence there. It is difficult to know what importance may be attached to his accounts of the alleged phenomena, as all of his statements were uncorroborated and he made no secret of his intense dislike of his mother. According to Marianne, Lionel Foyster was never aware of their true relationship. Ian claimed that d'Arles befriended him and informed him that his mother was a nymphomaniac. The question has to be asked as to whether or not Lionel Foyster was aware of the true relationship between Marianne and d'Arles. Years later, Marianne said that he was aware of the relationship and condoned it. In his book, Robert Wood has emphasised many times that Foyster was a pervert who seemed almost to enjoy such situations. We have to express our reservations about this. There is no evidence to support Marianne's claims and it has to be said that she did have relationships and could be untruthful. An equally likely explanation is that because of deteriorating health, physical and mental, Foyster was fooled easily and we remind ourselves that he would never hear a word spoken against Marianne. From all accounts he was infatuated with her and trusted her completely.

The other person who should be mentioned was a baby called John Evemond Emery. Tragically, he was only a few months old when he died in 1932 and he was buried in Borley churchyard. Marianne stated later that he was yet another adopted child. However, it was noticed that both she and d'Arles were very upset when the baby died and they used to make up floral tributes and place them on the grave. There must be the suspicion that the child was theirs and a qualified nurse employed temporarily at the rectory said that in her opinion Marianne's condition at the time was such as to indicate that she had recently had a baby.

It was shortly after the arrival of the Foysters at Borley Rectory that the alleged phenomena reached a pitch of intensity and volume not experienced previously[13]. In September 1931, two of the Bull sisters visited Harry Price at his National Laboratory of Psychical Research in Kensington and reported these disturbances to him. It was as a result of this visit that Price and some of his Council members, including the indefatigable Kathleen Goldney, went to Borley Rectory a month later and as we have seen, upset very much the Rev Lionel Foyster. This is the real reason why Price did not go there again until 1937 and well after the Foysters had gone. His critics have implied that he lost interest in the case and even that he did not believe in the haunting. We feel that they are wrong to do so. Certainly he did not trust Marianne, but in the long run he devoted an enormous amount of his time to his investigations at Borley. Relations with the Rev Lionel Foyster were patched up in the late 1930s due to the patient and diplomatic efforts of Sidney Glanville.

As to the phenomena themselves, they were said to consist of almost incessant bell-ringing; inexplicable footsteps padding around the place; the paranormal moving of household utensils; furniture being turned upside down in unoccupied rooms; the materialisation of bottles which would drop to the floor and cover it with broken glass; doors locking and unlocking themselves; stones and other objects being thrown about; sightings of the apparition of the late Rev Harry Bull; Mrs Foyster being tipped out of bed; François d'Arles receiving a black eye from a 'phantom'; outbreaks of fire in empty rooms; mysterious messages being written on the walls; and on one occasion (when Harry Price was present) a glass of wine turned into an inky fluid. The last mentioned 'phenomenon' occurred on one other occasion when Harry Price was present and utterly predictably, critics of the case have drawn attention to the fact that he was an accomplished amateur conjurer. All of this is dramatic stuff indeed and to discuss every one of these mysterious events individually would fill another volume. Frankly, it has to be said that the alleged phenomena did not occur under controlled conditions, which is natural enough, that many of them seemed to be centred on Marianne Foyster and that at this time the rectory was occupied by an assortment of very unusual people. They were a frail and possibly mentally ill rector, his extraordinary 'wife', a dodgy lodger and two small children who must have been bewildered and frightened by all of these strange events. Both of them came from unfortunate backgrounds and if they could have been examined by a present day child psychologist there is little doubt that they would be described as 'disturbed'. Nevertheless, some of the alleged phenomena cannot be explained away easily.

Lionel Foyster wrote at great length about the alleged disturbances and his work falls into three distinct sections. First, there was what he called his *Diary of Occurrences*. It covered the period from the time when the Foysters arrived at the rectory until July 1931. It described the phenomena during this time and the original purpose of the diary was to circulate the details of the haunting to other members of the family. It seems strange that the diary, which was written of course in instalments, was not kept up for very long. We wonder whether Foyster became tired of writing it, or if perhaps the more down-to-earth members of the family told him that they were fed up with reading it. The second item was entitled *A Summary of Experiences at Borley Rectory* written in 1938. This document covered the whole of the five years during which the Foysters lived at the rectory, although the later years are dealt with very briefly indeed. It was written whilst Lionel Algernon was living in the upstairs part of the chalet-bungalow near Ipswich and under the most peculiar circumstances. The *Summary* was produced at the request of Harry Price, who made considerable use of it in his *The Most Haunted House in England*. At first, Foyster refused to co-operate with the man who had made accusations against Marianne, but as we have seen Sidney Glanville interceded and gradually relations between the retired rector and Price became warmer. The third literary item from Lionel Algernon's pen was a novel called *Fifteen Months in a Haunted House*. It was a story based upon his experiences whilst at Borley and the various characters whom he knew there. All of the names of places and people were altered. Foyster spent many years working on his novel and he had great hopes that it would be published. However, it was really a very poor piece of work and it was not to be. He tried to persuade Harry Price to use his influence with the various publishing companies, but Price was not prepared to do so. It was a case of history repeating itself and we remember Mrs Smith and her *Murder at the Parsonage*.

In conclusion, we have to say that although Lionel Foyster may have been a good clergyman, the inescapable fact is that he was a poor writer. None of his three works were of the standard which one would expect from a Master of Arts out of Pembroke College, Cambridge. More to the point, his *Diary* and *Summary* included reports of many events which in all probability did not have any psychic aspect to them whatsoever. They could have been accounted for by a mixture of fraud by Marianne and possibly François d'Arles, by forgetful servants leaving household utensils lying about, by the children playing pranks and by Foyster's own appalling memory and declining mental health. If this is a correct interpretation of at least some of the alleged phenomena, then it would appear that the frail and ill rector was treated sometimes in a cruel fashion. To return to his actual writings, they have been quoted at great length in the other books to do with the alleged haunting of Borley Rectory and there seems little point in doing so again in this work.

In January 1932, the Foysters were contacted by the Marks Tey Spiritualist Circle, members of which felt that they might be able to rid the rectory of its 'evil spirits[14].' Their offer was taken up and the group, which included Guy L'Estrange, a well-known local medium, came to the house on 23 January and spent the night there. Apparently they were greeted with a barrage of phenomena, including the materialisation of bottles which would crash to the floor, leaving broken glass all over the place. They were subjected also to long outbreaks of the house bells ringing and various objects were said to have been thrown about. The members of the Spiritualist Circle stayed at the rectory until five o'clock in the morning. Then they felt that because of their work there would be no more disturbances in the rectory. With a few exceptions this appears to have been the case and we have noted already that the rector did not have much to report during the later years of his incumbency in his *Summary of Experiences at Borley Rectory*. Readers will have to make up their own minds as to whether the Circle's visit did have a beneficial effect, or perhaps if the phenomena were produced fraudulently, the perpetrators felt that they had gone far enough and that they had been presented with an excellent opportunity to bring down the curtain on their activities. We feel that there may have been a mixture of both of these possibilities.

We turn now to the involvement of the Whitehouse family, who were friends of the Foysters and became very concerned about their welfare during 1931[15]. Sir George and Lady Whitehouse lived at Arthur Hall, a Georgian house fronting onto the road between Sudbury and Long Melford. The property is still there and for some years it has been an Italian restaurant. The third member of the family to become involved was their nephew Edwin, who stayed frequently at Arthur Hall. Sir George and Lady Whitehouse had known well the Bull family and were aware of the Rev Harry Bull's leanings towards spiritualism and of his strong conviction that his house and garden were haunted. One day in May 1931, the Whitehouse family were at the rectory and during the course of the evening witnessed for themselves many manifestations which occurred whilst both the Foysters were in their presence. The phenomena included the familiar bell ringing, the throwing of stones and for the first time, an outbreak of fire in an unoccupied room. Both families were in the kitchen and the ladies remained there whilst Lionel Foyster and Sir George Whitehouse made a quick tour round the house. When they came back they reported that they had noticed an unusual smell, so they set off

Fig 27. Arthur Hall, Sudbury. It became Sudbury Hall and then an Italian restaurant with accommodation

again and on their return stated that the smell had become stronger. By this time the ladies had noticed it and Marianne said, "It's a fire!" The four people went upstairs and opened the doors of the rooms as they passed down the corridor. When they opened the door of the third room, it was filled with smoke and they could see that part of the skirting board was alight. They ran to get jugs of water and the flames were soon put out.

Critics of the case have said that the small girl Adelaide may have been responsible for the fire. They have quoted a Miss Gordon, who was living at the time at Borley Lodge and who stated in a letter to the authors of *The Haunting of Borley Rectory* that the little girl was always playing with matches and saying that she was going to burn down the rectory, thereby anticipating the threats of 'Sunex Amures' and Capt Gregson's fire by several years. It is really rather difficult to accept this as a possible explanation. On this particular occasion, the adults had noted the fact that the two small children were in bed and asleep. Also, at the time Adelaide was only three years old and had she said what she was reported to have said, then it would have been a simple matter to have kept matchboxes well away from her. We note in passing that in recent years there have been many well authenticated cases of spontaneous combustion, which type of phenomenon was not the subject of much investigation in the 1930s. There was no electricity supply to Borley, so faulty wiring cannot be blamed.

Later in the evening there was a further outbreak of bell ringing and stone throwing. The Whitehouses decided that it was not safe to be in the rectory under such conditions and it was agreed that the Foysters and the children should stay at Arthur Hall, which they did for several days. In fact, they stayed at Arthur Hall on other occasions because of the level of the alleged disturbances.

Shortly after the visit, Edwin Whitehouse (the nephew) was at Arthur Hall. He went to the rectory on many occasions, sometimes when the Foysters were in residence and sometimes when they too were at Arthur Hall. He claimed to have witnessed many phenomena at Borley. In 1938, he sent a report of his experiences to Harry Price and it became eventually chapter fifteen of *The Most Haunted House in England*. The authors of *The Haunting of Borley Rectory* and also Robert Wood who wrote *The Widow of Borley* were highly critical of Edwin Whitehouse's involvement in the case. In our view they were mistaken and unreasonable in adopting the attitude that they saw fit to do. The object of their attentions had served at the Battle of Jutland and what he had witnessed there had caused him to have occasional nervous breakdowns. Obviously he was a sensitive man, but he was also an intelligent person and the fact that he was unfortunate enough to have suffered these breakdowns after such an upsetting experience does not imply in any way that he was untruthful or fooled easily. Much was made of the fact that he described his adventures at Borley some years after the alleged events, but no mention was made of the more important point that his report was based upon notes which were written down at the time and whilst he was staying at Arthur Hall. Edwin Whitehouse was convinced that many of the alleged phenomena were genuine, was absolutely consistent about his experiences at the rectory and he defended himself vigorously against his critics. He was a deeply religious man; despite his poor health, he was ordained in 1940 and became a Benedictine monk, taking the name Dom Richard Whitehouse. He died in the late 1970s.

It was during the time that the Whitehouse family were drawn into the case that the famous (or infamous) messages appeared in Borley Rectory. This occurred in May and June of 1931. It all started with the discovery of pieces of paper lying about the place with 'Marianne' written on them. Then followed the mysterious messages on the walls. They were addressed frequently but not always to 'Marianne' and asked for Mass, light, prayers and help. Sometimes the messages were very jumbled, with one line of writing being superimposed upon another, which made them very difficult to decipher. They appeared to include various French words such as *trompée* and *ici* and it has been said that the messages had a Roman Catholic flavour about them. Harry Price described them in some detail in his first monograph about Borley, *The Most Haunted house in England*. There were several photographs and illustrations of them in the book and it is clear that not all of them seem to have been written by the same hand. This is an interesting point, because most of the sceptics believe firmly that Marianne Foyster was responsible for them. We have to say that the balance of probability is that this was the case, although there is an element of doubt. In *The Widow of Borley* there is a reproduction on page 99 of one of the wall writings together with an example of Marianne's signature, the implication being that the handwriting was very similar. However, it could be argued that there are considerable differences if one looks beyond the general untidiness of the writing.

After the publication of his first book, many people wrote to Harry Price and offered their interpretations of these jumbled messages. In several instances their comments were included in Price's second book about this case, *The End of Borley Rectory*. The most impressive of these came from Canon W J Phythian-Adams, the Canon of Carlisle. The canon had been involved in archaeology and the study of hieroglyphics in the Middle East and his report concerning the Borley wall writings is set out in full as chapter ten of *The End of Borley Rectory*. The report is a detailed and ingenious interpretation and led the canon to the conclusion that the cellars under the ruined rectory should be excavated. As we have seen already, he became a little impatient with Harry Price because the latter did not proceed to act quickly on his suggestion. When he did so eventually there was a remarkable result.

The Foysters left Borley Rectory in October 1935 and the place was never again occupied by a clergyman. It was during their five years there that the alleged phenomena reached a peak. It is very difficult to assess the events which were said to have occurred at this time. One of the problems is that they happened over 60 years ago and another is the conflicting statements of Marianne Foyster, who survived until 1992. She could be untruthful, given to indulging in fantasy and when questioned closely about the case in later years her answers varied on different occasions. Sometimes she was adamant that she did not 'haunt' the rectory and at other times she admitted that she had been responsible for fraudulent phenomena. There is the possibility that she was psychic and certainly Lionel Foyster thought that this was the case. There is also the possibility that some genuine phenomena were added to by one or more individuals for reasons of their own. We are inclined to take the latter view, but we cannot do other than leave it to readers to come to their own conclusions.

Fig 28. The Rev Foyster, Harry Bull's cousin, lies at rest in Campsea Ashe churchyard, Suffolk. The inscription reads: LIONEL ALGERNON FOYSTER, PRIEST, 1878 - 1945/THE LORD IS MY SHEPHERD

CHAPTER FIVE

The Henning incumbency:
What the rector had to say.

A
fter the departure of the Foysters, the next rector of Borley was the Rev Alfred Clifford Henning. At the time that he accepted the living he was married and had a son called Richard. Later on a second son was born, named Stephen. Henning was ordained as a deacon in 1911 and as a priest in 1919. He worked in several parishes before coming to Borley and was glad to leave an urban parish which, he complained, had a population of 4000, only about 20 of whom attended his services[1].

The Hennings never lived at Borley Rectory, although they were in the house frequently and they stored their furniture there. During the early months of his incumbency, Henning and his family stayed at Borley Place, next door to the church and immediately across the road from the rectory. They were the guests of Mr and Mrs Basil Payne. Mr Payne was a well-known local landowner and his family continue to be farmers in the Borley area.

In 1936 an Order in Council came into effect under the terms of which the parishes of Borley and Liston were united and at the end of that year the Hennings moved into the somewhat smaller and much older rectory in the latter village. The family had considered living at Borley Rectory, but like most people who had not seen it previously, they were astonished at its size and appalled at its broken down condition. Liston Rectory, on the other hand, was well-maintained and had electric light and generally better facilities. The choice was not difficult.

Nevertheless, Henning was responsible for Borley Rectory and was advised by the Bishop of Chelmsford to try to sell it. This was easier said than done and was not effected until the end of 1938, when Capt Gregson bought it and the rectory cottage for £500. This was after Harry Price's year long tenancy which commenced in May, 1937. However, it was possible to let the rectory cottage and from the time of the arrival of the Hennings until Capt Gregson purchased it, the

Fig 29. The rectory cottage. Borley Rectory stood immediately to the left

tenants were Robert and Maud Arbon.

Mr and Mrs Henning are remembered well by Alfred and Margaret Finch and also by their married daughter Kathleen King[2]. The Rev Alfred Clifford Henning was a quiet man, but he was not popular with all of the parishioners. He did not visit them very much and many of them felt that he neglected his duties because he became almost obsessed with the alleged haunting of Borley. His wife was popular and it appears that she undertook a lot of the visiting and other parochial work. Henning was an Anglo-Catholic who wore only rarely lay clothes. He was attired almost always in his clerical robes and wore a biretta, which is a square black hat favoured especially by High Church priests. He had a disagreement with his former hosts, Mr and Mrs Payne, over a dispute concerning a right-of-way and they took no further interest in Borley church during the rest of his incumbency. He upset some of the other churchgoers by introducing the use of incense into his services. He was well aware that most of his parishioners were agricultural workers, but (unlike his predecessors) he failed apparently to take into account the fact that they would have preferred a more simple and homely form of service.

Another controversial act on the part of Henning concerned the altar in Borley church[3]. He was told that the large stone under the wooden altar covered probably the entrance to the crypt or perhaps the Waldegrave vault. In 1943, Harry Price came to Borley again in order to organise the excavations under the cellars of the rectory, the house

Fig 30. Borley church interior, pre 1943, when the altar stone was reinstated. The Waldegrave tomb is on the left of the picture

itself being quite ruined after the fire four years previously. Henning thought that this would be a good opportunity to raise the stone under the altar and to carry out some investigations under the floor of the church. A mason from Sudbury was employed to raise partially the stone, but it was noticed with disappointment that it seemed to be resting on a bed of sand and certainly there was no exciting entry to a vault or tunnel. However, the mason suggested that the stone may be the original altar and Henning decided that he would seek expert opinion on the matter. For the time being, the stone was put back onto the bed of sand. At a later date the stone was raised again and examined carefully by experts. Their verdict was that it was indeed the original altar stone and that it had been placed on the floor upside down, presumably in order to prevent it from being recognised for what it was. Henning was determined that the stone should be returned to its rightful position and eventually this was done. Of course, he had to have the agreement of the diocesan authorities and also at least a majority of the Borley Parochial Church Council. However, not all of the faithful flock agreed with what had been done and their displeasure increased when the original wooden altar was taken to Liston church and installed there.

If Henning was not completely successful as the rector of Borley, there can be no doubt that he was enormously interested in the alleged phenomena there. He believed strongly that the rectory, the church and the area in general were haunted and Kathleen King remembers that

Fig 31. A recent photograph of Borley church interior. Note the new position of the pulpit in front of the organ
Fig 32. Detail of the Waldegrave tomb

he would become very annoyed whenever anyone expressed their doubts about the matter. He wrote and published a booklet called *Haunted Borley,* which included a foreword by the well-known authoress Elizabeth Goudge. Copies are now extremely rare, but we have managed to obtain one and it makes fascinating reading. Despite the title, only three of the ten short chapters are devoted to the alleged haunting. However, we feel that what the rector had to say is most important, not only because he has recorded various phenomena, but also because it has a bearing on subsequent attitudes towards the haunting. One of the complications of the whole case has been the accusations of dishonesty and bad faith on the part of Harry Price. These accusations came and continue to come nearly always from officials and members of the Society for Psychical Research. One is left with the distinct impression that he has never been forgiven for setting up a rival and arguably better equipped organisation. This was, of course, the National Laboratory of Psychical Research, which he founded in 1926. To return to Henning's booklet, he described his own experiences in the rectory,

Fig 33. Cover of the Rev Henning's booklet

the church and the surrounding area and reported also the first hand testimony of others. It has to be said that his writings support strongly the claims made by Price and they are well worth repeating.

In July 1937, the Hennings spent an evening at Borley Rectory with Mark Kerr-Pearse, who was one of Price's team of observers[4]. Henning emphasised that when they entered the building, they locked the front door, sealed all the windows and locked all the other doors. The only exception was the study (the 'base room') window which was the room where the party sat. The rector was satisfied that every precaution had been taken to ensure that no one else was in the house and that there were no opportunities for trickery. The three people were indulging in general conversation when they heard the sound of a door being opened. They sat and waited in silence and after a short interval they heard footsteps proceeding along the stone-flagged passage from the kitchen quarters and also a swishing noise, which reminded them of the sound of long trailing garments. The observers remained where they were, noting that the footsteps were coming towards the study. Then they moved quietly to the door and flung it open. The sound of the footsteps ceased immediately and no one was to be seen in the passage, not even the proverbial cat which has been so helpful to the sceptics. Once again the house was searched and there was no sign of an intruder. The Hennings went back to Liston Rectory and left Kerr-Pearse to complete his period of observation. The rector was adamant that he and the other two people heard exactly the same sounds and felt the same sensations of eeriness and tension.

Henning became very friendly with Kerr-Pearse and called often at the rectory for a chat when he knew that the latter was on duty. On one such occasion, Kerr-Pearse took the rector into the sewing room and showed him a piece of rotten wood which had appeared during the night and was not there the previous day. It was lying near the fireplace and Henning's first thought was that it had fallen down the chimney. He looked up the flue and noticed that there was a great deal of soot there, whereas the piece of wood had no trace of it and none had fallen into the hearth.

Henning reported first-hand on the peculiar affair of the women's coats, which was related by Harry Price in *The Most Haunted House in England* and was dismissed by his critics as nonsense[5]. According to the rector, his wife found one day a tattered coat hanging on the door of one of the bedrooms. It was obviously a woman's jacket and the Hennings asked Herbert Mayes to burn it. (We have met Mayes before; he was employed now by the rector as a chauffeur-gardener and we note with relief that he had managed to survive the advances of Marianne Foyster.) Then Harry Price visited the rectory in June 1937 and found a dark blue jacket hanging up in the Blue Room. He was confident that it had not been there during a recent visit and wrote to Henning about the matter. The rector thought that Herbert Mayes had forgotten to burn the coat, but was assured by the latter that this had been done. He showed the blue jacket to Mayes, who said that it was quite different from the one which he had destroyed. Also Henning remembered that the jacket which his wife had seen was hanging in a room adjoining the Blue Room. It would appear, therefore, that two old jackets were involved and that both of them had been deposited at some juncture in the rectory, despite the fact that it was supposed to have been locked and sealed and despite the frequent presence of the observers. We accept that there could be a perfectly normal explanation for this episode, but that it is all rather strange and we feel that if it was the result of trickery then the perpetrators would have had the opportunity to have arranged something far more spectacular.

Henning went on to describe an experience by Herbert Mayes in March 1939 which was related to him first-hand[6]. At this time, Mayes lived at Borley Green, situated at the far end of the parish from Liston and he was in the habit of cycling to and from his work at Liston Rectory each day. One evening, as he was cycling up Hall Lane towards Borley Green, he heard the sound of horses trotting down the hill. Thinking that some of the horses kept at the Paynes' farm had broken loose, he pulled his bicycle onto the grass verge at the side of the road and shone his lamp in the direction of the sounds. To his amazement, nothing was to be seen, but the sound of trotting horses passed closely by him and on down the lane towards the Stour. According to Henning it was not at all easy to persuade Mayes to talk about the incident, because the latter was afraid that most people would laugh about it. However, Henning claimed that he had questioned him closely about this experience on many occasions and came to the conclusion that he was telling the truth.

Herbert Mayes was one of the many villagers who claimed to have seen unaccountable lights in the rectory windows and he told Henning about one such sighting in 1937. He said that Mr and Mrs Payne saw the lights on the same night and all three of them were adamant that this phenomenon was not due to moonlight, nor to reflections from passing cars, nor the trains. Henning decided to do a little investigating of his own. The following day he visited Mr and Mrs Arbon, the tenants of the rectory cottage, as he thought that perhaps one of Harry Price's team of observers had been in the house during the previous night. Arbon assured him that this was not the case and that he had not handed over the keys of the rectory to anyone else. Then Henning thought that another possible explanation of the lights could be that some of the paintwork in the rectory had the quality of luminescence. Accordingly he asked a painter to carry out an inspection and was told that this was not so.

Herbert Mayes related details to Henning of two other experiences that he had had at the rectory when the Foysters lived there. When Mrs Foyster was away (either at her flower shop in London, or for other perhaps dubious reasons), Mayes looked after the ailing rector. On two such occasions he heard a loud crash, as if someone had dropped a tray loaded with crockery. He claimed that on both occasions he had searched the house, found that nothing had been damaged and that nobody else was about. We have to express our reservations about these claims, however; we remember that when Marianne Foyster was away from the rectory, the long suffering Lionel Algernon was left with the responsibility of looking after two small children. It could be the case that when Herbert Mayes said that there was no one else present, he may have overlooked the possibility that Adelaide Foyster and François d'Arles junior, both aged about four, were in the rectory and could have been playing tricks.

Henning described the experience of a personal friend, Alice Reid, during a visit to Borley Rectory in August 1937[7]. Miss Reid was interested in the alleged haunting and the Hennings decided to show her over the house. Although they went there on a warm summer evening, Miss Reid felt suddenly very cold on the landing outside the Blue Room. Then she moved away from this point and felt warmer, but when she returned to it she noticed again a feeling of extreme cold. In fact, she was standing on what became known as the 'cold spot'. Kerr-Pearce was in the rectory at the time as part of his duties as an observer. The three people felt Miss Reid's hands and noticed how very cold that they were, although they were not affected in a similar fashion. Nevertheless, Miss Reid was not the only person to undergo this experience at the 'cold spot' and later on, controlled experiments with thermometers indicated that at times this particular point was as much as 11 degrees Fahrenheit colder than the surrounding area.

Henning referred to his own experiences with regard to the famous messages and markings which appeared on the walls in Borley Rectory. He recalled being present there one night with Harry Price and some members of the team of observers. The entire group went round the house and noted carefully all of the marks which had been ringed. Then everybody waited together in the 'base room' and after an interval of about 30 minutes another tour of the rectory was made. Price insisted that the group should keep together and close to him so that no one could go ahead and prepare some new 'phenomena'. However, it was discovered that fresh marks had appeared. Henning accepted that the accusation could be made that someone was hiding in the house and marking the walls whilst everybody else had been in the 'base room'. Nevertheless, he rejected utterly this possible explanation and reiterated that the place was locked and sealed and had been searched thoroughly.

Henning did not report any more phenomena in Borley Rectory itself and after Harry Price's tenancy expired in May 1938, he was concerned mainly with the difficult task of trying to sell the house. He complained that it was a very costly business being responsible for the maintenance and repair of two large rectories. Of course, he did not own either of them and it would appear that the church authorities drove a hard bargain with their clergymen in those days. At last Borley Rectory was sold to Capt William Hart Gregson and he and his two sons took up residence in the cottage in December 1938. His time at Borley was short and not very happy because the rectory was ruined by the fire of 27 February 1939. Whether this was due to the entity 'Sunex Amures' carrying out his threat somewhat belatedly, or whether Capt Gregson was indulging in arson, as his insurers alleged, we shall never know now. Henning recorded merely that he was notified by telephone at midnight that the house was ablaze and that he could see the flames from the windows of Liston Rectory, which was about a mile away. He made no comment on vague reports that mysterious figures were seen in the building as the fire roared away. Capt Gregson (who reached an out of court settlement with his insurers) did not stay very long after the fire and what was left of the rectory was sold to a Mr Woods. During the following years the ruins were dismantled and the bricks and rubble were taken away.

Henning described many strange incidents in the church and the graveyard at Borley. Sceptics have lost no chance to draw attention to the point that when the rectory was destroyed by fire, the 'ghosts' transferred themselves conveniently across the road and into the church. This is not only an over-cynical view, it is also quite incorrect.

Fig 34. Kathleen King, née Finch

Claims were made over decades that the spectral nun had been seen in the general area of the rectory and the church, but never in the house itself. We remind ourselves that four of the Bull sisters stated that they saw her in the garden, as did their brother Harry, and Fred Cartwright claimed to have seen her at close quarters in Hall Lane on four separate occasions. There was another important sighting of her in the lane in June 1970, but we shall refer to this incident in a later chapter.

To return to Henning's booklet, he described the afternoon when the children in the village came to the church for Sunday school and were locked in[8]. The children sat down in the front pews and waited for their teacher. After a few minutes, they heard distinctly footsteps entering the porch and the key of the church door being turned in the lock. Kathleen Finch, who was about 13 years old at the time, called out, "We are here, Miss Byford." There was total silence; the children became increasingly frightened and alarmed even when Kathleen suggested that a joke was being played on them and said that everything would be all right in a few minutes. Fortunately, this was the case. Miss Byford arrived a little later and was astonished to find the door locked. Henning suspected at first that there had been a practical joke played and talked to Kathleen Finch about the incident later on. She told him that she had mentioned the matter to the girls who lived at the rectory cottage, but they denied strongly that they had been in the church porch and locked the door. Henning expressed the opinion that from his knowledge of these girls, they would not have bothered to come out of their home, cross the road, walk up the path in the churchyard, lock the door and then walk off again, simply in order to frighten a few children. He said that the sound of footsteps on the path and in the porch when nobody else was present occurred frequently and in his view the locking of the door was a paranormal experience. We have discussed this episode with Kathleen King (née Finch) and she told us that she never had been able to come to any definite conclusion. Trickery cannot be ruled out, but Kathleen King does not understand why footsteps were heard approaching the door before the key was turned in the lock, but that this was not followed by the sound of departing footsteps.

Henning described another occasion when the sound of unaccountable footsteps was heard on the pathway leading to the porch of the church and in the porch itself[9]. The date was 4 June 1947 and he was accompanied by Mrs Henning and Harry Price, who had expressed the wish to see the recently restored altar stone. Price had come from his home in Pulborough, Sussex, that day in order to deliver a lecture on the alleged haunting at Borley to an audience at the Town Hall in Sudbury. In the event, the meeting was packed and the proceeds went in aid of the funds of Borley church. This generous act on Price's part is referred to rarely if ever by those who are determined to belittle him. Reverting to the visit to the church, whilst the three people were looking at the altar stone, the birds in the trees around the small graveyard made suddenly a terrific screeching[10]. Harry Price enquired if 'they always went on like that'. The noise died down and in the ensuing quietness, footsteps were heard in the porch. Henning thought that visitors would be inconvenient and he and Price would not wish to be delayed because of the meeting at Sudbury. Nevertheless, he went to the porch and was surprised to find that nobody was there. He walked round the churchyard to look around the general area. Nobody was about and there had been insufficient time for anyone to have moved away hurriedly from the place, even if he or she had wished to do so.

Three days later, exactly the same phenomenon occurred. Henning had taken two young friends who were university students up to Borley church. After they had entered the building, the birds started screeching and when this had ceased footsteps were heard in the porch. The three people hurried towards it and the two students ran quickly round the churchyard. As on the previous occasion no one was about, nor would anyone have had the time to make themselves scarce.

Henning claimed in his booklet to have experienced personally another phenomenon: the sound of the church organ being played when the building itself was empty[11]. He reported that on 15 October

1947 he was telephoned by a Mrs Walrond who lived in a nearby village and who wished to see the stone altar. This lady was better known as the novelist Norah Burke. During the middle of the afternoon, Henning drove Mrs Walrond to Borley. They got out of the car and when they were halfway along the short path to the church, she said, "someone is playing the organ". Henning heard the music himself and thought at first that the instrument was being played by a local resident who had permission to do so. Then he remembered that that person was ill and that the regular organist would be away from the village following her occupation as a school teacher. The pair hurried to the church door and checked quickly that the building was empty and that the organ was locked. Henning was adamant that they had heard proper music and not the sort of sounds which would have been produced by a non-musician who was fooling about. In any event, the organ was of the old type which needed a second person to pump the blowing mechanism. Henning went on to say that villagers had reported from time to time that they had passed the church after it had been locked up at night and had heard the sound of the organ being played.

The matter was reported in *The East Anglian Daily Times* on 24 October and a few days later Henning received a letter from a Mr E W Jephcott, who lived in Alcester, Warwickshire. Jephcott wrote as follows:

'Dear Sir,

'I have read with quite unusual interest the account in "The East Anglian Daily Times" for October the 24th of the experiences of Mrs Walrond and yourself at Borley recently. It provided astonishing confirmation of what I believe to have happened on the afternoon of Tuesday, September the 16th.

'It was probably about 3.30 that day when I called with a friend to have a look at the site of the rectory. After doing this, we went across to the church and as we were walking up the pathway, my friend said "the organ's playing". I could hear no music and we passed on into the church where no one else was present and the organ closed. I though little more of the matter until I found in Mr Harry Price's latest book on Borley the statement that villagers claim to have heard ghostly organ music and singing from Borley church when no one was within it. My friend assured me he had not read Harry Price's book and that his impression of organ music was sufficiently strong to make him consider whether a funeral service was in progress and we had better not enter the church.

'You will see from this how remarkably similar this was to Mrs Walrond's experience. I should be much interested to know whether you yourself heard the music and whether any definite tune was apparent. If the playing should recur, it might be possible to take note of the melody and get it identified.

'I went to Borley again on September the 19th, but had no paranormal experience.'

We wish now to comment on these alleged phenomena and especially those involving the organ music. First of all, we have to acknowledge the possibility that the witnesses were not telling the truth. It may be that the reports of organ music coming from the church after dark were examples of the villagers testing each other's credulity. However, we feel that Henning, Jephcott and Mrs Walrond were in a different category and that the similarity of their experiences was remarkable. Two people were required to operate the organ and it would be difficult indeed for them to hide quickly in Borley church, which is a small building. Two explanations have been put forward which could account for sounds being produced from the organ without the assistance of human hands, or even the help of our old friend, that very useful stray cat. The first is that the sounds could have been the result of the building up of air pressure within the instrument and the second is that they could have been due to slight earth tremors. These 'explanations' are straw-clutching indeed and are bordering on the nonsensical. In the extremely unlikely event of one or other of them being correct, then all the odds are that meaningless and very discordant sounds would be produced and not properly constructed music. The other comment we would make about this matter is that in 1947 such all too real phenomena as portable radios and cassette players were not generally available; we do not feel that such gadgetry can be offered as an explanation of the mysterious organ music.

Henning described other incidents in his short book, but we have given a fairly representative sample of them. In addition to writing and publishing *Haunted Borley*, he and his wife gave many lectures on the subject to various organisations, some locally and some further afield. Henning died unexpectedly in January 1955 as the result of a spell of exceptionally cold weather. His widow outlived him by many years; first of all, she moved away from the area, but then she came back to the nearby large village of Clare. She was convinced of the genuineness of at least some of the phenomena and continued to lecture occasionally on the alleged haunting at Borley. One of us (CM) knew her and regarded her as a truthful and down-to-earth person.

We refer now to two matters which belong to the time of the Henning incumbency, although neither the rector nor Harry Price were involved in them. The first was a project which became known as the Cambridge Commission and the second was the experiences of the author James Turner, who owned the rectory site and lived in the rectory cottage from 1947 to 1950.

The Cambridge Commission was a well-organised venture led by Dr Andrew Robertson, MA, PhD, who became eventually a member of the Council of the Society for Psychical Research[12]. In 1939, he was a lecturer at St John's College, Cambridge and he arranged for groups of observers to visit the ruined rectory on 25 occasions, starting in that year and ending in 1944. Dr Robertson's speciality was physical chemistry and the reports of the visits were recorded with meticulous care. Never was the position overstated and when nothing of interest occurred, then this was duly noted. Full allowance was made for the fact that it was extremely difficult to move quietly around what remained of the rectory, due to large quantities of brick rubble and broken glass. Critics of the case have made the most of the points that Robertson was present at only eight out of the total of 25 visits and that all of his observers were under-graduates. They have implied that there may have been a certain air of levity surrounding the proceedings on some occasions and recalled with relish that on one visit the serious observers were entertained by some of their less earnest co-students who had arrived separately and secretly at Borley and one of whom flitted about the lawn with a white sheet draped over his head.

Although Harry Price was not involved at all with the organisation and work of the Cambridge Commission, Robertson wrote chapter nine of his (Price's) *The End of Borley Rectory*. The care and accuracy of the writing is all that one could wish for; there is a brief introduction, reports on the 25 visits to the rectory and a lengthy conclusion. As the book is still quite easy to obtain, we propose to relate only some of the alleged phenomena:

The first visit took place during the Easter vacation of 1939 and nothing of interest happened. During the course of the second visit, on 31 October 1941 (Robertson was present), a luminous patch was observed on the wall between the sewing-room and the corridor at a height of about a foot above floor level. The report of the observers stated definitely that the effect could not have been caused by moonlight, nor car headlights and that there was no one else about. An hour and a half later (at 2.10 am) distinct and heavy footsteps were heard descending the pantry stairs. During the third and fourth visits (again Robertson was present) the sound of knocks was heard, sometimes in response to questions asked out aloud. As previously, the observers were certain that they were alone. The fifth visit was uneventful, although it took place on 28 July 1942, the day of the year when the spectral nun was supposed to put in an appearance. Measured and steady footsteps were heard during the course of the sixth visit, which took place on 22 September 1942. The next two visits were uneventful, but on 23 March 1943 the observers heard the sound of horses' hooves on the road outside the rectory. The group was in the garden and was confident that there were no animals in the area. On the tenth, 11th and 12th visits there was little to report other than various noises for which rodents could have been responsible and on the 13th visit nothing of interest happened. On the 14th visit, dated 19 January 1943 temperatures were recorded on the 'cold spot' and at another point nearby and showed that there was a variation of 11 degrees Fahrenheit. However, it must be remembered that the rectory was a ruin and open to the elements. The next seven visits produced nothing of interest, although it was noticed that demolition work had been commenced on what was left of the house (this was during the period of late 1943 to early 1944).

The 22nd visit took place on 30 April 1944. One of the five observers noticed a white light which appeared, disappeared and then re-appeared at various points in what was left of the rectory, between 3.30 and 4.00 am. Checks confirmed that the light could not have been due to torchlight, moonlight or the presence of other people. The last three visits were uneventful and on the final date of 22 July 1944, the observers noted that the demolition of the rectory had been completed. It was on this night, also, that the hoaxers were present. As ever, we have to assume that the more serious participants were being truthful and on this basis we note two points: first, the alleged phenomena were growing weaker and second, they ceased altogether when the ruins were totally dismantled. We note also that the observers were concerned only with the seriously damaged building and the garden and not at all with the church across the road.

To obtain a more balanced view of the work of the Cambridge Commission, we note that in 1975, one of the monthly meetings of the Society for Psychical Research was devoted to the Borley case as a whole and one of us (EB) was present. The lecturer was none other than the indefatigable Mrs K M Goldney. By 1975 she was very elderly, but still forceful and was determined clearly to wield the axe in all directions, the integrity of the late Harry Price being selected for special treatment. All in all, she did not carry her audience with her and she was questioned vigorously for about an hour after she had concluded her lecture. Also present at this packed meeting was Dr Robertson, who was living by this time in retirement at Sevenoaks in Kent. He spoke with great authority and precision and was definitely of the opinion that at least some of the phenomena reported by his helpers could not be explained away by normal means.

Finally, we turn to two of the experiences of the poet and author James Turner, who lived at Borley for three years before moving to the neighbouring hamlet of Belchamp Walter and then on to the west country[13]. He had become increasingly irritated by the number of sightseers who arrived without notice and trampled all over his garden. His charming project of building a low brick wall indicating the outline of the rectory and planting a rose garden inside this area seemed destined not to be a permanent feature. During the course of a visit, Henning reversed his car into the wall, knocking some of it over and soon after Turner moved away from Borley, further excavations of the old cellars recommenced.

In June 1947 Turner spent several evenings clearing away the brambles which had grown over the Nun's Walk and on these occasions he heard the sound of laughter and talking, as if a garden party were in progress. Whenever he put his sickle down, the sounds would cease. He called his wife on some occasions and she heard also the sound of laughter and talking. They checked that no one else was about and that no social gatherings were being held in the area.

On 2 August of the same year, Turner strolled across to the churchyard soon after midnight and sat there for about three quarters of an hour. It was a warm night with brilliant moonlight and he felt completely relaxed. After a time, he heard footsteps coming along the path which leads to the porch of the church. He noted that one footstep was heavier than the other and that they were accompanied by a swishing sound as if the walker was wearing robes or a gown. No one was to be seen on the path which was only a few yards from where Turner was sitting. He said that the steps were very definite and had nothing to do with a courting couple who were saying a lengthy and no doubt tender goodnight to each other in Hall Lane. This experience seems to have been very much in line with similar alleged phenomena which had been reported many times.

CHAPTER SIX

The famous Harry Price

Harry Price was always a very controversial figure, but it can be argued that because of his experience and his technical abilities he was the right person to investigate the case. As we have seen, it was referred to him on 11 June 1929, by the editor of the *Daily Mirror* and we know now that this was after the matter had been reported to the Society for Psychical Research, who took very little action, at least as an organisation.

Harry Price was born on 17 January 1881, in rather poor circumstances in London, according to one of his biographers Trevor Hall (who was also one of the three authors of the highly critical book *The Haunting of Borley Rectory*)[1]. According to Price himself, he implied that he was born in Shropshire, where his father was a wealthy businessman. This seems not to have been true, but it is certainly true to say that his father came from that county, that many of his relatives continued to live there and that he spent long periods there during his boyhood. Trevor Hall's biography of Price is, frankly, a thoroughly unpleasant piece of work and no opportunity is lost to belittle the latter's many and varied achievements and to question the truth of his claims. We are reminded of the old proverb about people who live in glass houses: Trevor Hall had many contacts at Cambridge University, held the place in great awe and claimed to have graduated there himself. According to Robert Wood (who wrote *The Widow of Borley*), this claim was quite false. Harry Price was not the first person in the world to attempt to mask humble beginnings and he certainly will not be the last person to do so.

Harry Price was educated at Haberdasher's Aske's School in south-east London and appears to have been an average pupil. However, at an early age he developed interests in conjuring, photography and electrical and light engineering. His enthusiasm for conjuring had some most useful consequences. He became an accomplished conjuror himself and gave frequently performances for various charities. At a later period in his life he joined the Magic Circle and the Magician's Club. More importantly, his knowledge of the subject was invaluable

Fig 35. Harry Price, the original investigator of the Borley mysteries. He was an early motoring enthusiast. This photograph dates from the 1920s

when testing the claims of physical mediums, many of whom failed to measure up to his rigorous investigations and it went hand-in-hand with the idea of assembling his huge library of books and pamphlets to do with magic and the occult. This became known as the Harry Price Library of Magical Literature and he bequeathed it to the University of London; in fact it had been on permanent loan to that body for 12 years at the time of his death in 1948.

Harry Price's skills in the fields of photography and electrical and light engineering were also of considerable assistance in the testing of mediumships and the investigation of haunted houses. He claimed that he had over 200 photographs of Borley Rectory and he was capable of making various instruments and gadgets to a very high standard. He suffered severely from angina and was deemed to be unfit for military service during the first world war, but he was put in charge of a munitions factory in London. He had a first-class engineering workshop at his home in Pulborough, Sussex and produced many pieces of equipment which were put to good use at his National Laboratory of Psychical Research. This organisation was located in South Kensington and commenced to operate on 1 January 1926[2]. It was a rival body to the Society for Psychical Research, with whom Harry Price had fallen out and it was concerned largely with testing the claims of various mediums, many of whom were found to be fraudulent. Price was very impressed with the apparent genuineness of Eileen Garrett and also Stella Cranshaw (whom he discovered). On the other hand, he exposed the so-called spirit photographer William Hope, who had managed to fool the British College of Psychic Science and he had his doubts eventually about the famous young Austrian medium Rudi Schneider whom he brought to this country on three occasions.

In 1934, the National Laboratory developed into the University of London Council for Psychical Investigation. Many of those involved in it were lecturers at the University, but Price's critics have emphasised always that the Council had no official connection with the University. For that matter, neither had the Society for Psychical Research. However, we can see the way in which Price's mind was working and during the early 1930s he was trying to persuade the University of London to create a Department of Psychical Research; he offered to make an endowment for this purpose. When this possibility failed there were negotiations with other universities and in the case of the one at Bonn they reached an advanced stage, but they were frustrated because of the building up of the international tensions which preceded the second world war.

Price was a prolific author and about a dozen and a half of his books were published. Most, but not all of them, were to do with various aspects of psychical research and the last four were bestsellers. They were the two books about Borley Rectory, *Poltergeist over England* and his autobiography *Search for Truth*. Also, he wrote countless articles and he took part in many radio broadcasts. His experiments which tested an Indian fire-walker formed the basis of an early outside television programme from Alexandra Palace in 1937. For several years from 1925 he was the foreign research officer of the American Society for Psychical Research. In addition to all of these activities, he continued to live happily with the wealthy lady whom he had married in 1908 — and he investigated the alleged haunting of Borley Rectory. His critics have maintained that he should have been there far more often than actually he was, but in view of all of these other interests and commitments, we are not surprised and delegation must have seemed

Fig 36. Harry Price's laboratory in London with photographic gear and other equipment he used to test the authenticity of paranormal phemomena

the obvious solution to the problem. The main charge which has been made against him was that he was far too desirous of publicity and that later in life he lowered his high standards and even resorted to trickery in order to achieve it.

We have described already most of Price's early part in the alleged haunting, but we have done so in a piecemeal fashion. We feel, therefore, that we should cover briefly this period as a whole. His first visit to the hamlet of Borley (of which in all probability he had never heard previously) was on 12 June 1929, the case having been referred to him by the editor of the *Daily Mirror*[3]. He was accompanied by his secretary Lucie Kaye and on arrival they met the Rev Guy Eric Smith and his wife Mabel and also the reporter V C Wall, who was writing and sending sensational articles to the *Daily Mirror*. In the weeks and months that followed, Price visited Borley and district on several occasions, seeking out witnesses and taking statements from them. He interviewed the local people at Borley, including the Smiths' maid Mary Pearson and he saw members of the Bull family at Great Cornard. In Sudbury he met Mr and Mrs Edward Cooper, the former tenants of the rectory cottage and also Fred Cartwright, the carpenter who claimed to have seen the ghostly nun at one of the rectory gates on four occasions.

During a visit to the rectory on the evening of 5 July 1929, Price and some colleagues witnessed a further outbreak of poltergeist activity.

Fig 37. Lucie Kaye, Price's secretary and assistant. She became Mrs Lucie Meeker

After some bell-ringing and pebble-throwing (apparently without human assistance), several keys from various rooms were deposited in the hallway and among them was a small brass medallion. It was octagonal and on one side there was shown the head of a monk. There was a Latin inscription around the border. This piece was known as a St Ignatius medal and was fashioned out of brass. Price got into a muddle and into trouble with his accusers, when he referred to two different medallions appearing on this occasion in his first Borley book *The Most Haunted House in England.* However, he described the incident accurately in the Appendix of his book and surely would not have done so had he been intent upon deceit. At a later date Price's former secretary, who had become Mrs Lucie Meeker, confirmed that only one

Fig 38. St Mary's Church, Pulborough, where Price was a sidesman for 40 years

medallion, as described above, appeared during this visit. Other medallions were part of the Borley saga, but they come into the story much later. In fairness, we must add that one of Price's colleagues on this occasion was the hostile Lord Charles Hope. The latter distrusted the famous investigator, but in his own report he did not deny the appearance of the medallion. The reason for the bad relations between the two men had its origins in the fact that his lordship was one of those people (Mrs Goldney was another) who had a foot in both camps. He was a member of the Society for Psychical Research and also Price's National Laboratory of Psychical Research. Lord Hope was generous financially to the latter organisation and felt that in return he was entitled to have a say in the running of its affairs. Price was a quick-tempered man with strong views of his own and no doubt would have had none of it. Relations deteriorated even further a few years later when the two men became involved in a disagreement concerning the medium Rudi Schneider. They tried to belittle each other's efforts and Lord Charles Hope became loyal only to the Society for Psychical Research.

The next incident to do with Harry Price's early involvement with the Borley case is one in which there was a serious accusation of trickery on his part. There was another accusation of a similar nature much later in 1944 and we shall deal with the two together.

Fig 39. Interior of St Mary's Pulborough

In 1929, Charles Sutton, a reporter from the *Daily Mail*, asked Harry Price if he could be taken to see Borley Rectory[4]. This was agreed and Lucie Kaye drove the two men there on 25 July. In a book called *The Inky Way Annual*, published in December 1948 (nine months after Price's death), Charles Sutton wrote an article about his various experiences and he referred to the 1929 visit to Borley. He claimed that there was an outbreak of pebble-throwing and that after one had hit him on the head he seized hold of Harry Price and found that his pockets were full of bricks and pebbles. He claimed also that he rushed to the nearest village and telephoned the story to his newspaper, but that after taking legal advice, the news editor was not prepared to print it. He is alleged to have said to Sutton: "Bad luck, old man, but there were two of them and only one of you."

A storm was created when *The Inky Way Annual* of 1948 was published. Naturally, it delighted those people who had not trusted Price and who had been jealous of his virtual monopoly of the Borley case. Charles Sutton made much longer statements about the matter to various members of the Society for Psychical Research, including Lord Charles Hope and the three authors of *The haunting of Borley Rectory*. These statements did not clear the air at all. Sutton was not consistent and was vague when pressed for details; this is precisely what could be expected when an alleged event is described 20 years later by an individual who had spent his career in search of sensationalism rather than accuracy.

Lucie Kaye sent a long report to the Society for Psychical Research

Figs 40 & 41. The pair of Jacobean chairs donated by Price to St Mary's in 1923 in memory of his parents for the use of distinguished visitors such as the Bishop

three months after *The Inky Way Annual* went on sale. She stated that she knew Sutton before the visit to Borley as he had been present at some of the sittings with Rudi Schneider. She had no recollection at all of an exposure or any other sort of upset during the time spent in the rectory, but she said that both Price and herself were extremely annoyed with Sutton when he insisted upon leaving the house after having been in it for only an hour. They told him that normally they would not have undertaken such a long journey for such a short period of observation. They felt that he was scared, but he said that he had to telephone his newspaper before midnight in order that his report could be printed in the next day's edition. Miss Kaye drove the two men to The Bull Hotel at Long Melford. They chatted for some hours in the lounge and had some drinks, but the secretary said that Sutton did not use the telephone. She concluded her report by stating that she remembered having lunch with Charles Sutton in Fleet Street in 1940 and would definitely not have done so if there had been any trouble or acrimony during the course of the visit to Borley Rectory or afterwards. Referring to Harry Price, she said that she had worked for him for five years and had remained friends with him until his death; she considered him to be an honest person who did not resort to faking 'phenomena.'

The second incident which called Harry Price's integrity into question occurred on 5 April 1944[5]. On that day Price visited what was left of Borley Rectory together with Cynthia Ledsham and David Scherman, both of whom were in the employ of the American magazine *Life*, the former as a journalist and the latter as a photographer. The object of the visit was to gather material for an article for that publication. By this time the ruins were in the process of being demolished and there were workmen on the site. According to Price, the group stood about 100 feet away from the wrecked building in order that Scherman could frame all of it in a photograph. At the precise moment that he released the shutter of his camera, a brick shot up about four feet in the air in the old kitchen passage and was recorded in the picture. Both this photograph and an enlargement of the 'flying brick' were reproduced in *The End of Borley Rectory* and in the accompanying paragraphs Price stated that this may have been a genuine phenomenon. David Scherman took many photographs that day, mainly for the benefit of his magazine, but some of them are included in Price's above-mentioned book.

In an undated letter to the Society for Psychical Research, but which was written probably in early 1950, Cynthia Thompson (formerly Miss Ledsham) said that she had witnessed the 'most barefaced hocus pocus' on the part of the late Harry Price. She claimed that the brick which Scherman had photographed had flown through the air (and so had others) for the simple reason that one of the workmen had thrown it. Mrs Thompson is said to have repeated this charge during the course of a lunch with the omnipresent Mrs Goldney on 17 October 1950. The latter prepared a report based on this discussion, which Mrs Thompson signed. One cannot help wondering if Mrs Goldney wrote her report with a certain relish and it seems extraordinary that a professional writer and researcher (that is, Mrs Thompson) should not have been invited to submit her own statement.

All of this may seem to be very serious with regard to Harry Price's reputation, but there are some questions which need to be addressed and we refer again to the visit in April 1944 to the remnants of the rectory. First, Price stated that the brick shot up in the air and not that it was moving in a downward direction. Second, David Scherman's original picture showed a workman on the extreme left, but experienced photographers have expressed the view that it would not have been possible for him to have thrown the brick to the point at which it was shown.

Both the 1929 and the 1944 alleged incidents are now over half a century away and it is very difficult to decide today whether Harry Price lowered his standards in the interests of publicity and high sales of his books, or whether his critics and detractors were determined to discredit him. From all accounts he was a strong-willed person who perhaps did not find it easy to work in co-operation with others and there is no doubt that he had his enemies. We think that it is a general truth to say that people are not indifferent to an individual who happens to have a forceful personality; such a person is usually either very much liked or disliked. We wish to make one final point about these two alleged incidents which have much in common and which is the reason why we have considered them together. In both cases the accusations of trickery were made by journalists and moreover by journalists who were in the employ of popular and not particularly intellectual publications. Frankly, sensationalism is part of the stock-in-trade of some newspaper reporters and although many people felt that

Price was far too concerned with publicity, there is the possibility that in regard to these two alleged incidents it may have been a case of being sinned against rather than sinning.

We have described already Harry Price's visits to Borley Rectory on 13 and 14 October 1931. He took a small group of colleagues with him, which included Mrs Goldney and it was on the second day that he informed the Rev Foyster that Marianne, his 'wife', could have been responsible for the manifestations. As we know, this made the clergyman extremely angry, the two men parted on very bad terms and that was the position until well after the Foysters left Borley. This was the reason why Price did not go there again until 1937; it was not because he had lost interest in the case, but it was the end of his early involvement in it.

Before we move on to Harry Price's later investigations, we must refer to a strange occurrence which took place during supper at the rectory on 13 October 1931[6]. The Foysters had prepared some food and one of Price's friends had provided a luncheon basket which included two bottles of wine. When the corks were pulled it was discovered that the burgundy looked like ink and that the sauterne smelt like eau-de-cologne. One suspects that someone with a knowledge of conjuring may have been at work and the sceptics have emphasised that this was one of Price's many skills. However, he did not open both bottles and if he had tampered with the one which he may have uncorked, then he did so under the gaze of the observant Mrs Goldney, surely a trained and serious investigator if ever there was one. Price, a wealthy man who liked to live in style, was rather annoyed about the matter. He accused openly the Foysters, who had provided the glasses and tumblers. This did not make for a relaxed atmosphere at the table and perhaps was a foretaste of the confrontation which was to come on the following day. If Price had wanted to present the incident as a genuine phenomenon, it seems rather strange that he made such an accusation. Perhaps the condition of the wines may have had more to do with a long journey in a pre-war motor car than with the paranormal.

Harry Price went to Borley again in May 1937, although it must be said that during his long absence he had been receiving reports from local residents, describing alleged phenomena. This time he met the Rev Alfred Clifford Henning (who had succeeded Lionel Foyster) and the two men established quickly a good rapport. As we have seen in the last chapter, Henning was extremely interested in the alleged haunting and also that as he lived at Liston, he had been advised by the Bishop of Chelmsford to try to sell or at least to let the rectory at Borley. Price claimed that he could have bought the house very cheaply and toyed with the idea of doing so. He wanted to have the opportunity to resume his investigations and felt that perhaps the place would have a long-term future as a study centre for psychical researchers. In the end good business sense prevailed and he realised that a low purchase price would be far outweighed by the huge cost of bringing the place up to a reasonable state of repair, let alone any attempts to provide modern facilities. In the time of the wealthy Bull family, the house and grounds had been kept in an excellent condition and the owners had been protected from problems which were related to the lack of basic amenities (there was no electricity, nor piped water supply) as a result of the efforts of a squad of full-time maids and gardeners.

When Harry Price went back to Borley on 19 May 1937, he met Henning. The former had decided already that the best procedure would be for him to rent the house for the purposes of observation and investigation and he discussed his plan with the rector[7]. It was agreed that there would be a tenancy lasting for one year for the sum of £30. Price's next problem was how to organise his project. Rightly or wrongly, he decided to delegate the work to others and to keep out of it himself. The facts must not be forgotten that he was very involved with other aspects of psychical research at his office (the former National Laboratory was known now under the grand and rather inaccurate title of the University of London Council for Psychical Investigation), his literary output continued unabated and it was said that he disliked having to sleep away from home and avoided doing so whenever he could. He placed an advertisement in *The Times* on 25 May 1937. The wording was as follows:

'Haunted house. Responsible persons of leisure and intelligence, intrepid, critical and unbiased, are invited to join rota of observers in a year's night and day investigation of alleged haunted house in Home Counties. Printed instructions supplied. Scientific training or ability to operate simple instruments an advantage. House situated in lonely hamlet, so own car is essential. Write Box H989, The Times, EC4.'

Price said that he received over 200 replies to his advertisement. Some were obviously from cranks and sensation seekers, but he selected and interviewed those applicants who appeared to be suitable and they became the team of observers. There were 48 of them and they were clearly the professional type of people whom Price had hoped to attract. We have met already the Glanville family, Dr Bellamy and his son and Mark Kerr-Pearse, who was a senior official in the diplomatic service; they were fairly typical of the other observers. All of them were issued with an instruction pamphlet which became known as *The Blue Book* relating to the colour of the cover[8]. (It would have been almost impossible to have chosen a more unfortunate name for the booklet. We can only hope that Harry Price was unaware of the fact that another publication bearing the same title had been produced and sold quite openly some 30 years earlier in New Orleans. It was in effect a trade directory of the city's notorious red light district.)

Critics of the case have alleged that *The Blue Book* was not intended to supply helpful information, but rather it was a 'barrage of suggestion' and the real purpose of it was to encourage the observers to attach undue importance to anything that they may see or hear. Sceptics have complained also that no log-book was kept at the rectory, that the observers had to send their reports direct to Price who would edit them to suit his own purposes and that none of the participants had had previous experience of such investigations. We feel that, all in all, these criticisms are invalid and we would make the following points: **first**, the calibre of the observers was underestimated and seriously so; **second**, early entries in a log-book at the rectory may well have influenced the comments of later contributors; **third**, Price wanted and got in most cases, detailed and independent reports, rather than a few lines in a dog-eared and tea-stained book which could have been lost or stolen; **finally** and with every justification, he had no intention of allowing his project to be taken over by other psychical researchers, not even trained and serious ones. With regard to the final point, it was after all Price who had taken up the one-year tenancy of Borley Rectory. Presumably, the Society for Psychical Research could have done the same if it had wished to do so; what it did eventually, as we know, was to ask three of its leading members to write a report and this predictably critical and carping piece of work, *The Haunting of Borley Rectory*, was not published until eight years after Price's death.

The year long operation got under way. The library at the rectory was fitted out as a 'base room' for the observers and their reports started to flow. The pro-Borley camp regard the reported incidents as good and carefully recorded evidence of paranormal activity. The antagonists claimed that they did not amount to very much at all. We do not propose to go into the matter in detail and we refer to Price's *The Most Haunted House in England*, copies of which are fairly easy to obtain. Appendix A of this book is a copy of the declaration form which the observers were required to sign, Appendix B is the wording of *The Blue Book* and Appendix C is a lengthy digest of the observers' reports. Our own view of these reports is that they included many incidents which defy a normal explanation (such as unaccountable footsteps and other noises, the movement of objects from marked positions, fresh wall-markings, the appearances of strange lights and possibly a sighting of the spectral nun), but undoubtedly the alleged phenomena were growing weaker. This is precisely what one would expect to happen eventually in any alleged haunting and this tendency was confirmed by the observation and reports of Dr Robertson and his Cambridge Commission, which commenced its investigations just after the rectory was consumed by fire on 27 February 1939[9].

We turn now to the excavations of the cellars under the ruined rectory, which commenced on 17 August 1943 and carried on for two days after that date[10]. Dr W J Phythian-Adams, the Canon of Carlisle, had offered a suggested interpretation of the wall-messages in the house and had urged Harry Price to have the work done. The former felt that the writings indicated that there may be human remains buried under the cellars, that this possibility should be investigated and indeed he had become rather impatient because a start had not been made at an earlier date.

The first work which was carried out on 17 August was the unsuccessful attempt to find the entry to the crypt under Borley church. Then the group, which consisted of Harry Price and his secretary, the Rev and Mrs Henning, Capt Gregson, Dr Eric Bailey (a pathologist) and his brother, Flying Officer Creamer and a local workman named Jackson, crossed the road to the rectory ruins and commenced the main work of digging up the cellar floors and excavating the wells there. The task was not an easy one, as the cellars were full of debris from the ruined house which had to be moved around constantly in order that digging could take place at various points. The first really interesting item that came to light was the Sheffield plate cream jug which Jackson discovered at a depth of five and a half feet in one of the wells.

In the early afternoon digging was started under the so-called well tank. This was a shallow cement trough and presumably it owed its existence to the need to keep the cellars reasonably dry. They had always been very damp and slimy and provided residential accommodation for dozens of frogs, lizards and other amphibians. The soil under the brickwork was of a very heavy type of clay, but Jackson struggled on and at a quarter to two he found part of a jawbone. Most of the group thought that it belonged to an animal, but Dr Bailey identified it immediately as being human. A few minutes later Jackson handed up part of a skull and this also was identified as being human. Bailey stated that the piece of jawbone was the left mandible, with five teeth in situ and belonged probably to a woman and that the other bone was the left part of a human skull. Nothing else of interest was dug up on the first day, but the pieces of bone were indeed an exciting discovery. The local coroner was notified that human remains had been found, but he took the view that as they were so small there would not be the need to hold an inquest. Eventually the bones were put in a casket which was buried by Henning in the graveyard of Liston Church on 29 May 1945. It may seem strange that they were not interred at Borley, but one of us (CM) remembers being told several years later that there were considerable local objections to this course of action. It seems that some people in the hamlet were less than enthusiastic about the alleged haunting of their rectory and the subsequent investigations, not to mention the constant stream of sightseers, some of whom were not well-behaved.

Digging recommenced the following morning and the area was extended by several yards and to a depth of three feet. We must emphasise again that this was very difficult and hard work, because it was necessary at every stage to shift tons of debris from the ruins above in order to start digging up a different part of the floor. Also, the earth which was brought up from below the brick floors had to be sifted. At a quarter to twelve, a piece of metal with a loop attached to it was discovered. A few minutes later a small plaque, also with a loop attached, came to light. When the clay was scrubbed off these objects it was found that the former was a pendant of poor quality gold which had been damaged by acids in the soil. The second object was found to be made of copper. It was covered with a green patina and it too had been damaged because of contact with the soil. Later on, Harry Price had both objects examined by experts in London, who stated that the copper plaque was about 60 years old, that the gold pendant was much older and that both were of French origin. Nothing else of interest was discovered during the second day's digging.

The third day's digging took place after a slight interval on 30 August 1943. This time the group consisted of Harry Price, the Hennings, Sidney Glanville and his son Roger and the sturdy Jackson, whom we suspect did most of the hard work. Unfortunately, nothing of interest was found on this occasion. In his second book on the subject (*The End of Borley Rectory*), Price put forward the question as to whether or not the fragments of bone were indeed the remains of a murdered nun called Marie Lairre and commented that the French origin of the pendant and the plaque could be in the nature of a clue or 'pointer'. His detractors thought otherwise and stated that there could be a different and very discreditable explanation, which we must discuss at some length.

Messrs Dingwall and Hall and Mrs Goldney, the authors of *The Haunting of Borley Rectory,* implied in that book that Harry Price may have 'planted' the bones in the earth under the well-tank in order that Canon Phythian-Adams' theory, based upon his interpretation of the wall messages, could be proved[11]. These authors mentioned a letter dated 2 January 1945 from Henning to Price in which the rector said that a Mr Woods, who had bought the rectory ruins for demolition, was surprised to find some wiring and electrical switches in the cellar; we remember that at this time there was no electricity supply at Borley. Whilst they were about it, the three authors might have said just as well that this equipment was in place in order to illuminate the cellars so that Price could dig away under the floor like an anxious terrier and bury the bones, which could be 'discovered' sensationally at some future date. Robert Wood says outright in his book (*The Widow of Borley*) that Price had almost certainly buried the bones. The reality is that almost certainly he did nothing of the sort and if readers are somewhat surprised at the lack of trust and charitable feeling between these trained and serious investigators, then all that we can do is to remind them that we have cautioned them already about this unfortunate state of affairs.

We feel that these serious allegations against the conduct of Harry Price do not stand up to a close examination. First, if they should be correct, he would have had to have run the risk of discovery by members of the Cambridge Commission, or the tenants of the rectory cottage, or other local residents, or one of the many visitors to the site. Second, the condition of the bones (and the pendants) was such as to indicate that they had been in the soil for a very long time. This comment applied especially to the fragment of the skull which was very delicate and the clay had to be removed from it with great care. Third, any resident of north Essex will know that the local soil is really very heavy clay and that without additives it is more suitable for the building of mud huts rather than for any attempts at horticulture. They will know also that the deeper one digs the worse it gets. In August 1943, Price was 62 and he had suffered from angina for most of his life. He had been classified as unfit for military service during the first world war, he had sustained at least one heart attack later on and he was unable to carry out any of the digging when the excavations were under way because of his poor health. Frankly we find the notion that an elderly and unwell man would carry bits and pieces of human remains of the correct sex and age up to Borley (presumably from London), dig up the cellar floor, attack the heavy clay underneath, bury the bones and then replace the soil and the bottom of the well-tank, to be absolutely absurd. And all of this was accomplished, so the sceptics would have us believe, by the light of the silvery bulbs attached to a battery set. Unfortunately, the skull fragment was broken later. It was dropped by a London photographer, who complained of strange occurrences whilst it was in his studio.

With regard to the wiring and switches which Mr Woods (the demolition contractor) saw in 1945, we can say only that it seems very strange that nobody noticed nor commented upon the presence of such equipment during the excavations of August 1943. We feel that the most likely explanations of it being there after that date are that it was used by sub-contractors during the course of their work, or by Woods' employees and without his knowledge, or just possibly during the later visits of the Cambridge Commission.

However, assuming deceit (which we do not) the elderly and unwell Price may have had an accomplice who buried the small fragments of human bone. This is not a likely scenario and our opinion is based on one of the less worthy aspects of human nature — greed. In 1943, when the bones were discovered, Price was a wealthy man and his first Borley book, *The Most Haunted House in England* (1940), had been a best seller. In early 1948 he died, having published in 1946 his second Borley book, *The End of Borley Rectory*, which was also a best seller. If there had been (literally) skulduggery and an accomplice, then that accomplice would have been in a position to blackmail Price whilst he was alive, or to have gone to the national press with a dramatic exposure after his death. There is no evidence to support the first possibility and the second did not happen.

Harry Price gave several lectures about the alleged haunting during the 1930s, which does not appear to have pleased some people. Lord Charles Hope, an old antagonist, wrote to Price some days before a proposed lecture in 1932 and asked that the latter should either refrain from mentioning his name at all, or say that he was not impressed by the phenomena. The Rev Lionel Foyster, who was extremely angry with Price after the visits to Borley Rectory in October 1931, threatened legal proceedings in an attempt to prevent a lecture (possibly the same one which caused concern to Lord Charles Hope) being delivered.

Perhaps the best known lecture which Harry Price gave on the subject of Borley Rectory was the one which was held at the Town Hall in Sudbury on the evening of 4 June 1947. The meeting was organised by the Rev Alfred Clifford Henning and its purpose was to raise money for the Borley church funds; to be exact it was an attempt to make good some of the cost of the reinstatement of the stone altar. The Town Hall was packed and people had to be turned away. It was usual for Price's lectures to be well attended, mainly because people were very interested in what he had to say, rather than because he was an impressive speaker. Although an experienced lecturer, he was not a natural orator. It was his custom to speak in an informal manner, without the use of notes and he liked to illustrate his talks with lantern slides. He was an expert photographer and prepared the slides himself. We have spoken to Olive Marshall, a resident of Sudbury, who attended Price's lecture there and it appears that he followed his usual procedures on this occasion[12]. He was 66 by this time and within a year his heart condition would claim his life. Mrs Marshall remembers that he was short, stocky and what little hair he still had was white. He looked much older than he really was and no doubt his poor health was the cause of this. (He does not appear to have been the type of person who would have been suitable for heavy manual work, such as clandestine grave-digging.) Rather surprisingly, Price spoke with a slight stammer; nevertheless he commanded the rapt attention of his audience, although it was clear after the lecture that a small minority were not convinced of the genuineness of the alleged haunting at Borley Rectory. Be that as it may, it cannot be said that Price was motivated only by the desire for publicity on this occasion. He had been invited to come and speak at Sudbury by Henning and had travelled the considerable distance from his home at Pulborough, Sussex, in order to do so. Both of Price's books about Borley Rectory had been published already. Both of them were best-sellers and there was no need at all for any further advertisement.

In addition to the two books which he devoted entirely to the alleged haunting of Borley Rectory, Price wrote numerous shorter pieces about the place for other publications. Probably the first of these was the one which appeared in the journal of the American Society for Psychical Research in August 1929; as we have said, for many years Price was the foreign research officer for that organisation and he travelled all over Europe in that capacity. One of the last pieces which he wrote about Borley was a chapter in his penultimate book *Poltergeist over England*. At the time of his death he was planning to write a third book on the subject; he referred to it in correspondence as *Borley Three* and had he been able to finish it, there is no doubt that *Borley Three* would have been a best-seller. However, Price was found dead in his study at his home in Pulborough on 29 March 1948; he was only 67 and he had suffered the final heart attack. Although he had been a man of abounding energy and enthusiasm, angina had been a serious problem for much of his life.

Price broadcast about Borley Rectory in 1935, 1937, 1938, 1941, 1946 and 1947. Guy L'Estrange (the Essex medium) broadcast in 1936 about his experiences at the house and Capt W H Gregson (who owned the place when it was destroyed by fire) broadcast on the subject in 1939. Many of these broadcasts formed part of the *In Town Tonight* programmes. There have been several television programmes about Borley Rectory, two of which were transmitted as recently as 1994.

Fig 42. Harry Price's grave in St Mary's graveyard. His is the one with the tilted cross. The inscription reads: IN LOVING MEMORY OF / HARRY PRICE / PASSED AWAY 29TH MARCH 1948 / AGED 67 / AND OF HIS WIFE / CONSTANCE MARY / DIED 25TH APRIL 1976 AGED 94

CHAPTER SEVEN

The last rector of Borley and Liston
(by Claudine Mathias)

I married the late Rev Edward Lanfranc Morgan Mathias MA, on 3 July 1946 and on 28 July (of all dates) 1955, he was inducted as the last rector of Borley and Liston. Lanfranc was born in Hampshire, but was descended from a Welsh family. When he was at school, his only ambition was to become a clergyman. He studied at Cambridge in due course and left with two degrees and a well deserved reputation as a sportsman, his specialities being rugby union and badminton. From Cambridge he went to Cheshunt Theological College and after his ordination he took up his first curacy at the Church of the Holy Redeemer, Lamorbey, Sidcup, Kent. From there he moved to the Church of St Michael and All Angels, Barnes, Surrey, this being his second curacy. It was at this stage in his career that we met and then married. A year later our son was born and three years later we had our first daughter.

After serving as a curate for several years, which was the usual procedure in those days, Lanfranc was offered his first living. He became the vicar of St Philip's, Sydenham, in south-east London, the patron of the living at that time being the late King George the Sixth. We lived happily at Sydenham for several years and our second daughter was born there. St Philip's was a busy London parish and our holidays consisted often of Lanfranc acting as a locum for priests in rural areas when they wished to have a break.

One such locum, which lasted for a month, was in the small parish of Belchamp St Paul. This remote hamlet is located in north Essex, about five miles away from Borley. The incumbent of Belchamp St Paul was the rural dean, the late Canon Edward Powell. His residence was a huge Victorian vicarage, which is now a private house known as 'Mulberry House'. Whilst we were living in the vicarage, we made many local expeditions in the village bus to the nearby market town of Sudbury. In addition to the usual variety of shops, the town had and has still, a good library. In it we came across a copy of Harry Price's first Borley book, *The Most Haunted House in England*, so, of course, having

Fig 43. Rev Lanfranc Mathias and his three children during the incumbency at Borley and Liston. Francis Mathias (left) grew up to be a popular schoolmaster but was killed in a mountaineering accident. His sisters are Mary Louise (right) and Rosemary (centre), the youngest

read the book we went to have a look at Borley. There was little left to see of the rectory and the church across the road seemed tiny when compared with the ones that we knew in London. However, the atmosphere in it was quiet and peaceful as was the countryside surrounding it. We spent a happy month in Belchamp St Paul, but did not expect to see the area again.

In the early part of 1955, the then bishop of Southwark was giving consideration to the possibility of offering a second living to my husband. Unfortunately, Lanfranc became extremely ill and

Fig 44. The old vicarage at Belchamp St Paul in the early 1920s

underwent major surgery at Beckenham Hospital. It was really doubtful as to whether or not he would pull through, but after many anxious weeks he managed to do so. However, from this point onwards he was always in delicate health and he had to take medication for the rest of his life. Another busy London living was out of the question and the choice for the future lay between early retirement on the one hand (he was only 41), or trying to find a quiet living on the other. Fate took over; Canon Edward Powell, of Belchamp St Paul, who knew of our predicament, told us that there was a vacancy at Borley and Liston, following the unexpected death of the Rev Alfred Clifford Henning in January and the bishop of Southwark recommended that Lanfranc be offered the incumbency.

The patronage of the Borley living was still with the Bull family, who were well known in local ecclesiastical circles. To be precise, the patron was Alfred Richard Graham Bull. He was a retired schoolmaster and a brother of the late Reverend Harry (he who had spent so many nights in the rectory garden waiting and watching for the spectral nun). Lanfranc and I were invited to luncheon by Alfred Bull and his sister Ethel; it was all very genteel and somewhat amusing. At this time there were the usual consultations with the parochial church councils; the members appeared to like us and all went well. They were made fully aware of the fact that Lanfranc was in a delicate state of health, but they were very understanding and welcoming. All we had to arrange was our move from the new

Fig 45. The Rev Alfred Clifford Henning's grave in Liston churchyard

vicarage in Sydenham to the (old) rectory at Liston. We were determined to put Lanfranc's traumatic illness behind us and we looked forward to our new life in the country.

It was the beginning of twelve and a half years of a very happy ministry for Lanfranc and for his family. Lanfranc was well-liked and was acknowledged as being a very 'spiritual' man. He had never learned to drive a car but had been always a keen cyclist and in a very few months I became an experienced cyclist as well. Often, after he had completed his pastoral visiting, he would go and rest in Borley church before cycling home to Liston Rectory. He felt that the church had a very peaceful atmosphere and he believed that this was due to the cumulative effect of generations and centuries of prayer and worship, which one would hope to find in any ancient church.

With regard to the alleged haunting at Borley, Lanfranc kept always his cards close to his chest. I shall describe his service of institution and induction in the next chapter. For the time being, I will say merely that on this occasion the then bishop of Chelmsford, Dr Faulkner Allison, had expressed the wish, albeit in a firm yet friendly manner, to Lanfranc that his first loyalty should be to the pastoral care of his parishioners and not to the investigation of the paranormal. It was not that Lanfranc refused to discuss the matter of the alleged haunting when other people wished to do so, or that he did not believe in it; for example, he said that on some occasions when he was 'alone' in Borley church, he had the feeling that there was another presence there. I think that he took note of the bishop's concern and also that he felt that the alleged haunting, like party politics, was a controversial subject in which the village priest should not become involved.

During the years when we lived at Borley and Liston, Lanfranc had many requests from various groups and individuals for permission to stay in Borley church at night, to take photographs in the building and to keep vigil in the churchyard. He had an open mind on the subject and when considering such applications he would use his discretion.

Fig 46. The Rev Lanfranc Mathias (nearest camera) at a Christmas party for parishioners of Borley and Foxearth, held in Foxearth village hall in the late 1950s. There are many Borley residents in the photograph

He felt that it was his duty to try to achieve a proper balance in the matter; on the one hand, he had no wish to interfere with the investigations of genuine and responsible people, but on the other hand, he had the task of endeavouring to ensure that no damage was done, nor nuisance caused, by sensation seekers and amateur ghost hunters, who may have been in contact with spirits of the alcoholic variety immediately prior to their arrival at Borley. Unfortunately, local residents have been subjected to rowdy behaviour from time to time ever since 1929, when the case first attracted national attention[1]. Even more regrettably the problem seems to be getting worse; in recent years, the church has been broken into and damage done, the graves of some of the Bull family have been vandalised and the windows of nearby residences have been broken.

Of course, during the whole of the time of Lanfranc's incumbency, numerous articles about the alleged haunting were appearing in various journals and the Dingwall-Goldney-Hall book, *The Haunting of Borley Rectory*, was published in 1956, the year following our arrival. Lanfranc was approached by various television companies, including one from Germany, who sought permission to film at Borley. On 11 February 1962 there was an Independent Television programme called *About Religion*; in fact, it was about Borley. One article about the programme said that Borley Rectory, near Sudbury, Suffolk, had been rebuilt partially in the studio and another article stated that there would be a reproduction of the famous Blue Room shown for the benefit and education of the viewers. Unfortunately, this room was set up as being on the ground floor and the ghostly nun was shown gliding through it. The truth is that nobody had claimed to have seen this particular apparition in the rectory itself and she is said to have confined her appearances to the garden, the lane and the surrounding area. Furthermore, the Blue Room was one of the first-floor bedrooms and was the one in which the Rev Harry Bull breathed his last. It is up to the producers and programme-makers to strive for accuracy and the rector could not be held responsible for basic errors such as this.

During the early years of Lanfranc's incumbency at Borley and Liston, a considerable amount of digging and excavating took place on the site of Borley Rectory. Before discussing the digging in detail, it may be useful if I describe the background and legends concerning all of the subterranean activity which is said to have gone on at Borley over a period of many centuries. If it were all true, one could reach the conclusion that the place was built upon a complex labyrinth of underground passages and tunnels; this is an overstatement of the case.

To deal with the legendary aspects of the matter first, it was said that Borley Rectory was built on the site of an old monastery and the latter building was connected by means of an underground tunnel to a convent at Bures. This belief may have had something to do with the tale of the eloping monk and nun, but it is almost certainly a tale and nothing else. Harry Price's friend and helper, Sidney H Glanville, was in correspondence with the Essex Archaeological Society in 1938 and that organisation confirmed that there was never a monastery nor any other ecclesiastical building at Borley except for the 12th century church itself[2]. There seems to be little or no real evidence to suggest that there was at any time a convent at Bures, a larger village which straddles the river Stour (one half in Essex and the other in Suffolk) and which is approximately eight miles away from Borley. The construction of an ancient underground tunnel linking the two communities would have been a formidable accomplishment and would have needed to avoid the Stour, which is a large and winding river in this area, and be made impervious to the groundwater. That there are no written records, indicates fairly clearly that such such a major feat of engineering, even by 21st century standards, never took place. It is perfectly possible to walk for miles underneath a large city using the routes of underground railways or main sewers, but it is not possible to do so in the rural area of the Essex-Suffolk border where many of the smaller villages and hamlets (including Borley) are without main drainage even today.

To return to the real world, it is certainly true to say that there were and are still, many wells in Borley because there was no mains water supply to the hamlet until long after the second world war. In the case of Borley Rectory, there had been confusion as to how many wells there were, partly because Harry Price made a mistake in his first book about Borley, which he acknowledged and corrected in his second work *The*

Fig 47. Excavating the cellars in the early 1950s with a cine film crew recording the proceedings

End of Borley Rectory, and partly because in the latter book he stated that there were four wells, while his colleague Sidney Glanville referred in correspondence to the existence of only two wells. The position is a little confused, but if one consults the other books about the rectory wells it seems that Price's second assessment was correct. There were three wells and there was the so-called 'well tank', under which the human remains were found. Readers will remember that this was of a fairly shallow construction and almost certainly it was to do with keeping the cellars relatively dry.

I should like to make two points about the circular wells. The first is that descents were made down them (by James Turner and others), which was rather dangerous in view of their deteriorating condition; no tunnel entrances were found in the sides of the shafts, thereby disposing of one of the legends. The second point concerns the claims of the sceptics with regard to one of the alleged phenomena. They maintain that at least some of the loud noises and unaccountable footsteps which were heard inside the rectory had a perfectly normal explanation — they were caused by the tenants of the cottage when they were operating the wheel pump to the main well, both of which were located in the courtyard. It will be remembered that the huge house was built around the almost totally enclosed courtyard and it was claimed that this arrangement produced some peculiar acoustic effects inside the building itself. What the critics do not say is that there were several windows overlooking the courtyard and that it would

Fig 48. Len Sewell with the old well and pump (in the former courtyard) circa 1955

have been a simple matter to have seen (with the aid of a torch, if necessary) whether or not someone was indeed in the enclosed area when unexplained sounds were heard inside the rectory. On some occasions such sounds were found to have a normal explanation as indicated above, but on many other occasions they did not.

The digging and excavation on the site of Borley Rectory re-commenced in 1954, the year before Lanfranc had been appointed as rector and the work was carried on for about three years[3]. The three main participants were Messrs Philip Paul, L G Rayner and Leonard Sewell, although they were assisted by a number of other people. Unlike the last two, Paul was not a local resident; he was a London journalist and my co-author remembers seeing him appear on the popular television programme *What's my Line*. (This particular edition was transmitted on 12 April 1953.) Paul claimed that he was continuing Harry Price's work at Borley and he felt that the way ahead was to press on with the digging there. He had written an article called 'Ghosts still walk at Borley', which was published in *The Star* a few weeks before his television appearance; in this article he maintained that the content of one of the wall writings in the rectory had led to the discovery of human remains underneath the cellar floor and proved the existence of ghosts. As argued in the previous chapter, the first point is acceptable, but the second point seems to me to be somewhat obscure. Whilst not denying the existence of ghosts and poltergeist activity in general, in the Borley case in particular there may not be necessarily a direct link between them and the wall messages and the human bones which were found.

Paul interested himself in the matter between October 1954 and August 1956. He said that as the result of further digging he hoped to

*Fig 49. L G Rayner (always known as 'L G')
rediscovers one of the wells in the cellars in 1957*

find the rest of the skeleton, the lost plate from Borley church, some of the tunnels which were said to exist in the area and some evidence to support the theory that the rectory garden was established on the site of a former plague pit. It is certainly true to say that in many instances the old plague pits were dug out in the shape of a long thin triangle and that the outline of the very large rectory garden followed the same pattern. Paul supervised a considerable amount of digging in the general area of the rectory and the work went on for nearly two years. At one stage he appealed for help and was offered the use of a mechanical digger. I am sure that this gesture was made with the best of intentions, but I do not think that the machine was appropriate for the task in hand. It enabled large quantities of rubble to be moved around quickly and this was done, but if two of the objects of the exercise were to unearth old and fragile bones and valuable pieces of metalware, then it seems that there was a considerable risk that they could have been damaged very seriously, or overlooked altogether. In fact, nothing of interest was discovered and Paul came to the conclusion that there was no point in continuing with the project. I should explain that Lanfranc was well aware of all this activity, but he did not regard it as being of any direct concern to him, because the rectory site had ceased a long time ago to be church property.

Fig 50. Stained glass window in Borley church dedicated to Susanna Herringham. The inscription reads: IN LOVING MEMORY OF / SUSANNA JACKSON HERRINGHAM / LATE OF OLD CLEEVE SOMERSET / WHO ENTERED INTO HER REST OCTOBER 5TH 1883 AGED 85

Rayner and Sewell and a few other volunteers, wished to continue with the digging and the work carried on for about another year until the autumn of 1957. Unfortunately, from the point of view of any further discoveries which may have been relevant to the alleged haunting, their painstaking and patient labours were not rewarded; there were no more human remains, nor church plate to be seen. However, from the point of view of local archaeology and local history, their work was of some interest. They unearthed many old walls and pipes of varying ages, which indicated that Borley Rectory had been built upon the site of more than one former house, but not of the legendary monastery. Sewell discovered some good documentary evidence which supports this theory. He obtained a copy of a tithe map of the area dated 1841. It showed a building of approximately the same size as the rectory cottage and in the same position and another house which occupied part of the site of the huge rectory which the Rev Henry Dawson Ellis Bull had had built in 1863. Almost certainly this

Fig 51. A mechanical excavator was used to help with the digging, circa 1955

was the home of the Herringham family who also produced two rectors of Borley, who were father and son. William was the incumbent from 1807 until 1819 and his son John was in post from the latter date until 1862[4]. It appears that the Herringham rectory did not exist for very long, because in 1848 it was described as being a modern building. Sewell found also another map of the area dated 1772 and this showed that at that time there were three buildings on this site. One was located where the Bull rectory was, another one was where the rectory cottage is still and a third where the present day farm barns are. The position of the last mentioned building is of some interest, as will become clear shortly.

The legend according to which there were underground tunnels in the Borley area had at least some basis in truth and it was during Lanfranc's incumbency that one of them was discovered. To be exact, it was rediscovered because it was broken into by a local labourer called Farrance, whilst he was working in the front garden of Borley Place. In fact he was repairing a wall and he was in the employ of the Rev Harry Bull at the time, which would appear to indicate that the incident must have occurred at some point during the second decade of the century. It has been said that Farrance endeavoured to explore the tunnel, but was unable to do so as he was driven back by the presence of foul air.

Two years after Lanfranc became the rector of Borley, the local authority arranged for the mains water supply to be brought to the hamlet. Not everybody benefited from the service and even today the occupants of some of the outlying properties have to rely upon

Fig 52. Excavating the cellars circa 1957

rainwater butts and hand pumps. However, the scheme had interesting consequences. On 12 September 1957, workmen were digging a trench in Hall Lane (and just outside the farm buildings which are located immediately across the road from Borley Place) when they broke into a tunnel with their mechanical digger. Leonard Sewell was contacted and he went up to Borley immediately, accompanied by a reporter from *The East Anglian Daily Times*. Sewell explored the tunnel to some extent on that day and also on subsequent days with his colleague, L G Rayner. To a very great extent this was made possible by the co-operation of the former Halstead Rural District Council and also the firm of contractors, Biggs Wall.

The discovery of the tunnel confirmed the belief of many local people that the road at this point had a hollow sound to it. Unlike Farrance, Sewell and Rayner had no problems with foul air and they were able to examine the tunnel in great detail and for some distance. They reported that the tunnel was constructed of red two-inch thick Tudor bricks which were still in good condition, although the floor was covered with earth[5]. The width of the tunnel was 32 inches, the height of the walls was 12 inches and the height of the arched roof at its central point was 28 inches. The tunnel ran at approximately right angles to the road and its northern end terminated in the front garden of Borley Place. At this point the condition of the tunnel had deteriorated somewhat and its progress was blocked by a brick wall, but its direction indicated that it would have linked up with the cellars of Borley Place. There is an alcove in the cellars at an appropriate point

Fig 53. Len Sewell in the tunnel, 1957

which could have been the position of the entrance to the northern end of the tunnel.

The tunnel went under the roadway at a depth of about a foot and its southern end emerged in the farmyard, or to be more exact, it petered out there. It was not possible to explore very far in this direction because the deterioration was more advanced than at the other (Borley Place) end and the tunnel was packed with hard clay. Nothing was found in the tunnel, but it was observed that it dipped under the roadway, with the result that the northern section was about a yard lower than the southern section. This appeared to be a deliberate feature of the construction and not the result of subsidence; the brickwork of that part of the tunnel which was under the road was in good condition and showed no signs of cracking.

I am puzzled as to the reason for the existence of the tunnel. I do not think that it was an old culvert and in any case the hamlet is still without main drainage. I feel that the tunnel was too large and elaborately constructed to be a land drain and in any event, both types of such subterranean passages need to be gently sloping and would be unlikely to have been constructed with a marked change in level at one point. Was the tunnel a secret link between Borley Place and the house which stood at one time across the road, as indicated on the map dated 1772? If this is the case, what was its purpose and why did somebody go to a considerable amount of trouble constructing it, let alone crawling through it? In view of its measurements, I cannot help thinking that this is perhaps what the tunnel was there for. On the other hand, I wonder why it was not possible nor perhaps prudent for somebody or other to do things the easy way and walk across the road from one building to the other? Was the existence of the tunnel something to do with the troubles of the Reformation? Did it have in any way a bearing on the alleged haunting? I doubt if we shall know ever the full answers to these questions and it remains to be seen as to whether or not any more such tunnels will be discovered at Borley.

Lanfranc would never initiate a discussion about the alleged haunting at Borley, but I propose to conclude this chapter by describing the experience of another priest, the late Canon Leslie Pennell and his wife Ursula[6]. James Henry Leslie Pennell was a tall, elderly Scotsman and not at all the sort of person who would have allowed his imagination to get out of control. The high peak of his career was his appointment as provost of St Andrew's Cathedral, Inverness from 1949 until 1965, when he reached the age of 60. He had decided already that when he achieved that age he would resign from this position and seek another one that would carry perhaps somewhat lighter responsibilities. It was partly as a result of that decision and partly due to the fact that Ursula was a native of East Anglia that they left Inverness in November 1965 and Leslie became the rector of Foxearth and Pentlow, residing in the former village. These two small parishes are located in north Essex and are very near to Borley and Liston.

The Pennells moved to Foxearth at the end of November and a few days later, on 3 December 1965, they drove down to the railway station at Long Melford in order to meet their son David and to take him back with them to their new home. The time was approximately eight o'clock and it was a wet evening. When they were driving away from the station and reached the point on the road to Foxearth between the turnings to Borley and Liston, they saw a hooded figure walk out immediately in front of them and had circumstances been normal, there is no way that an accident could have been avoided. The figure stepped into the road immediately in front of their vehicle. Ursula shouted out "you fool" and Leslie braked hard. Their vehicle at that time was a *Dormobile*, a small camper van with a very short bonnet, and the figure was only a few feet away from them. However, there was no impact and when they got out into the lane and searched the area there was nobody about. Both Leslie and Ursula saw the figure, which had crossed the roadway from right to left. They described the figure as bowed and wearing a hood and long robe which appeared to be dark grey in colour. They accept fully the fact that the headlights of a car can have a distorting effect upon colours.

I shall now comment upon a couple of minor points to do with this remarkable incident. One is the fact that David Pennell did not see the figure, although this is hardly surprising. He was sitting in the back of the *Dormobile*, there was no need for him to concentrate upon the driving conditions and he was quite unaware of anything untoward until his father applied the brakes so quickly. The other and slightly amusing aspect of the matter is that when it was written up in the local press, the reporter created the unfortunate impression that when

Fig 54. Ursula Pennell and the late Canon Leslie Pennell in the sitting room of their home in Hundon, a village not far from Borley

Ursula Pennell shouted out "you fool", she was addressing her husband. This was not the case, she was directing her remarks to the mysterious figure, who may or may not have been the phantom nun. I believe that the Pennell's extraordinary experience defies a normal explanation.

After having been the rector of Borley and Liston for twelve and a half years, Lanfranc took the living at Gestingthorpe, which is yet another nearby village in north Essex. He was truly the last rector to look after the two small parishes of Borley and Liston, because after our departure the church authorities decided to combine the living with that of Foxearth and Pentlow. Canon Pennell became the first of several priests to be responsible for the pastoral care of the group of four parishes.

CHAPTER EIGHT

The last widow of Borley
(by Claudine Mathias)

Fig 55. Claudine in 2002. Borley church in the background

Robert Wood wrote a book about Marianne Foyster called *The Widow of Borley*, published in 1992. My co-author and I feel that his title is misleading and rather illogical. As my late husband was the last rector of Borley and Liston, I trust that readers will feel that the title of this chapter is reasonably appropriate and will allow me to indulge myself a little in this regard.

After early consultations with the parochial church councils at Borley and Liston, my husband and I received an invitation to 'luncheon' with Miss Ethel Bull and her brother Alfred, who was still the patron of the living. We were to meet at The Four Swans Hotel in Sudbury. This very comfortable hotel was situated in North Street and coincidentally immediately across the road from The White Horse public house where the carpenter Fred Cartwright told Harry Price, and no doubt many other people, about his experiences at Borley, where he claimed that he had seen the phantom nun on four separate occasions. I felt that the use of the word 'luncheon' implied correctness and formality, so I decided that I ought to wear a hat and gloves and in the event I was proved right to do so. Of course, we knew that we were going to be 'put under the microscope' and that the Bulls wanted to assess their prospective new rector and his wife. However, it was also an opportunity for Lanfranc and me to observe two members of this by now famous family. Ethel Bull was one of the four sisters who had claimed that they had seen the spectral nun in the garden at Borley rectory on 28 July 1900 and she said that she had seen her on other occasions as well[1].

Ethel and her brother Alfred were elderly, very much gentlefolk and seemed to be rather like characters out of a Victorian or Edwardian play. Ethel was a small, bird-like lady and on this occasion she wore an enormous hat and also the obligatory gloves. She chatted away happily, but I remember that she had a slightly hesitant manner in her speech. She was very kind to us and seemed to be anything but a cantankerous old spinster, which description Robert Wood has applied to her and her sisters. Her brother Alfred was a tall, thin man and was slightly stooping. He was the less talkative of the two, but after we had finished our meal and were chatting away in a relaxed fashion, he began to say (although these were not perhaps his exact words): "How do you feel about the Borley gh.......?" He was not allowed to finish his question. Ethel interrupted swiftly and admonished him: "Shush! They don't know anything about it!" Alfred was somewhat deflated and did not refer to the matter again. It is of interest to students of the alleged haunting, possibly, that Ethel did not say anything to the effect that it was a hoax which she and her sisters had invented when they were young. We thought that the Bulls were charming people, although they gave the general impression that they had stepped out of a bygone era. In due course, they attended my husband's induction ceremony at Borley, but they did not take much part in parish affairs after that. Alfred died on 17 March 1956 and Ethel passed away on 29 April 1961,

Fig 56 (above). A contemporary photograph of the Four Swans Hotel in Sudbury. It was altered over the years and then gutted by a disastrous fire in March 1997 but the facade survived

Fig 57 (below). Thanks to planning legislation, the two shops now on the site were required to retain the facade more or less as it was before the fire. A 2002 photograph

Fig 58. The White Horse, almost opposite the Four Swans Hotel, is still a popular public house in Sudbury

at the age of 93. I remember her with a mixture of affection and a little amusement and cannot agree at all with Robert Wood's assessment of her.

In 1955 the then bishop of Chelmsford, Dr Faulkner Allison, was asked to choose a date for the induction service which was convenient for him, in view of the fact that (like all other bishops) he was committed to a very busy schedule. He selected 28 July and he could hardly have chosen a more controversial date if he had tried to do so. It was arranged that the service would be held at Borley church during the evening. Almost to the hour, this was the 55th anniversary of the occasion upon which Ethel Bull and three of her sisters maintained that they had seen the phantom of the nun in the rectory garden, which was situated on the other side of the narrow road and immediately opposite to the tiny church. Local tradition had it that the spectral lady appears always on this day of the year, but there is no valid reason to support such a belief at all. The irony of the situation was that the bishop was blissfully unaware of this aspect of the alleged haunting. It is clear from the advice that he gave to Lanfranc that he felt that the previous incumbent had spent too much of his time investigating the supernatural, perhaps to the detriment of his parishioners. Lanfranc's

Fig 59. The Old Rectory at Liston undergoing comprehensive refurbishment in 2001

first responsibility was to his official duties, an important part of which was the pastoral visiting. It was all put in a tactful and diplomatic way by the bishop, but the meaning was clear and Lanfranc was in full agreement with it anyway.

As always, the service of instituting a new incumbent to a living is a very moving and happy occasion. After the ceremony, everybody welcomed us and with much bell-ringing we walked out of the ancient church with the bishop to find ourselves face to face with a small army of newspaper reporters and photographers. Our first thought was that in country parishes the arrival of a new rector is big news. Of course, this was not the reason for so much excitement. The gentlemen of the press were well aware of the significance of 28 July. As we went to the car, several of the journalists tried to question us, but the bishop dealt firmly with the situation by saying to them: "I have nothing to add to my sermon, good evening!" And that was that. We were driven back to our rectory at Liston and to the best of my knowledge the elusive lady did not put in an appearance on that day.

People ask me very often if I have had any unusual experiences at Borley, to which question the short answer is that I have not. This should not be taken to mean that I do not believe in the paranormal in general and in this case in particular. The reality is that I was kept very busy as the wife of a country parson and the mother of three schoolchildren, and the rectory at Liston was a large Georgian house which had to be looked after. The two hamlets are situated about a mile apart and I never went up to Borley for the specific purpose of observation for long periods. We did not own a car and if I needed to go to Borley it was a matter of cycling or walking up the long hill which separates the two communities. Another aspect of the matter is whether or not one is sensitive to psychic activity and it is difficult to assess one's own degree of ability in this field. Perhaps the position is that some people would not see a ghost if it was standing right in front of them, whereas others could be very aware in such a situation; undoubtedly, yet other people suffer from hyperactive imaginations and their claims have to be treated with caution. It is very difficult to take a balanced view of the subject, but in this book my co-author and I are trying to do so.

We received many enquiries from people who were interested in the alleged haunting but it may help to put the matter into perspective if I describe some of the other aspects of my 12 1/2 happy but busy years at Borley and Liston. Parishes which have been combined have a 'time-share' in their clergyman. In the case of Borley-cum-Liston, the parochial church councils continued to operate separately and were responsible for their own programmes of financial management. The result for us was that my husband had to chair two parochial church council meetings at set intervals and had to look equally enthusiastic about two sets of fund-raising events in the two parishes. We had to cope therefore with a double dose of summer fêtes, garden parties, jumble sales and Christmas bazaars and, needless to say, Lanfranc avoided showing any bias in favour of one of the two parishes to the detriment of the other; any favouritism would have been noticed quickly. Everything went well in the two parishes and, although the money-raising events involved a lot of hard work, they created a lot of enjoyment and a good community spirit among the organisers.

There was also a lot to do in connection with running Liston Rectory. In his booklet, *Haunted Borley,* Mr Henning wrote that the house which became our home, enjoyed the benefits of electricity supply. This is not really very accurate. The rectory was not connected to the grid and our electricity, such as it was, came from an old generator which was housed in one of the outbuildings. For lighting we depended in the main on our collection of oil lamps. My husband made it his responsibility to attend to their cleaning and maintenance. There was no mains water supply in Liston when we moved there and water had to be pumped from a well up to the tanks in the attic.

One of the very irritating factors in our small rural community was that part of Lanfranc's stipend consisted of the rents in respect of the glebe land. He did not own this land (the church did) but owing to the system which was in force at the time, the procedure was that the tenant farmers paid the money directly to him. The problem was that some of them were very slow to pay which left us with the annoying and embarrassing task of having to keep sending out reminders to people who were our own parishioners.

One of the parishioners, who became a great friend of our family was the late Miss Violet Oates. She was one of two sisters of Capt Lawrence Oates, a member of the ill-fated Scott expedition to the Antarctic in 1911-1912. The family home was the Hall at nearby Gestingthorpe but, following the death of her mother, Violet Oates sold this huge house to a London business man and came to live in a more modest establishment at Liston. The Oates family were very wealthy and Violet was very generous to, and did a great deal of work for, Liston church. It was through her that I met the sister of Dr Wilson, another member of the Scott expedition who failed to return. We moved to Gestingthorpe not long after Violet Oates died and this was to be my husband's last incumbency.

Fig 60. The brass tablet dedicated to the memory of Capt Oates on the north wall of Gestingthorpe church. The badge is that of the 5th Royal Inniskilling Dragoon Guards. The inscription reads: IN MEMORY OF / A VERY GALLANT GENTLEMAN / LAWRENCE EDWARD GRACE OATES / CAPTAIN IN THE INNISKILLING DRAGOONS / BORN MARCH 17 1880 DIED MARCH 1912 / ON THE RETURN JOURNEY FROM THE SOUTH / POLE OF THE SCOTT ANTARCTIC EXPEDITION / WHEN ALL WERE BESET BY HARDSHIP HE / BEING GRAVELY INJURED WENT OUT INTO / THE BLIZZARD TO DIE IN THE HOPE THAT BY SO / DOING HE MIGHT ENABLE HIS COMRADES TO / REACH SAFETY. THIS TABLET IS PLACED / HERE IN AFFECTIONATE REMEMBRANCE BY / HIS BROTHER OFFICERS AD 1913

Although there was and is still, a constant stream of visitors who are aware of the alleged phenomena in varying degrees, nevertheless Borley is populated by ordinary people, most of whom are either involved with the farming industry or are retired. To the best of my knowledge they do not spend hours of their time in nocturnal vigil and some of them are sceptical of the whole matter. On the other hand, many people whom we shall meet later remain firmly convinced that they have had supernormal experiences there.

The ruins of the rectory and the garden were purchased by a Mr Woods, a demolition contractor. His objects in doing so were, first, to dismantle what was left of the rectory and sell the materials and second, to resell the land itself, obviously for profit. It was at this point, in the mid-1940s, that the huge garden was divided, because the south-eastern (and lower) part of it was bought by a local farmer, Tom Gooch. He built the first of the four bungalows which appeared eventually on the site for his own occupation. I came to know his wife well, as she was the church organist at Borley. The family were involved in what could be regarded as the later events at Borley. Gooch took part in a radio programme which consisted to a large extent of recordings which were made in the village and which included the sound of knocking, emanating apparently from the rectory cellars. They were full of rubble and the noises could have been caused by settlement, but it was claimed that these sounds commenced and ceased on request. The programme was broadcast on 29 June 1947.

A few years later, on 20 August 1949, Mrs Gooch claimed that a figure, dressed in light-coloured robes, was seen in her garden, the observer being a friend[2]. The figure vanished and did not reappear; a search revealed nothing and it is a matter of speculation as to whether or not this was another sighting of the phantom nun. Mrs Gooch claimed also that she had personal knowledge of the fact that on various occasions relatively heavy objects had been moved about inside Borley church during the night, when the building was locked. One of the former churchwardens, Mrs Pearson, was also aware of this apparently paranormal activity. These alleged events took place before Lanfranc became the rector, but Mr and Mrs Gooch did not seem to me to be at all the type of people who possessed unduly vivid imaginations, or were publicity seekers; indeed, they were practical and sensible country people. Tom Gooch died on 13 February 1974 and his wife Mabel passed away three years later.

The rectory cottage at Borley was not damaged by the fire which consumed the main building in February 1939; this was rather remarkable and fortunate in view of the fact that the two properties were only a few yards apart from each other. As we have seen, the well-known author James Turner purchased the cottage and most of the rectory garden in 1947, Tom Gooch having bought part of it a few years previously. The Turners lived there for nearly four years and moved partly because they were irritated by the constant stream of visitors, some of whom wandered around the grounds without permission. In 1951, the cottage and land were purchased by the Bacon family who lived there for over 20 years; in other words they were there during the whole of Lanfranc's incumbency. I knew Mr and Mrs Bacon quite well and my co-author met them on two quite separate occasions and discussed the alleged haunting with them. The family consisted of Robert and Betty Bacon, their son Terry, their daughter José and Mr and Mrs Williams, who were Mrs Bacon's parents. Mrs Williams died about four years after we came to the district. From time to time, there were foster children at the rectory cottage as well.

Bob Bacon as he was known locally, turned the place into a small-holding and he had sheds full of battery hens. Gradually, Bacon reduced the size of his business and it was he who sold most of the old rectory gardens as three separate plots. The family were very interested in the subject of the alleged haunting and were always willing to talk about the matter to visitors, once they had been assured that such 'visitors' were not in fact newspaper reporters who were short of good copy. Mrs Bacon had leanings towards spiritualism and many seances were held at the rectory cottage. Both her son and her father claimed to have seen the spectral nun on several occasions, although they did not discuss the matter with me.

Another person who claimed to have had some unusual

Fig 61. Betty Bacon in 1960

Fig 62. Bob Bacon, Philip Paul, who obtained the excavator, and Harry Williams, circa 1955

experiences at Borley and who became a good friend to us, was our family general practitioner, the late Dr Margaret Abernethy. She was the senior partner in a medical group based at nearby Long Melford and was very caring and efficient, but she was also a blunt, no-nonsense Scotswoman.

Dr Abernethy claimed that she saw the spectral nun on 26 July 1949 (was the lady two days early?), when she was driving up Hall Lane towards Borley in order to attend to one of her patients there. When she reached the part of the lane which was outside the rectory garden, she saw the figure of a nun standing by the hedge. The doctor continued on her journey for a few yards and then felt that perhaps she should have stopped and offered to give a lift to the nun. She reversed her car back to the point at which she had noticed the figure, but no one was to be seen. Margaret Abernethy said that the lady was solid in appearance and not in the least wraith-like. She said also that she had a good view of her face and that she seemed to be about 40 years old. Apparently, both the doctor and our predecessor, the Rev Alfred Clifford Henning, made local enquiries to try to find out if a nun had

Fig 63. Terry Bacon (left) with a friend on the Nun's Walk in the early 1950s

been in the Borley area on the day in question, but they met with no success. Dr Abernethy took part in a television programme about the alleged haunting at Borley and described her experience. The programme was transmitted on 31 October 1955, but the recently appointed rector and his wife were not invited to appear.

In addition to the television programme, the above incident was recorded in the Tabori-Underwood book *The Ghosts of Borley.'* However, Dr Abernethy told me that she had had a second uncanny experience at exactly same spot some years later and to the best of my knowledge this occurrence has not been reported elsewhere[3]. Not long after we had moved to the area, but following the television programme, Margaret Abernethy said that she had driven up the hill towards Borley and when she reached the point where she had seen the nun, she noticed that there was something lying on the road. The object was shining and when she drew close to it she saw it was a rosary. She stopped her car and got out with the intention of picking up the object. When she went to do so it had vanished. Dr Abernethy was not at all the type of person who would imagine things and I feel that it is very difficult to find an acceptable explanation for such incidents. Was the 'rosary' a trick of the sunlight which may have streamed suddenly through the trees, or was it a genuine supernormal phenomenon which linked up in some way with the doctor's previous experience at this spot? Certainly, there have been many comments to the effect that, working on the hypothesis that at least some of the phenomena were genuinely paranormal, there seems to have been a strong Roman Catholic theme attached to them. If the phantom nun had been a real person at some time, then she would have been a Roman Catholic and we remember the facts that Borley church would have been a Roman Catholic place of worship originally and also that the Waldegrave family, who were lords of the manor of Borley for approximately 300 years, were strong supporters of that faith.

Having written about the experiences of Dr Abernethy, I am reminded of a curious episode which involved her partner, Dr Margaret Hamp and myself. Whilst living at the Old Rectory at Liston, I suffered for a year or more from warts, which had appeared on the knuckles of both hands. Dr Hamp prescribed various lotions and treatments, but they had no effect on the condition. The warts were very unpleasant as well as being somewhat embarrassing and consequently I wore gloves frequently to cover them up. One day, Mr Ling, one of the elderly villagers, appeared at the rectory door with some flowers and I removed one of my gloves in order to take them from him. He saw the warts on my knuckles and asked how long I had had them. I told him that I had suffered from them for a very long time. "I can get rid of they", said Mr Ling. Within a few weeks the warts withered away and then they vanished altogether, leaving neither

Fig 64. An early 20th century photograph of Liston church

marks nor blemishes on my knuckles. Some time later Dr Hamp enquired about the warts and I told her what had happened. She showed no surprise at all and said in a matter-of-fact way, "Oh, he's a white witch." It would seem that the alleged haunting was not the only strange thing about Borley-cum-Liston and I am pleased to report that the warts never reappeared.

I shall conclude this chapter by relating some more details of some of the people who resided at Borley Rectory during the 1920s and 1930s. This information has been given to me by my friend Nancy Goodale (née Fisher) and sheds light on the quality of the reports of alleged phenomena[4]. Her father and grandfather were the rectors of Liston before that tiny parish was combined with Borley. The Rev Thomas Ruggles Fisher was the incumbent from 1857 until his death in 1893 and he was succeeded by his son, the Rev Stewart Travers Fisher, who remained in office until the amalgamation of the two parishes in 1936. Thus they held continuously the living for nearly 80 years and in the sense that there was a Bull dynasty at Pentlow and to a lesser extent at Borley, there was a Fisher dynasty at Liston; in the case of the latter two, it will be seen that they ran concurrently. However, Nancy did not live at the Old Rectory, which became eventually our home. Her father had spent his boyhood there and felt that he would like to live in his own modern house. Therefore he had one built and in due course he and his family occupied their private home which was known as the New Rectory. This house exists still and today is called 'Highfield'; Violet Oates lived here after the death of her mother.

Fig 65. A 2002 photograph of Liston church. No young ladies with their pony and trap — just the author on the churchyard wall

Fig 66. 'Highfield,' Liston

When Nancy Goodale was young and living at Liston she came to know very well the Bull family at Borley and briefly the Rev Guy Eric Smith and his wife. My friend described in some detail the many members of the Bull family, although she did so from a somewhat different vantage point from that of Margaret Finch. They were very old-fashioned people, but courteous and sociable and they loved to hold tennis parties in the summer. Some of the Bulls spoke in a rather hesitant way and all of them indulged in the peculiar habit of adding 'er' to their names when they were addressing each other. Thus Ethel would become 'Ethel-er', Harry would become 'Harry-er' and so on. Only Alfred appears to have escaped — he was known to the others as 'Ally'. This curious custom was noticed with much amusement by their friends, who referred to the family as the 'Bull-ers'. Nancy Goodale was well aware that their tranquil and congenial life style had been disrupted abruptly when the Rev Harry married Ivy Brackenbury. She remembers the 'new' Mrs Bull and her daughter very well. They were smart and up-to-date in appearance and manner and the contrast between them and the old-fashioned and rather frumpish Bull sisters could hardly have been greater. The two sets of women did not like each other and there is little doubt that this factor put pressure on the marriage. My friend feels that it may not have been a very happy one, which supports rather the views of Margaret Finch.

Nancy Goodale's mother experienced an apparently supernormal incident at Borley Rectory; as many other people had done before, she heard mysterious footsteps when no one else was about. The Rev

117

Fig 67. The Bull family graves in Great Cornard churchyard

Stewart Fisher and his wife had spent an evening at the rectory as the guests of Harry and Ivy Bull, which dates the visit as being in the early or middle part of the 1920s. It seems that it started to snow heavily and it was decided that the Fishers would sleep at Borley and return to Liston on the following day. When the time came for them to leave in the morning, Mrs Fisher was the first to move away from the front door of the rectory. As she walked towards the main gate at the lower end of the driveway, she heard the sound of footsteps crunching in the snow behind her and assumed that they were those of her husband. When she turned round he was not there and neither was anybody else. No doubt he was having a brief parting conversation with his hosts and he had not left the rectory at the time when Mrs Fisher thought that he was following her. My friend said that her father and Harry Bull knew each other very well and that the latter spoke frequently about his paranormal experiences at Borley. He claimed that he saw the phantom of the nun and saw and heard the mysterious coach on many occasions. The unaccountable ringing of the house-bells used to upset him greatly, as he believed that this was a precursor of bad news for himself and/or his family. There is no doubt that he was somewhat eccentric, as were his many brothers and sisters. However, there were a few nods in the direction of the 20th century. It seems that Harry Bull and his youngest sister, Kathleen, bought and learned to drive motor cars. One can hope only that they did so in not too eccentric a fashion.

Nancy Goodale's recollections of Mrs Mabel Smith are somewhat at variance with that lady's nervy and shy image. According to my friend, who met her on only a few occasions, Mrs Smith said that she was 'going to make Borley hum!' It would appear from this remark that she may have had more than a little to do with her husband's letter to the editor of *The Daily Mirror* seeking help with their paranormal problems; and also that she may have felt that the ensuing publicity would have assisted with the placement of her novel (*Murder at the Parsonage*), with one of the major publishing companies. If this was the case, then her letter to *The Church Times* in 1945 appears to make her seem hypocritical, unless she had become indeed vague and forgetful by that time. Perhaps she should be given the benefit of the doubt.

Nancy Goodale's only memory of the Foyster 'family' is that she met the Rev Lionel Algernon on one occasion and that he seemed to be a very sick man. The occasion was a garden party at Borley Rectory and Nancy recalls that the food was awful.

CHAPTER NINE

The vanishing lady and other reports.

Assuming that at least some of the reported phenomena were genuine, one of the truly remarkable facts about the Borley saga is that they have continued for such a long period of time. The destruction of the rectory itself had an effect on the volume and frequency of such reports, but we have to remember that many of them were concerned with incidents in the general area and not in the building itself. This had been the case always and most definitely it was not a matter of the ghosts transferring themselves conveniently across the road to the church after the rectory was destroyed by fire in 1939 and the last traces of the house were removed by Mr Woods and his demolition workers in 1944, as the sceptics have claimed. Sightings of the spectral nun have been reported as having occurred in the rectory garden, the churchyard and at many points up and down Hall Lane. We shall consider now some more of these alleged sightings and we have to emphasise that they are only a few out of many such reports.

In the early 1970s a small research group based at Harlow in the western part of Essex decided to concentrate their efforts upon the Borley case. The group was led by Geoffrey Croom-Hollingsworth and Roy Potter and together with their friends they spent many cold nights waiting and watching at Borley[1]. They decided also to make use of modern technology and their considerable amount of equipment included tape-recorders and short-range radio transmitters and receivers ('walkie-talkie' sets). The group claimed to have heard and recorded many sounds emanating from the secured and unoccupied church and which could not be accounted for normally. They included music and voices, rappings and sounds rather like heavy furniture being moved about. On one occasion, at approximately three o'clock in the morning, they heard the sounds of voices and laughter as if a party was being held and the noises appeared to originate from the lower end of Hall Lane. Potter cruised down the hill in his car, but with the engine switched off and could see no one about, nor find any reason to account for these sounds. He reported this to his colleagues by means of his radio transmitter and it was agreed that they would carry out an experiment. As he returned back up the hill, he stopped at various points and shouted. His friends could not hear his cries at the farthest point and he became audible to them only when he was relatively near to them. This experience seems to be very similar to the ones reported by James Turner and his wife in June 1947 (see chapter five). To return to the 1970s and to Roy Potter's experiment, the night was said to be a misty one and we wonder if one of the local insomniacs, or perhaps a furtive poacher, reported solemnly in due course that he had heard the sound of anguished cries near to the site of the 'haunted rectory'. We are not being totally flippant in making this observation, rather we are drawing attention to the fact that there is always the need to exercise caution in regard to reports of alleged phenomena.

There is another aspect of the Harlow group's experience which should be discussed. It is an established fact that sound travels for long distances in fog and mist when conditions are still, as indeed they must be otherwise the fog would be blown away. Foggy conditions are often due to a temperature inversion which means that instead of the air becoming colder the higher above the ground one goes, it becomes warmer. This effect causes sound waves to bend downwards and return to earth, rather than being bent upwards and being lost in space. However, on this occasion, and assuming for the moment a normal explanation for the sounds, we wonder where the source was and we remind ourselves that Roy Potter was unable to locate it . For the benefit of readers who are unfamiliar with the district, Borley is situated in a very thinly populated farming area. The place itself a tiny and scattered community, hardly worth calling a village, notwithstanding the presence of its church.

The high point of the investigation by the Harlow group came during the night of 19 June 1970, when three of the members claimed to have seen the ghostly nun and to have kept her under observation for a period of about 12 minutes. Geoffrey Croom-Hollingsworth was the first to see her at ten minutes to two (am). He felt suddenly extremely cold as he watched the figure proceed across the gardens of the bungalows towards the rectory cottage. The nun passed through an old fence as if it were not there and appeared to be gliding along just above the ground rather that walking on it. Croom-Hollingsworth contacted his two colleagues on his short-wave radio and told them that he had seen an apparition which was approaching them. At this time they were standing in Hall Lane by the churchyard. Then the mysterious figure turned round and moved back towards the bungalows and one of the observers who had been alerted by radio saw two people near to each other. One of them was Croom-Hollingsworth and the other was the nun. As noted during previous sightings, her robes appeared to be grey rather then black. Croom-Hollingsworth said that she was facing him at a distance of about 15 feet and that he was able to observe her appearance carefully. Her eyes were shut and her expression was sad; she looked elderly and had a mole or some such blemish on her left cheek. Her head and shoulders were covered by a cowl and she wore dark grey robes which reached down to and covered her feet. The other two observers experienced also the feeling of intense cold, which is hardly surprising and one of them (Roy Potter) moved to a position in which he was only about 20 feet away from the figure. Finally, the spectral nun turned again, glided away towards the farmland at the back of the bungalows (that is, in a south-westerly direction) and vanished.

As ever one has to be cautious, but this would appear to have been one of the most remarkable sightings of the apparition of the nun since the famous occasion on 28 July 1900, when four of the Misses Bull claimed to have observed her simultaneously. On both dates the figure was visible for relatively long periods of time. On the first occasion, it was possible for one of three sisters to go to fetch a fourth one and the spectral nun was still on view when she arrived; on the second occasion it was claimed that the elusive lady's perambulations were observed at very close quarters for about 12 minutes by the three men. Interestingly, Croom-Hollingsworth's assessment of this nun's age does not seem to support the legend of the eloping nun and monk, nor the 'Marie Lairre' theory. Readers will recall that according to a planchette message this young lady was a novice who claimed to have been murdered in 1667 by a member of the Waldegrave family when she was only 19 years old. It will be remembered also that Dr Abernethy claimed to have seen the nun's face and thought that she looked about 40 years of age. One possibility is that the planchette information was quite incorrect and that the relationship between the mysterious lady and the Waldegrave family may have been far more harmonious than indicated by that source. The Waldegraves were aristocrats, wealthy landowners and they were staunch Roman Catholics. It is perfectly reasonable to postulate that the Borley branch of the family may have included a nun among the members of the household.

To revert to the experience of the Harlow psychical research group, Croom-Hollingsworth is reported to have said of the Borley case that the issue is not about the authenticity of some of Harry Price's early claims, rather it is about the possibility that the hamlet may be indeed a haunted place; hardly surprisingly, he came to the firm conclusion that it is. Following the investigations of the Harlow group, several interesting tape recordings were made in Borley church during the 1970s, some of which were used as the basis of a BBC television programme. However, permission for this type of research is granted only on rare occasions now, because of the regrettable amount of vandalism that has been inflicted upon the church itself and some of the graves (including that of the Rev Harry Bull) in the churchyard.

Another reported sighting of the spectral nun has come to us from Mrs Hilary Wright[2]. She is a former resident of Borley and lives now in a small Suffolk town. We interviewed her about her experiences on two

Fig 68. Official opening of Borley bridge (or Rodbridge as it is now often called) in 1911 with a parade of steam traction engines

occasions in 1995 and she told us that she saw the figure of the nun one night during the autumn of 1971. Perhaps we should say at this juncture that we feel sure that readers will understand that many responsible witnesses are unable to be precise about dates. In our opinion this does not detract from the value of their reports and we feel that critics of the case are incorrect to maintain that it does. Even residents of Borley, so far as we are aware, do not announce at their breakfast tables that they propose to see a ghost at some time during the course of the day. When sightings take place, usually the people concerned are so shocked and surprised that they neglect to make detailed notes of what they have seen and it is only reasonable to make allowance for the fact that most of them do not enjoy the benefits of being trained and serious investigators.

To return to Mrs Wright and the autumn of 1971, she was being driven home at about two o'clock in the morning, after having attended a social function. It was a clear moonlit night and the visibility was good. Her companion drove from Rodbridge Corner and over the bridge itself into Essex. Both of them saw the figure of a nun standing just beyond the end of the bridge and to their left, slightly before the turning which leads up to Borley. This is known as Lower Road and it becomes Hall Lane at the sharp curve near the entrance to Borley Mill. Mrs Wright told us that she was not able to discern any details of her features, but she said that the figure was dressed in long grey robes and appeared to be either rather tall, or "standing upon high ground which is no longer there." Presumably because they were in the

Fig 69. Pond Cottage, Borley, in 2002 with the church tower showing over the roof

car, she and her companion did not notice any sudden drop in temperature, but over and above being very surprised Mrs Wright experienced a most unpleasant feeling which she described as 'bad vibes'. She is a former nurse and seemed to us to be a reliable witness.

In August 1974 Mrs Wright was living at Pond Cottage, which is situated very near to the site of Borley Rectory and took part in a BBC television programme which was filmed at her home. The host of the programme was Peter Underwood and Mrs Wright and others (including her mother, whom we shall meet shortly and the late Canon Pennell and Mrs Pennell) related their experiences at Borley. For their efforts the participants received the generous reward of £10 each.

The late Marie Poore was Hilary Wright's mother and is our next witness[3]. The two ladies who lived fairly near to each other, were frequently together and we discussed the alleged haunting at Borley with both of them on the same occasions. Mrs Poore moved to Borley with her late husband upon his retirement. They came from the Middlesex area and purchased a bungalow which they called The Willows and which is situated in Lower Road. When they lived there, theirs was the first residence as one approached the hamlet of Borley from the direction of Rodbridge Corner. This is no longer the case, but Mrs Poore told us that they were disturbed frequently by strangers who asked to be directed to the church and even to the haunted rectory. This was 30 and more years after the place had been destroyed by fire.

Mrs Poore told us about a remarkable experience which occurred

Fig 70. The late Marie Poore (left) and Hilary Wright
in Mrs Poore's home in Lavenham.

one autumn evening during the early 1970s. At the time she was involved with a local dramatic society and was in the process of producing a pantomime which was to be performed at the Theatre Royal in Bury St Edmunds. After a rehearsal, she was being driven home by her husband and when they reached Rodbridge Corner it was approximately midnight. It was a clear night and the visibility was good. As they crossed the bridge and were about to turn to the left into Lower Road, both of them saw what appeared to be an old-fashioned coach coming across the large and sloping field which is to the rear of The Willows. The coach was travelling towards them and before it vanished suddenly Mrs Poore was able to take note of the facts that it was horsedrawn and had small lamps attached to it. Mr and Mrs Poore were astonished at what they had seen and they felt quite sure that it was not a modern tractor being used at night with the aid of powerful headlights, which is a fairly common practice in the autumn. Mrs Poore was aware of the Borley legends, but her husband was completely unable to find an explanation for what he had seen. There were two strange consequences to this experience. First, Mr Poore examined the field on the morning after they had seen the apparition of the coach; there were no tyre marks, nor wheel marks, nor hoof marks in the area at all. Second, when Mrs Poore was relating her experience to an elderly resident a few days later, she was told that there was an old belief to the effect that originally the road between Borley and Rodbridge was straight and did not follow the present route of Hall Lane and Lower Road, which is approximately L-shaped. It would appear therefore that the mysterious coach was travelling on the line of the old road. It is interesting to note that there is and always

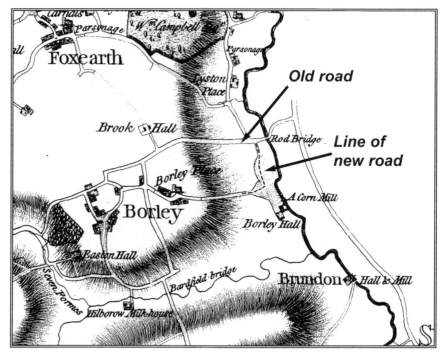

Fig 71. This map dated 1777 shows the original route of the road from Rodbridge to Borley

has been a public footpath on this line and a map dated 1777 confirms that it was indeed the original highway to Borley.

Mrs Poore told us about another fascinating link with the Borley saga. Whilst living there she had many friends, including the Payne family who lived at Borley Place and others. Through one of her contacts she met a lady called Eileen Livock, who lived at Sudbury and who had known the Bull family well. She showed Mrs Poore a diary which had been kept by Ethel Bull when she was young. Apparently the diary was more like a school exercise book than a pocket book and the entries were written in pencil. They included comments to the general effect that 'we saw the nun in the garden today.' We have tried, unsuccessfully so far, to locate this document which obviously would be of the greatest interest.

Another possible sighting of the Borley nun was related to us by Dorothy Lane (née Tabbart) whom we interviewed in November 1995, at her home in a Suffolk village[4]. She told us that her experience took place in the early part of the summer of 1944 just after the invasion of Europe by the Allied forces, which commenced on 6 June. During the war, she served in the NAAFI[5]. and was stationed at Liston Hall, most of which is no longer in existence. At this time, most of the service personnel were accommodated in Nissen huts[6] erected in the Hall grounds. Mrs Lane, who was then 20 years old, slept in one of the huts with three other young ladies. She awoke suddenly at five o'clock one morning and saw that a shadowy figure dressed in long grey robes was standing at her bedside. She was very frightened, but did not get any sensation of malevolence from the presence. She put out her hand and would have touched the figure if it had been solid. She felt nothing and then she screamed and woke up the other three young ladies in the hut. She told them what she had seen and they believed her because it was clear to them that she was very shocked. She remained so for several days and had the feeling that what she had seen may have been some sort of a premonition, but in fact nothing untoward happened to her. Mrs Lane told us that at the time that she saw the figure the black-out screens were in position and that because of this factor, she was unable to make out any details of the features. She said that the figure, which was of average height, stood still for about ten seconds, then faded away gradually — it did not vanish suddenly.

Mrs Lane informed us that a few years after this experience, she learned from a radio broadcast about the alleged haunting at Borley that the human remains which were discovered under the floor of the cellars of the former rectory had been buried by the Rev Alfred Clifford Henning in the graveyard at Liston; naturally, this information made her wonder if the figure which she had seen was the Borley nun. On the one hand, we explained to Mrs Lane that the remains were not interred until 29 May 1945, that is, almost a year after she had seen the figure by the bed[7]. On the other hand, we have to remind ourselves that the accounts given to us by Canon Leslie Pennell and his wife, and also by Hilary Wright, would seem to indicate that the phantom of the nun has been seen in the district in general and not only in the vicinity of the rectory grounds. It is very difficult to come to any definite conclusion and we can report only that Mrs Lane is adamant that her experience was real and not imagined. It was something which she will never forget.

During the course of our investigation we interviewed Thomas Musk in November 1995[8]. He has lived not far from Borley for many years and was very interested in the alleged haunting there. He told us of an experience which he and three friends had had near to Borley church during the late autumn of 1987. He and his friends decided to carry out a little investigating of their own and to spend a whole night at Borley, watching and listening for anything unusual. They took with them a tent and camping equipment and set it all up not too far away from the church. To their disappointment they neither saw nor heard anything of interest during the early part of the night, so they decided to try to get some sleep. At four o'clock in the morning they were awoken by the sound of footsteps walking around their tent. It was still dark and Mr Musk said that it was a cold, frosty morning and that the footsteps produced a crisp sound on the whitened ground and leaves. He calculated that the sounds lasted for about one minute and then ceased. The flap of the tent was unfastened immediately, but no one else was about. The four friends were rather alarmed, first of all because they thought it was possible that they may have been asked to pack up their camping equipment and leave and second, because after a few moments they realised that there seemed to be no normal explanation for the footsteps which they had heard. We do not know if the friends noticed any footprints in the frost or not.

Thomas Musk and his friends tried to get back to sleep again, but their adventure was not over yet. Approximately half an hour later they heard the sound of music coming from the church, which was locked. The music lasted for between five and ten minutes and Mr Musk described it in some detail. He said that it was properly constructed music rather than jumbled sounds, that it was instrumental and not vocal and that it sounded like an old gramophone record. We feel that this is an interesting description; the organ in Borley church is a relatively small and old instrument and originally it had to be pumped by hand, before eventually an electrical device was fitted to it. It occurs to us that this organ would sound indeed like an old gramophone record if one was listening to it from a distance outside the building, the doors and windows of which were closed. We suppose that it is possible, but extremely unlikely at that hour in the morning, that somebody was operating a gramophone with the object of trying to frighten Mr Musk and his friends away. Our comments on this particular experience are two-fold: first, that the sounds of the footsteps and then the music were heard by all four members of the group and second, that there is nothing new about these alleged phenomena. With regard to the second point, the sound of footsteps in the area when nobody else was about have been described by many different people on many different occasions and there has been a number of reports of the sound of music emanating from Borley church when the building was locked and empty (see chapter five).

The organ in Borley church seems to have behaved in a perverse manner on a number of occasions, We have another account of its eccentricities from the late Mr Gerald Hazell, who lived in a small Suffolk village not far from Borley. He told one of us (EB) that he knew the late Mrs Maud Stearn, who was a relief organist in the area and who lived at The Vicarage, Lindsey, Suffolk[9]. She described an unusual incident which happened at Borley. She had been asked to play for a service there and when she was walking towards the church she was surprised and very annoyed to hear the organ being played, apparently by someone else. However, when she reached the porch the music ceased and when she entered the building, there was no one else present. This incident was confirmed later by Mr Hazell's brother and it can be dated to 1955; shortly afterwards Mrs Stearn moved away from Lindsey. The phenomenon may have caused her to have been surprised and annoyed but it was an exact repetition of the experiences of Mr E W Jephcott and also the Rev Alfred Clifford Henning and Mrs

Walrond in September and October 1947 (see chapter five).

CM remembers Mrs Stearn very well and we remind ourselves that the Rev Lanfranc Mathias was the rector of Borley and Liston when the above occurrence took place. Mrs Stearn drove an Austin *Seven* from Lindsey to the various churches where she played for the services. She played sometimes at Borley but more frequently at Liston church which did not have a regular organist at the time. CM also remembers Lanfranc's reaction when Mrs Stearn described her experience to local residents: "It would be best if the children did not hear about this," he said.

Another person who claimed to have seen an apparition in Hall Lane, Borley, and just outside the rectory grounds, was the late Canon Edward Powell, who died on 14 November 1994[10]. Canon Powell was a well-known and much respected figure in the north Essex area. He was the vicar of the parish of Belchamp St Paul, which is only a few miles from Borley, until his retirement (at the age of 80!) in 1989. He was for many years the rural dean and in addition to his ecclesiastical duties he was active in local government. He was the chairman of the parish council (the local government unit) and also he was elected to

Fig 72. Canon Powell (second left), at his retirement celebrations at Belchamp St Paul Community House, December 1988. Also in the picture are the Ven Ernest Stroud (left), Archdeacon of Colchester, Mrs Anne Powell and Mrs Mary Cutts, head teacher at the village school. She retired in 1969 after 60 years at the school as pupil and teacher

serve on Braintree District Council. It is said to be largely as the result of his recommendations that the remote and isolated hamlet of Belchamp St Paul has a fine community centre and enjoys the facilities of main drainage; the latter is not the case in nearly all of the surrounding villages and hamlets, including Borley. In addition to all of this, Canon Powell ran educational courses, the purpose of which was to prepare young people for entry into the various public schools and similar establishments. In other words, the Canon was one of the old style 'crammers'. He described himself as 'the last of the autocratic clergy' and we can imagine that his pupils, and perhaps some of his parishioners, regarded him as being a somewhat awesome character.

It was on one afternoon during the early 1960s that Canon Powell cycled over to the Rodbridge area of Borley in order to visit a friend who was ill. He knew the sick person well and was not 'poaching' in Lanfranc's parish. After having seen his friend, Canon Powell set out on his journey home and his route took him past Borley church, which would have been to his right and the old rectory grounds, which would have been to his left. When he had cycled up Hall Lane and reached this point, a shadowy figure dressed in long robes moved out onto the road in front of him, coming from his left and then 'melted' back into the hedge from whence it had appeared. After overcoming his surprise, Canon Powell got off of his bicycle and went into the former rectory garden in order to see if anybody was there. Despite a careful search he could find no one and he noted that there was not much cover because the area had been cleared in preparation for the commencement of the building of the bungalows which stand there today. Tom Gooch's bungalow was there already, but it is situated at the eastern (lower) end of the original garden and the Canon had cycled well past that point. He noted that although there were no workmen on the site, the light was still quite good. We hope that we have given the correct impression that the Canon was a redoubtable personality; he was definite that 'he saw what he saw,' he was at a loss to find a logical explanation for this incident and he expressed the firm opinion to his acquaintances that Borley was indeed a haunted place.

Whilst we were preparing this work, we were contacted by Mrs Gillian Cook, who lives in a large town in Essex[11]. She reported to us that she had had a curious experience in the churchyard of Borley on 6 August 1991; she was able to be precise about the date because she suffered a family bereavement on the following day. A friend, Mrs Cook and her two children decided to visit Kentwell Hall, which is one of the two Elizabethan mansions at nearby Long Melford, the other one being Melford Hall. Their route took them through Borley and they thought that they would have a look around the church and graveyard as they had heard about the alleged haunting there. Their friend parked the car near to the churchyard and the four people got out. They wandered about for a short while and for no apparent reason Mrs Cook found herself drawn to one of the graves marked with a rusty

Fig 73 (above). Kentwell Hall. This fine Tudor house is now open to the public and many events are held here, ranging from Elizabethan days and farmers' markets to Glenn Miller style big band concerts

Fig 74 (below). Melford Hall. Lucky Long Melford has two Tudor halls; this one is also open to the public and is in the care of the Nationanl Trust. Queen Elizabeth the First stayed here

iron cross, situated to the north side of the church, adjacent to the farmland. Then the two friends and the children returned to the car and had a picnic lunch. After they had eaten, Mrs Cook went for a stroll in the cornfield; she was rather frightened when a pheasant flew up just in front of her, so she turned round with the intention of walking back through the churchyard to the car. She found herself by the grave which had attracted her attention earlier and was astonished to see that at the foot of the metal cross, there was a gold-coloured bracelet lying on the ground. She was convinced that it had not been there when she had stopped by the grave on the first occasion. She picked it up, returned to the car and the group drove to Kentwell Hall.

There was a sequel to this strange incident. As there was no means of identifying the original owner of the bracelet, Mrs Cook decided to keep it and to wear it, but about a week later she lost it temporarily. Whilst walking with her children to school, the delicate chain of the bracelet snapped and it slipped off of her wrist without her noticing it. Mrs Cook did notice, however, that it was missing when she got to the school. On her return journey she was very surprised to see the bracelet lying on the pavement. This was on a busy route and she felt that it was extraordinary that no one else appeared to have seen the shiny object, nor to have picked it up. Mrs Cook retrieved the bracelet and has it still. It consists of a fine chain and a small heart-shaped lock; the whole article is gold coloured and similar items can be seen frequently. This is a curious affair and we regard the discovery of the bracelet on the grave as the more remarkable part of it, although the temporary loss of and the finding again of the object, is also rather peculiar. With regard to the first part of the experience, we consider that it may be excessive to claim that the bracelet was an apport, that is, a solid object which has appeared, or re-appeared, without the

Fig 75. Mrs Cook and the bracelet in 2002. She has never had it repaired and says she would never wear it

Fig 76. The grave where Mrs Cook found the bracelet. The chances of spotting it in such an overgrown environment were very slim

assistance of normal agencies. Nevertheless, it is a strange business and we felt that it should be recorded in this book.

The final section of this chapter could be accorded the sub-title of 'pets corner'. There have been reports over a period of many years of 'vanishing' cats at Borley. In their book *The Ghosts of Borley*, Peter Underwood and Paul Tabori related experiences to do with mysterious cats which were reported by two well-known authors, James Wentworth Day and James Turner, the second of whom owned and occupied the rectory cottage during the latter part of the 1940s.

Mr Wentworth Day (also a resident of Essex) said that he spent a night at Borley about four months after the fire which destroyed the rectory, which would date the incident as having taken place in late June or early July 1939[12]. He was accompanied by a friend and the night was clear with good visibility. The two men explored the ground floor of the ruined rectory, but when Wentworth Day suggested that they should go upstairs and have a look at what was left of the first floor, his companion refused to do so and said that he felt that there was an evil presence up there. Instead, they went out into the moonlit garden and after a short time during which they kept the ruins under observation, a huge black cat jumped between Wentworth Day's legs and ran into the rectory. They did not see the animal come out again, but it may have left by another route (most of the windows were smashed), or quite simply it remained in the huge building.

Wentworth Day told the authors of *The Ghosts of Borley* that a colleague of his, a London journalist, had exactly the same experience on another occasion. When that gentleman made some local enquiries about the huge black cat, he was told that no such animal was kept in the area, but that there had been many reports that the creature had been seen, always rushing into the ruined building but never coming out of it. Of course, it is quite possible that it could have been a feral cat, but these incidents could link up with some previously unpublished statements which we shall come to shortly.

James Turner and his wife kept two cats during the years when they lived at Borley and in addition to these flesh-and-blood specimens they were convinced that there was a phantom cat around the rectory cottage as well and claimed that their pets reacted to its presence on a number of occasions[13]. The Turners noted the date of one of the later incidents which took place; it was during the early hours of the morning of 6 March 1950. At the time they had a friend staying with them. He was the Rev John Dening, who was very interested in the alleged haunting at Borley and who took part in some of the later excavations there. On the night in question, he had retired soon after midnight and the Turners were preparing to do the same. One of their cats was indoors with them and the other had been let out a few moments earlier. Suddenly, there was a loud noise of a cat squealing; the sound came from within the rectory cottage and the Turners felt sure that it had originated from upstairs. They checked that their cats were not on the landing; one continued to doze on the settee and the other one was still outside. The following morning, Dening reported that he had fallen asleep immediately after he went to bed and had not been disturbed. We do not know if he suffered from nightmares and was responsible unwittingly for the squealing sound. Also, we must draw the attention of readers to the fact that the rectory cottage is not situated in a central position in its garden. It is only about six feet from the road and it is perhaps the case that a stray cat, or possibly a fox, was responsible for the noise and that due to some acoustic quirk the sound appeared to come from the first floor of the building.

The authors of *The Ghosts of Borley* said that after the Turners left the hamlet (in 1950), there were no further reports of any spectral cats. However, we are able to offer what we feel was an extraordinary experience which occurred approximately two years after that related by James Wentworth Day. It was reported to us by the late Russell Herbert, BEM[14]. He was born in 1922, spent his early years in Sudbury and dates the following incidents as having occurred in 1941. One hot and sunny summer day, he and some of his friends (of both sexes) decided to go for a long hike across the fields and out into the countryside. Their route took them past the attractive Brundon Mill, which is still in existence and then up the hill towards Borley. When the group reached the hamlet, the young Russell Herbert felt the need to answer the call of nature, so he went into the rectory grounds in order not to be visible from the road. He remembers well opening one of the main gates, which at that time was painted a creamy colour and walking down the gravel driveway which was lined with tall trees, most of them firs and cedars. He told us that as he approached the ruined rectory, he became aware suddenly of a feeling of intense cold

Fig 77. This lovely old mill at Brundon is one of many along the river Stour. Moving north, the next two are at Borley and Liston at intervals of about a mile

and an awful smell which reminded him of rotting vegetation. Then, as he looked towards the house, he saw three large cats which were arching their backs and hissing. He continued to walk in their direction and they vanished. Herbert was very definite that they did not run away into the undergrowth; one second the animals were in front of him and the next second they were not there.

Herbert was so scared that he forgot his rather pressing problem and ran back to join his friends in Hall Lane. They said to him, "You look awful. Don't you feel well?" Then one of the girls asked him if he had seen the Borley ghost, which remark caused the others to laugh. Herbert told us that his experience had made him feel very frightened and that he would not like to go through it again. He said that when he went into the rectory grounds he had had only one thought in mind and that it was nothing to do with the alleged haunting.

We noted with interest that Herbert said that when he was a boy and living in Sudbury, there was much talk of the 'Borley ghost'. He told us that the general view was that some of the accounts were 'a bit far-fetched, but that sensible people all believed that there was something awry at Borley.' We feel that if this statement were to be couched in official terminology, then the balance of probability is that it would be acceptable to the majority.

With regard to the mysterious cats, the fundamental question is, of course, whether they were of psychic origin or whether there was a normal explanation for their presence. We are impressed especially with the testimony of Russell Herbert, but in every case of a visual experience, the witnesses are very definite in their statements to the effect that the animals vanished instantly and that they did not run away quickly to the nearest cover.

As a footnote, two later accounts were reported to us by Hilary Wright and Marie Poore[15]. Mrs Wright said that during the summer of 1974 she was being driven through Borley at dusk in good weather and visibility. Driving from Rodbridge corner towards the church, a large cat dashed out into the road and then vanished. The driver did not see the animal but Hilary Wright remembers the exact spot at which the sighting occurred, Marie Poore claims also to have seen a cat on a different occasion which vanished, at the same location and during the same year. Again the night was clear and visibility good.

In March 1937 the then Archbishop of Canterbury instituted an enquiry into the questions of psychical research and spiritualism. It was not the first time that the Church had considered these matters and nor was it the last time. However, on this particular occasion, the Commission debated the premise that if it were possible for human beings to survive physical death, then there was no reason to assume that animals could not do likewise[16]. Flowing from this line of argument and if we are prepared to accept the possibility that from time to time the dead are able to appear to us, then it is reasonable to assume that departed animals may be able to do the same. We suggest that there are three hypotheses: first, the cats which have been under discussion were indeed phantoms; second, their presence was due to the fact that some of the Rev Harry Bull's many pets of this species were afflicted from time to time with 'spring fever'; and third, taking the alleged phenomena as a whole, there may have been a mixture of the first and second possibilities.

CHAPTER TEN

Further experiences and an exciting discovery

Dr Margaret Abernethy was not the only local medical practitioner who claimed to have witnessed paranormal phenomena at Borley. Dr Alec Ritchie, who had a practice at another nearby village, Cavendish, alleged that further apparently inexplicable events had occurred there in his presence.

Both Dr Ritchie and his son Ted have died. Our friend Nancy Goodale knew Ted well and he described his own and his father's experiences at Borley to her. Indeed, she discussed the case with him on our behalf[1]. When Ted Ritchie was in his late 'teens, sometimes he would go out with his father when the latter was visiting patients at their home addresses. One of Dr Ritchie's patients at Borley was Marianne Foyster, so it is possible to date these experiences as having taken place between October 1930 and October 1935. These were the dates of the Foyster incumbency, although as we know, it was frequently the case that Marianne was absent because she hated the boredom and loneliness of Borley. On the other hand, her elderly and frail 'husband,' the Rev Lionel Algernon, considered it to be his duty to stay there and look after his flock, notwithstanding the coldness and lack of comforts in the huge rectory and also the activities of what he called 'the goblins.'

Dr Ritchie claimed to have experienced two examples of paranormal phenomena in Borley Rectory. On one occasion, when he was in Marianne's bedroom and the patient herself was in bed, a medicine bottle which was placed on a bedside table rose up into the air and then came down again, without breaking and without any human assistance. Dr Ritchie is quite definite that Marianne remained in bed and neither stretched her arm out nor touched the bottle in any way. Sceptics have drawn attention to the fact that when Marianne was interrogated many years later by a tough American private detective about her life at Borley Rectory, she admitted that she had faked phenomena there. However, on other occasions she denied having done so flatly; telling the truth was not one of her major accomplishments. One is driven to the conclusion that sometimes she was playing tricks and that sometimes she was not; the episode of the airborne medicine bottle would appear to come into the latter category.

Dr Ritchie's other experience inside the rectory occurred on another occasion after he had called there to see Marianne Foyster, who was ill and confined to bed. She was suffering in all probability from psychosomatic disorders. After Dr Ritchie had seen his patient he left her room and then descended the main staircase, which led down into the entrance hall. Later on, he told his son that whilst he was coming down the stairs, he experienced the feeling that he was being forced and pushed down them and that it gave him the very strong impression that some entity or unseen presence wanted him to leave the house; needless to say, there was nobody else on the staircase at the time.

Dr Ritchie told his son about another strange experience that happened to him at Borley, although not inside the rectory itself. The doctor said that when he was driving along Hall Lane and reached that part of it which was between the church and the rectory, the engine of his car cut out for no apparent reason but when he managed to get the vehicle moving again, he had no further problems with it elsewhere. Of course, sceptical people may argue that this was merely bad luck, or that the engine may have been affected by temperature variations. We feel that these possibilities are most unlikely, although it has to be accepted that this part of the hamlet is located on high ground and is a rather cold and windswept place. On the other hand, many people have reported similar difficulties with their vehicles at Borley, but that they have performed efficiently once that they were away from the place. One such person was Ted Ritchie, the doctor's son; years later when he had his own car, he had engine failure problems at Borley which were not repeated elsewhere[2]. In fact there have been many instances of mechanical gadgets working erratically or not at all whilst they were in the village and then behaving themselves when removed from it. We shall describe more of these mechanical eccentricities in the final chapter and we shall offer a possible explanation for them; to the best of our knowledge it has not been discussed in the other works on the subject of the alleged haunting at Borley.

Another such aberration may have occurred towards the end of 1954. The managers of the then popular but now defunct magazine, *Picture Post,* decided to concentrate their attention and at least some of their resources upon an attempt to solve the riddle of the 'Borley ghost[3].' They dispatched a reporter and a photographer to the by now famous hamlet in order that at least some local research could be carried out and then used as the basis of an article. The reporter was the late Kenneth Allsop, who became very well known in later years as a television presenter and interviewer, and the photographer was Godfrey Thurston Hopkins, who took a remarkable picture which has been the subject of much controversy. Hopkins' photograph is a picture of one of the two entrances to the gravel driveway which went past the front door of the rectory. It is said to be the point at which the spectral nun was standing when she was alleged to have been observed by many people including the journeyman carpenter, Fred Cartwright, who claimed that he had seen her on four separate occasions. The picture shows one of the four tall gateposts and a short section of the picket fencing which at one time went along the full length of the rectory garden where it had frontage onto Hall Lane. The stakes of the picket fence were of three different lengths, were arranged to form a pattern and were joined together by horizontal strands of wire. However, the photograph included also a wispy and shadowy outline of a figure which was not visible when the picture was taken. Hopkins was at a loss to provide an explanation and commented to the effect that when he took his photograph it was mid-afternoon and that the visibility was good. He said that he wanted to emphasise the outline of the gatepost and the fencing against the clear sky and when the film was developed the dark shadow was found in the centre. He stated definitely that the dark mass was not visible in the viewfinder and that he could not understand why it had appeared in the picture.

The editorial staff of *Picture Post* were mystified by Hopkins' photograph and all the more so when their photographic department assured them that the negative was genuine and that it had not been tampered with. It was decided that another photographer should be sent to Borley, with instructions to take a picture from exactly the same position. This was done and the second photograph showed the gatepost and the fencing only. In their issue dated 1 January 1955 the editors of *Picture Post* printed an article entitled 'Is this the Borley Rectory ghost?' It was accompanied by both pictures. As we write, we have before us a copy of the photograph taken by Hopkins. There is indeed a shadowy figure shown where the picket fencing is and it appears to be superimposed upon, or standing in front of the stakes. In other words, the figure, if it was such, was standing outside the fencing and at the point where so many people claimed to have seen the phantom nun.

The whole episode creates problems. On the one hand, *Picture Post* was a reputable and respected magazine, its photographic experts were of the opinion that Hopkins' picture was genuine and it is difficult to accept that those responsible for this publication would have stooped to trickery. On the other hand, so much so-called 'spirit photography' has been found to be fraudulent. There have been many examples of this over the years and we recall especially the affair of the 'Cottingley fairies', in which two young cousins claimed during the 1920s that they had taken photographs of gossamer-winged little people cavorting about at the bottom of their garden. Several decades later, one of the cousins (by this time an elderly lady) admitted on television that the whole matter had been a hoax. Nevertheless, it fooled Sir Arthur Conan Doyle (then a prominent figure in the Society for Psychical Research) at least for a time; perhaps he should have enlisted the services of Sherlock Holmes, who may have seen some significance in the fact that one of the cousins worked for a firm which manufactured birthday and children's cards. To return to the question of Hopkins' photograph, was this another mechanical 'hiccup' at Borley, or did his camera record a figure which was there, but not obvious to his eyes, nor to those of the reporter?

Now let us turn to some more experiences, which did not involve the use of any gadgetry. The first of them was alleged to have occurred in the autumn of 1947 and was reported by Miss Edna Backhouse[4]. She was the headmistress of the Church of England Primary School at nearby Foxearth and one of us (CM) remembers her well, if not with any excessive degree of affection. Miss Backhouse was the old type of authoritarian teacher with her favourite and unfavourite pupils. If you were unfortunate enough to be in the latter category, then the chances were that you would not have been inclined to agree with the old adage to the effect that 'schooldays are the happiest days of one's life.' Almost incredibly by the standards of today, the Rev Lanfranc Mathias was barred from giving religious instruction on a voluntary basis at what was in theory a church school, because of the pettiness of the then headmistress.

To return to Miss Backhouse's alleged encounter with the paranormal, she had gone up to Borley church to have a look at the

Fig 78. The former primary school at Foxearth in 2002, with its tasteless functional extension, had a sad history in its final years. With a declining number of pupils, it became less and less viable and finally, in 1998, 181 years of education in the place were ended by closure and sale

recently restored stone altar, which the Rev Henning used to refer to as the *mensa*. As she entered the church and walked towards the altar she felt conscious of a 'presence' near to her and then she heard footsteps following her. When she turned round and walked away from the altar, she heard the footsteps following her again, but the sound ceased when she left the church. The aisle was carpeted, she was convinced that no one else was present in the building and she reported that the footsteps were uneven, as if whoever was responsible for them walked with a limp. There are people living still in Foxearth who remember the formidable Miss Backhouse. They may well agree that she was far too inflexible in matters of discipline, but this does not mean that she was a fool or a liar and as ever we have to leave it to individuals to come to their own conclusions in the matter.

We have another first hand report of an alleged paranormal phenomenon from a gentleman who lives not far from Borley, but who wishes to remain anonymous[5]. We can say, however, that one of us (CM) has known his family well over a period of many years and that the other (EB) interviewed him in December 1995, discussed the matter in detail with him and was impressed by his genuineness and his ability to recall a lot of detail. Our informant said that his experience took place in June 1977. It happened at approximately 11 o'clock at night; the weather was dry but the night was a dark one. He was interested in the alleged haunting and had been discussing the matter with some of his friends. They agreed that on the evening in question they would go to Borley church, with the object of spending a period of observation in the graveyard. The group consisted of six people in all and our informant drove up to Borley alone in his own car. He reached the churchyard and parked there before his friends arrived in the other vehicle. He decided he would play a trick on them when they appeared, so he hid behind one of the gravestones. He remembers that it was to the right of the footpath which runs from the gate to the graveyard up to the porch of the church. The proposed prank went badly wrong, however. Whilst hiding behind the gravestone, he heard footsteps coming towards him. They appeared to come from the far (north) side of the church and then round the end of the building, that is, outside of and below the altar window. He described the footsteps as being heavy and loud and of a slow and even pace. There was no one else present who could have been responsible for the footsteps and when our informant was asked whether the sound of them had stopped abruptly or if they had faded away as would have been the case if they had gone past him or changed direction away from him, he replied very definitely that he had not waited to find out. He was very frightened and ran out of the churchyard. At this moment the other car arrived and his friends noticed with concern that he was in a shocked condition.

We were impressed with the honesty of our informant, who is a religious person and we wonder what sort of entity could have been responsible for the heavy footsteps which he described. They do not seem to be what one would expect from a phantom nun, which leads us on to the obvious suggestion that she does not appear to enjoy a monopoly in the alleged haunting at Borley. This is pure conjecture, but seems to us to be a perfectly reasonable theory if one accepts the possibility of survival (which is a key factor in nearly all religion) and also that the dead are able (at least sometimes) to make their presence known to us. For the time being we note merely that on this occasion the sounds were ponderous; on some other occasions, but by no means all of them, it has been reported that the footsteps were like those of a person who walked with a limp. In his last years, the Rev Henry Dawson Ellis Bull had a pronounced limp and incidentally he was only 59 years old when he died. However, many people have suffered from lameness and do still and we have no intention of putting forward facile and over-sensational suggestions.

We have met the Bacon family (see page 112), who lived in the rectory cottage. Bob Bacon bought it and most of the rectory garden from James Turner in 1951. The family consisted of Bob, his wife Betty, his son Terry, his daughter José and Mr and Mrs Williams, who were Mrs Bacon's parents. Mrs Williams died in 1959 but the rest of the family remained at Borley until 1972.

One of us (EB) interviewed José Simmonds (née Bacon) in 2002, who described two curious experiences which happened to her at the cottage[6]. The first occurred during the late 1950s. There is a window at the foot of the stairs at the cottage and, on one occasion whilst descending the stairway, José saw the lower half of a person walk past the window. The view was rather limited because of the angle. No one should have been there and when José investigated, there was no one there. Her description of the half of the figure which she saw was that it was clothed in a full-length black skirt and was striding in a masculine fashion. This seems incongruous and we suggest that what José thought was a long black skirt may have been a priest's robes.

José's second experience happened in the early 1960s. One evening she and a young man friend were sitting on the settee in the living room of the rectory cottage; the lights were switched off. Suddenly deep and heavy breathing was heard from a corner of the room. They were frightened by it and José's friend ran out of the room, at which point the breathing stopped. The sounds were never explained, the only other living creature in the room being a budgerigar, which could not have been responsible.

Over a period of many years, several psychical research groups have done a great deal of work at Borley (and no doubt, a great deal of fruitless waiting and watching as well). One such group took a local clairvoyant to Borley church on 30 August 1986 in order to see what impressions could be picked up. A report was typed on the following day and we have seen this account. Not all psychical researchers are enthusiastic about the subject of clairvoyance as they feel that it is linked far too closely to spiritualism. Indeed it is but it is also a proper subject for the attention of those who study the paranormal. One of us (EB) has discussed the matter with the clairvoyant on a number of occasions[7], who has been kind enough to provide us with an up-to-date account of the visit, as follows:

'The leader of a local psychical research group asked me to visit Borley church to see if I could pick up any presence there. I went with an open mind and on entering the building I felt nothing until I was half way down the aisle. Then I became aware of what I have always known as 'spirit coldness,' which comes when someone from spirit joins us and this is very normal to me. The rest of the group were in front of me, near to the altar. A lot of talking and movement was going on, which can be distracting when I am trying to concentrate. I sat in one of the pews to the right and about the third one from the front. Suddenly I saw the back of a lady waiting to play on an old-fashioned harmonium type of organ. Her hair was mostly grey and she had on a straw hat. She wore a costume, sat upright and gave the impression that the instrument was 'hers' and not to be played by others. I became aware of the prescence of other people around me, including a lady who was weeping and I felt that she was grieving over a loss.

'The other impression I picked up was that of a man standing between the altar and the altar rail. He was wearing a jacket with pleated patch pockets, the pattern of the material being a large check of black and tan squares. He had dark hair parted in the centre, well marked brows and a squarish face and was of medium height. He was listening to and looking downwards at someone else and he gave the impression of being an intruder into this time and place.

'Then I walked to the area around the font at the back of the church and noticed another cold spot. I was asked for my reactions. I felt that there should have been a door there and was told that the entrance to the crypt used to be at this point.

'As at 2003, this is the only time that I have visited Borley church.'

We found this report to be of the greatest interest and it would be difficult to say anything other than that the clairvoyand had performed well. The impressions fall into two categories; first, those to do with the characters who were described in some detail and second, those to do with the building.

With regard to the former, we wonder who the gentleman with the patch packets and who was standing near the altar was. Regarding the latter, the person in charge of the group confirmed that the descriptions of the former layout of the church, and especially of the font area, were correct. We have met the leader of the group, who has an extensive knowledge of Borley, and we have had detailed discussions with him.

To return to the question of the possible identity of the man with the patch pockets, there may be an indication in the clairvoyant's own choice of words and in all probability given quite unwittingly. In the third paragraph of the report there is a reference to this man as giving the impression of 'being an intruder into this time and place.' Broadly an intruder is one who intrudes, that is, one who insists upon being in a certain location even if his or her presence is unwelcome or illegal.

More specifically, during the time of Oliver Cromwell's Commonwealth, an 'intruder' was a clergyman who was imposed upon a parish if the existing incumbent was unable or unwilling to come to terms with Puritanism. East Anglia was an important area during the Civil War and was a stronghold of Puritanism. Oliver Cromwell was associated closely with the eastern counties. He was born at Huntingdon into a family prominent in local political affairs. He was educated in his home town; the school is still there and is now the Cromwell Museum. He became the member of Parliament for Cambridge and Huntingdon and eventually the Lord Protector.

Our friend with the patch pockets, whose shade the clairvoyant became aware of, may have been one of Cromwell's intruding priests. They disliked intensely the paraphernalia and trappings of High Church and wore their hair cut short. The Civil War and the Commonwealth lasted from 1642 until 1660 and during that period exactly, the rector of Borley was one John Deeks[8]. Legend has it that he was a stern character and a local historian has described an intruder as 'one who enters without welcome or right' and 'an obnoxious minister imposed by a patron.' John Deeks replaced the former rector, Robert Warren, who had been in office since 1607 and who was dismissed abruptly from his duties. When the national rule of the Commonwealth and the local rule of John Deeks ended in 1660, Robert Warren was reinstated but he carried on for one year only, presumably because of his age and perhaps because poor health was an additional factor. All in all, we feel that it is likely that John Deeks may have been our man and we repeat that in our view the clairvoyant's impressions seem to have been of considerable significance and should not be dismissed lightly.

In 1988, an exciting and important discovery was made. There was a legend to the effect that there was a crypt under Borley church and that various members of the Waldegrave family had been laid to rest in it. On the assumption that it existed at all, there had been some attempts to find the entry, but all of these had been unsuccessful. Harry Price claimed in his first Borley book, *The Most Haunted House in England*, that Ethel Bull had told him that there was a crypt under the church and that on a number of occasions it had been noticed that the Waldegrave coffins had been disturbed. However, on 4 April 1953 she was interviewed at her home at Chilton Lodge, Great Cornard (near Sudbury), by Dr Eric Dingwall and Trevor H Hall, two of the three authors of *The Haunting of Borley Rectory*. Readers will recall that this book was commissioned by the Society for Psychical Research and that it was highly critical of Harry Price's investigations. Dingwall and Hall claimed that when the subject of the crypt and the coffins was raised,

Fig 79. This statue of Oliver Cromwell (1599 - 1658), sculpted by F E Pomeroy in 1900, stands in St Ives where he lived from 1631 to 1636

it was clear that Ethel Bull had no knowledge of the matter. In view of the extraordinary lengths to which some people were prepared to go in order to discredit Harry Price's work and in view of the discovery of 1988, we have to express our doubts about this claim. We think that the likelihood is that Harry Price had persuaded Ethel Bull to say rather more than she had wanted to about the crypt, that she may have regretted having done so and that she had decided to be very cautious during the interview which she gave in April 1953. Dingwall and Hall commented warmly on the hospitality that they received on that occasion, but we suspect that they may have been kept short of certain information[9]. In view of what we shall reveal soon, we feel that readers will agree with us.

Before describing what happened at Borley in 1988, we shall discuss some earlier attempts to find the entrance to the church crypt. In chapter five we referred to the discovery and identification of the original altar stone in 1943 and how in due course it was restored to its former position. To the disappointment of Harry Price and the Rev Henning, it was found that the stone was resting on a bed of sand, not covering an entry to an underground chamber. As the main task in hand was to commence the excavations of the cellar floors beneath the ruined rectory, no further attempts were made on this occasion to search inside the church for the access to the crypt; however, the stonemason hired to assist remarked, prophetically as it transpired, that the entry might be in the churchyard.

In 1947 the ecclesiastical authorities granted a faculty (that is, permission) for the stone altar to be reinstated and for the replacement of the wooden flooring of the sanctuary with flagstones. Officially, the view was that this would be an appropriate exercise in restoration and unofficially Henning wanted to find out what, it anything, was under the floorboards[10]. On 26 May, Whit-Monday, Mr and Mrs Henning, accompanied by James Turner and John Durrant, a Sudbury resident who was interested in the Borley case, went into the church and work

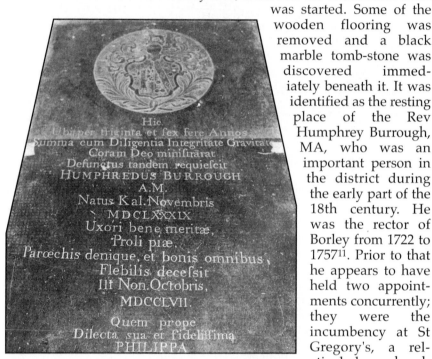

Fig 80. Tomb of the Rev Humphrey Burrough, found under the altar in Borley church

was started. Some of the wooden flooring was removed and a black marble tomb-stone was discovered immediately beneath it. It was identified as the resting place of the Rev Humphrey Burrough, MA, who was an important person in the district during the early part of the 18th century. He was the rector of Borley from 1722 to 1757[11]. Prior to that he appears to have held two appointments concurrently; they were the incumbency at St Gregory's, a relatively large church in Sudbury (the parish adjoins Borley) and the headmastership of the local grammar school. One of his pupils and his nephew was the famous artist Thomas Gainsborough.

Borley has never been anything other than a small hamlet and scattered rural parish and it is a reasonable assumption that the Rev Humphrey Burrough's appointment as the rector there in 1722 was in the nature of a semi-retirement. Nevertheless, he managed to hang on for 35 years. After the discovery of his tombstone under the

Fig 81. An early 20th century photograph of St Gregory's church, Sudbury

Fig 82. Statue of Thomas Gainsborough which dominates Sudbury's market place

floorboards in the church, the sandy soil was dug and probed by Henning and his helpers and many old and presumably human bones were found. They were re-interred later in the churchyard. On the same day, James Turner broke into a vault, which was presumed to be that of Humphrey Burrough. There was no escape of foul air and the brickwork was in excellent condition. With the aid of a powerful torch, it was observed that there were three skeletons in the vault, that they were lying in about three feet of water and were on top of each other. It was assumed that they were the remains of the Rev Humphrey Burrough and his daughters. On the following day the aperture was filled in and the new stone flooring was put into place. This was a most interesting discovery, but it was after all only a small vault located immediately under the church floor; fairly obviously it was not the crypt, so that the doubt concerning the existence of the latter remained.

That doubt was not removed until more than 40 years later. The entry to the crypt was discovered in somewhat bizarre circumstances on 6 July 1988[12]. A small local psychical research group had been studying and investigating the Borley case since the middle of the 1970s, as no doubt similar groups and individuals had been doing over the years. We know the leader of the group in question, who told us that he and his friends had been considering, among other associated matters, the possibility of trying to find evidence which would establish the existence of a crypt under the church.

On 6 July 1988, five members of the group including the leader, were at Borley. They noticed that one of the larger tombstones in the graveyard had no inscription upon it; it was not that the surface of the horizontal stone had deteriorated due to the passing of time and

Fig 83. This early photograph shows the railings enclosing what was thought to have been a grave but was later found to be the entrance to the crypt

erosion caused by weather conditions, rather it was completely plain. The grave was barely two yards from the altar window and it was surrounded by an iron fence approximately four feet in height. The absence of any writing on the stonework intrigued the group, so one of them scaled the fence, tapped sharply on the stone and was surprised to note that a hollow sound was produced. The next step was to see if it was possible to lift the stone and when this had been accomplished, a flight of steps was revealed. In other words, the grave was a dummy. This was extraordinary enough in itself and we cannot conceive why somebody, or some group of people, should have gone to such lengths to disguise in such an eccentric fashion the entrance to the crypt, for it became clear almost at once that this was what it was.

The group descended the flight of stairs, which was a long one; it was calculated that it went down into the earth to a depth of about 25 to 30 feet. The sides of the stairway were lined with bricks, but the walls were in very poor condition, large sections of the brickwork had fallen down, revealing bare earth behind and the steps were littered with the rubble. As the group went down the stairway, they noticed a human skeleton embedded in the earth to their right. Only a few feet away from the bogus grave there is a memorial stone dedicated to a member of the Herringham family, who provided the two rectors of

Fig 84. A later photograph (2001) of the entry to the crypt in Borley churchyard. Note the regrettable damage to the railings

Borley immediately prior to the Bull incumbencies. However, it is assuming too much perhaps to suggest that the skeleton was the remains of a member of the former family in view of the fact that down the centuries it was a common practice to use the same grave spaces over and over again. Coffins were not always provided and sometimes the bodies were buried after having been wrapped up in material.

At the foot of the flight of stairs there was a small chamber, the floor of which was littered with brick rubble and opposite to the stairs there was a large and ancient wooden door. It was heavily barred both vertically and horizontally and etched into the woodwork were the initials 'H F B' and the date '1921.' The initials are, of course, those of the Rev Harry Foyster Bull who was still the rector of Borley in 1921. In this instance we feel that he was responsible for having the door barred and that this was done during the year indicated. Obviously he knew all about the crypt and it seems highly likely that at least one of his sisters (Ethel) had some knowledge of it also. The door was locked, but fortunately there was a large old-fashioned keyhole which was not blocked by a key and with the aid of torches it was possible to see a good deal of what proved to be a huge underground chamber. The members of the research group were of the opinion that it extended for at least the length of the church and possibly further; the ceiling appeared to be arched and grooved. Near to the door and to the right there was a small altar, which may have been simply a table. It was covered with a purple cloth and a crucifix was standing on it. To the left were some old coffins which appeared to have been made of lead and which were encrusted with a green patina. They were resting on stone supports; it was possible to count four of them, but in view of the size of the crypt the probability is that there were others as well. One possibly important feature which the group observed was that the brickwork at the far end of the crypt looked as if some repair or replacement work had been carried out at a later date, as compared with the ancient wall surfaces elsewhere. The metal fencing, which is now very rusty and which surrounded the bogus grave, it still in position, the stone has been removed and the stairway down to the crypt appears to have been filled in, at least partially. The ground inside the fencing is roughly level and covered in ivy and weeds. One of us (EB) observed that three large iron bars were lying in this undergrowth.

The discovery of the crypt in 1988 was clearly an exciting and important accomplishment, but it has not solved any of the mysteries of the Borley saga. To the contrary, it has raised even more questions to which it is difficult to find the answers at the present time. For example, although it is not unusual for a crypt to be laid out as a chapel, what would account for the secret entry to it, hidden under a false grave in the churchyard? In view of the initials and the date etched on the ancient door and assuming that the Rev Harry Bull arranged for it to be heavily barred in 1921, why did he do so and why did he do it in that year? Was the crypt used for some purpose until 1921 and if so, what was it? Were there other and hopefully more orthodox entries to the crypt?

We are able to offer two possible answers to this question, at least. First, we recall the impressions of the local clairvoyant who had felt that at one time there had been an entry to the crypt near to the font and after this statement had been made, it was confirmed that this had been the case[13]. Second and literally in more down-to-earth fashion, the group who found the entry in the churchyard noted that the far (western) wall of the crypt showed signs that the original and ancient brickwork there had been repaired or altered at a later date. To the western side of the church only a few yards away from it is situated the large house known as Borley Place, which property has extensive and very old cellars under it and the east wall of these cellars (that is the side adjacent to and very near to the church) shows similar signs of later alterations. An inner wall has been built which does not extend quite to the cellar ceiling. As stated in chapter seven, there is evidence on the south wall of the cellars that the substantial tunnel which was discovered under Hall Lane in 1957 terminated there. We have put forward already the theory that the other end of the tunnel terminated in the cellars of the ancient house which stood at one time across the road from Borley Place where there are farm buildings today. We have stated also our reasons for believing that the tunnel was neither a land drain nor a sewer. It seems very likely therefore that there was an underground link between the crypt and the two large houses which

Fig 85. Borley Place

were situated very near to the church. Why should there have been such a connection? We believe that it is likely that it may have had something to do with the upheavals of the Reformation. Before the age of materialism people as a whole took religion much more seriously than is the case today and for a long time it was illegal for Roman Catholics to hold Mass. Nevertheless, many of them did so secretly; the Waldegrave family, who were the lords of the manor of Borley for three centuries, were ardent Catholics and Sir Edward Waldegrave, notwithstanding his political eminence, was imprisoned in the Tower

Fig 86. The tower of Borley church from the grounds of Borley Place. It is very close, as can be seen

of London for permitting the celebration of Mass at Borley.

The crucial question is, of course, whether or not all this subterranean activity has any bearing on, or any connection with, the alleged haunting of Borley. It is true to say that the affair has a backcloth of Roman Catholicism and it may be the case that a nun prayed in the crypt under Borley church, or perhaps was ill-treated, incarcerated or even killed there. At the present time there is no firm evidence to support such theories; all we have to date are the planchette and seance messages which indicated that a young French novice was tricked into going to Borley and was murdered there by a member of the Waldegrave family. Until and unless more definite information does come to light, we feel that it is a matter of balancing the various possibilities, one against the other.

CHAPTER ELEVEN

The documents and what they tell us

We are fortunate in having access to many documents to do with Borley Rectory and the people who lived there. The earliest document is that part of the 1871 census return which listed the occupants of the rectory in that year. They were the Rev Henry Dawson Ellis Bull, aged 38, described as the rector of Borley and born at nearby Pentlow, followed by Caroline Sarah Bull, aged 34, described as the rector's wife and born at Harrow Weald in Sussex. (There is an error here; Mrs Bull was formerly a member of the Foyster family of Hastings, but Harrow Weald is situated in the north west outskirts of London and not in Sussex). Then eight children are listed; the first five of them are described as scholars and the last three were too young to have commenced attendance of school. They are Harry, aged eight, Caroline (Dodie), aged seven, Winifred (Freda), aged six, Alfred, aged five, Basil, aged four, Ethel, aged three, Adelaide (Mabel), aged two and Edward (Gerald), aged five months. All of these children were born at Borley Rectory except for Harry who was born at nearby Gestingthorpe and we shall refer to this point again shortly. Other occupants of the rectory were Mary Peters, aged 67 and described as a nurse, Maria Baker, aged 34 and described as a cook, Mary Stapley, aged 48 and described as a housemaid and Elizabeth Howell, aged 19 and described as a nursemaid. There were also George Sharp, aged 51 and described as a coachman, Eliza Sharp aged 50 and described as the coachman's wife and Sarah Sharp, aged 15 and described as a scholar; no doubt the Sharp family lived in the rectory cottage. Clearly it was a large household and there were six more children yet to come. We have referred to the fact that the eldest son, who became eventually the Rev Harry Bull, was born at Gestingthorpe. Mrs Bull was originally one of the genteel Foysters of Hastings, but we are informed reliably that she was slightly simple-minded and that she was employed for a time as a resident helper at Gestingthorpe Rectory. It appears that she gave birth to her first child at this address.

We have before us the wills of the Rev Henry Dawson Ellis Bull and of his son, the Rev Harry. The former was only 59 years old when he died in 1892 and his will was dated 22 March 1877. It is a very lengthy document covering three pages of foolscap. It has been copied out in the most beautiful copper-plate handwriting, full of flourishes and curls. It is almost a work of art and must have taken a Dickensian clerk a long time to complete. The outstanding features of the will are as follows: The executors were Mrs Caroline Sarah Bull, the Rev George Alfred Foyster, of All Saints Rectory, Hastings and a London solicitor named Walter Scadding. The contents of the house were bequeathed to Mrs Bull and the sum of £500 which was to be paid to her as quickly as possible; also, Mrs Bull had the right to continue to live at the rectory; £100 was bequeathed to the eldest daughter (also Caroline Sarah, but known as Dodie). The patronage of the living and the rectory, the rectory cottage and the grounds passed to the Rev Harry Bull, who was clearly the main beneficiary. The will laid down the most precise instructions as to how the estate should be managed in the event of the rector dying before his son Harry had attained the age of 21 years. However, there were two surprising features in this will. The first was that a codicil, dated 5 June 1887, was added, under the terms of which Mrs Bull had the use of the contents of the house, rather than the outright ownership of them, as indicated earlier in the will. The second was that the gross value of the Rev Henry Dawson Ellis Bull's personal estate was shown as being only £3132.

We have described fairly briefly a lengthy and complicated will, but it raises some most interesting points. First, one of the executors and trustees, the Rev George Alfred Foyster, who was the rector and patron of the living at All Saints Church, Hastings, from 1862 until 1904, was none other than the father of the Rev Lionel Algernon Foyster. As we have seen, after several years of missionary work in a remote part of Canada, the latter was the rector of Borley from 1930 to 1935, during which half decade an exciting time was had by all. Whilst on the subject of family connections, we have been informed reliably that the Bulls and Foysters were related to each other before the Rev Henry Dawson Ellis Bull married Caroline Sarah Foyster. If this is the case, then it has to be said that it may have accounted for the eccentricities of the 14 offspring. The second point is the codicil to the will, which appears to us to have operated to the disadvantage of Mrs Bull. We wonder if this was to do with some disagreement within the family and/or perhaps with the belief to the effect that the rector's wife was slightly simple-minded. At this distance in time, it is almost impossible to ascertain the truth of the matter. The third point which interests us is the gross value of the personal estate (no net value is indicated). A reliable method for converting the value of the Victorian pound into present day currency is to multiply the former by 50. If this is done in this case, then the Rev Henry Dawson Ellis' £3132 becomes £150,600. This sounds better, but it is still not good enough. In today's terms, this sum is nowhere near to the value of the huge rectory which was well-maintained and filled with Victorian and antique furniture, the rectory cottage and extensive grounds. We must remember also the cost of retaining five or six resident servants. The Bull family was said to have been wealthy and to have owned property around the Borley and Sudbury district; one is driven to the conclusion that there must have been a lot more money which was kept out of probate, probably by means of a trust, or trusts. There is a legend to the effect that the Bulls and their wealth, were descended from Anne Boleyn and although no definite connection has been established, we know that the family had lived in north Essex since the middle of the 18th century at least. We know also that Anne spelt her name sometimes as Bullen and that she too was a resident of north Essex. She lived at the Great Lodge, Great Bardfield and this large property is still in existence. Interestingly it is said to be linked to the village church by means of an underground tunnel of considerable length, which is reminiscent of the subterranean passages which were discovered at Borley. It is almost as if a secret access to the local church was par for the course for the upper classes in 'Tudorbethan' times.

We turn now to the will of the Rev Harry Bull, which is a much shorter and simpler document than that of his father and we were relieved to see that it was typewritten. Harry Bull was only 64 when he died in 1927 and his will was dated 31 January 1912. The executors

Fig 87. The Great Lodge, Great Bardfield

were his brother Alfred Richard Graham Bull, who was a schoolmaster who lived for many years near Broadstairs, Kent, his cousin Bernard Brereton Foyster, who was a London solicitor and one of Lionel Algernon's brothers, and Henry White who was also a solicitor, with offices at Winchester. The main provisions of the will were to the effect that one hundred pounds was to be paid as quickly as possible to his widow (Ivy Bull) and that all of his assets should be sold and converted into money. This was to be used to form a trust, the three executors were to be the trustees and the investment income was to be paid to Mrs Bull for the rest of her life, unless she should remarry. In that event, the income from the trust was to be paid in equal shares to Harry's siblings. The gross value of the estate was £6643 and the net value was £5983.

There is not a great deal to comment upon in the case of the Rev Harry Bull's will. First, he left more money than his father, which must confirm the view that in the case of the latter's will, a lot of money was kept out of probate by one means or another. Second, it was after Harry Bull's death that the rectory, which had been also the family home since it was built in 1863, was sold to the church authorities. Finally, Ivy Bull did not remarry. She survived until 1955, when she died in a nursing home in Hastings.

The next document which we shall consider follows on logically from Harry Bull's will, under the terms of which Borley Rectory had to be sold. In the year following his death the church authorities decided to amalgamate the two small parishes of Borley and Liston. This scheme was not implemented until the Rev Alfred Clifford Henning arrived upon the scene in 1936. However, it was planned eight years earlier. We have before us a copy of *The London Gazette* dated 23 November 1928, in which it was reported that:

'At the Court at Buckingham Palace, the 20th day of November 1928. Present, the King's Most Excellent Majesty in Council. Whereas the Ecclesiastical Commissioners for England have, in pursuance of the Union of Benefices Measure, 1923, duly prepared and laid before His Majesty in Council, a Scheme bearing date the 11th day of October, 1928, in the words and figures following, that is to say:

'We, the Ecclesiastical Commissioners for England, acting in pursuance of the Union of Benefices Measure, 1923, have prepared and now humbly lay before your Majesty in Council, the following Scheme for effecting the union of the Benefice (being a Rectory) of Liston and the Benefice (being a Rectory) of Borley, both of which Benefices are situated in the County of Essex and in the Diocese of Chelmsford:

'Whereas Commissioners appointed at our request by the Right Reverend Guy, Bishop Chelmsford, pursuant to the provisions of the said Union of Benefices Measure, 1923, to inquire into and report (*interalia*) upon the Union of the said Benefices of Liston and Borley duly made their report to the said Bishop of Chelmsford and therein recommended the Union of the said two Benefices and the terms for effecting the union and the said Bishop of Chelmsford signified in writing his approval of the said Report:

'And whereas we, the said Ecclesiastical Commissioners for England have prepared this Scheme for the Union of the said two Benefices based upon the terms recommended in the said Report:

'And whereas the said Benefice of Liston is now full the Reverend Stewart Travers Fisher being the present Incumbent thereof and the said Benefice of Borley is at present vacant:

'Now therefore, we, the said Ecclesiastical Commissioners for England, with the consent of the said Guy, Bishop of Chelmsford (in testimony whereof he has signed this Scheme), do humbly recommend and propose to your Majesty as follows. . . . .'

What follows this preamble is the scheme itself, set out in four numbered paragraphs. We will summarise what in today's jargon would be called a four-point plan. The first paragraph laid down that the benefices should be united, but that the two parochial church councils would continue to operate separately. The second paragraph stated that if the scheme was ratified and published in *The London Gazette*, then it would come into effect immediately. The third paragraph laid down that the incumbent would reside at Liston Rectory and the final paragraph stated that the patrons of the two original benefices would take turns alternately at nominating a new incumbent as and when necessary.

We wish to make several comments upon this document. First, we have met previously the Rev Stewart Travers Fisher who was mentioned in the preamble; he was the father of Nancy Goodale (see chapter eight). Regarding the second part of the scheme, notwithstanding the fact that it was ratified and published in 1928, it was not implemented until several years later. As for the third part of the scheme, it is interesting to note that the church authorities felt and rightly so in our opinion, that the lovely old rectory at Liston would be a much more comfortable residence for the incumbent than the huge Victorian house at the top of the hill at Borley. And the former did not have the reputation of being haunted. The Rev Stewart Travers Fisher had confused the issue somewhat by having had built and then occupying his own new house at Liston, but his successors, the Rev Alfred Clifford Henning and the Rev Lanfranc Mathias lived in the old rectory there in accordance with the provisions of the scheme.

Now we shall turn to a copy of *The Suffolk and Essex Free Press*, dated 13 June 1929. The editorial comment in that copy, entitled 'The Borley Ghost', is a thoughtful piece of work and reads as follows:

'Myers, in *Human Personality* says: 'Whether through reason, instinct or superstition it has ever been commonly held that ghostly phenomena of one kind or another exist to testify to a life beyond the life we know'. This week we record certain strange experiences at Borley Rectory and, after weighing all the facts which are in our possession, we do not propose, as some no doubt will, to treat this matter with ridicule or turn it down as the phantasm of disordered mental processes. In view of all the circumstances and the mass of corroborative evidence there is in existence, we think the subject is one for thorough investigation from the scientific and spiritual points of view. If such an investigation is sincerely made there is no doubt that much valuable information for psychical research can be adduced. That there is phenomena that has shown itself at periods for years at Borley Rectory there is little doubt. What is it?

'It is remarkable that people who have seen it agree in essential details with what has been the experiences of others in years past, although one set of observers have not been connected in any way with the others. There is the London domestic who, two days after entering the rectory and knowing nothing of past legend, almost goes off in a dead faint as she informs her mistress that she has seen a nun dressed in black. The mistress makes light of it, yet later is convinced that years ago exactly a similar 'something' had been seen. This is not mere coincidence when there is an accumulation of evidence which all tends in the same direction, that something like a nun and a coach and horses passes.

'True, from many points of view, to the ordinary man or woman, the whole story seems preposterous, but we repeat, the whole circumstances, as we know them, warrant careful investigation over a considerable period of time'.

The article went on to draw a not very accurate analogy between public attitudes towards paranormal phenomena and the alleged powers of witches. However, the piece concluded, fairly enough in our view:

'It is an accepted fact that there is some phenomena, not understood, which for want of a better definition is called a 'ghost'. There is nothing extraordinary in it, the eeriness comes in our lack of knowledge of what it is and the terror of the unknown and mysterious still grips us humans.'

Although it contains a few grammatical problems, we feel that this article is a most interesting piece of work. The first point to be noted is that it is quite clear from the context that the alleged haunting at Borley was common knowledge in the Essex/Suffolk border area and had been for a long time. If one argues that this contention is incorrect, then we can say only that the local press seems to have been very quick off of the mark. The article was published only three days after the first of V C Wall's sensational reports appeared in *The Daily Mirror* on 10 June 1929 and only one day after Harry Price's first ever visit to Borley; in fact he was still there on 13 June. The next point which may require some explanation is that the piece commenced with a quotation form Myers' *Human Personality*. The author was Frederick W H Myers, born in 1843 and educated at Cheltenham and Trinity College, Cambridge. He was one of the founding members of the Society for Psychical

Research, which was set up originally in Cambridge in 1882 and which transferred to London as its centre of operations fairly soon afterwards. Myers was a prolific author and poet and for the benefit of those readers who may wish to try to obtain it, the full title of the book mentioned in the article is *Human Personality and its Survival of Bodily Death* (London, 1903).

The last comment which we shall make on the article in *The Suffolk and Essex Free Press* is concerned with the reference to early witchcraft, which we did not quote in full. The writer stated that the alleged powers of the witches had a lot to do with hypnotism and the naïveté of country people in centuries past. He reported that these unusual ladies were said to have surprised even themselves sometimes with the effectiveness of their spells. In the long run they did not benefit from their supposed talents. Inevitably the time came when the country people felt that they had had enough of the witches and many hundreds of them were burned to death. If you were unfortunate enough to be female, ugly and the possessor of more than the standard number of nipples and a black cat, then you were likely to suffer a most fiery and terrible end. Perhaps Mr Ling (see chapter eight) was lucky to have been a male, a white witch and to have belonged to the 20th century. All this may be very interesting and it is true to say that hypnotism is a proper subject for the attention of psychical researchers, but we feel that, all in all, mediaeval witchcraft has very little to do with the modern scientific study of alleged paranormal phenomena. Surely the more enlightened attitudes and advanced techniques of today are a far cry from the era of these poor old ladies and their incantations. However, we have to say that, taking it as a whole, we were impressed by the article.

The next document takes us into the 1930s. We have before us the 1935 electoral roll for the parish of Borley. The hamlet was polling district "Z" in the parliamentary constituency of Saffron Walden; at the time the lower-tier local authority was the Halstead Rural District Council and Borley has been always in the administrative county of Essex.

There were 91 electors listed, including some (by now) familiar names. There were three Misses Byford, who were sisters and who lived in Brook Hall Road. One of them, Helena, was the church organist who found the members of the Sunday school locked in Borley church (see chapter five). There were three gentlemen called Farrance and no doubt it was one of them who discovered part of the tunnel which ran under the roadway whilst repairing a well in the grounds of Borley Place when the Rev Harry Bull was living there (see chapter seven). Electors numbered 23 and 24 were Alfred and Margaret Finch, who were shown as living 'near the Green.' The only people listed at the rectory were the Rev Lionel Algernon Foyster and the flamboyant Marianne Emily Rebecca Foyster; obviously the days of resident staff were over and in view of the fact that nobody was shown as living at the rectory cottage, we may assume that that property was unoccupied at the time when the electoral roll was under preparation. The Foysters were followed alphabetically by eleven Gardiners, all of whom were related to one another. Herbert Mayes (see chapters four and five) was shown as living in Hall Lane. Six members of the Payne family were listed, but in 1935 none of them was living as yet at Borley Place. Miss Marion Pitt, the village schoolmistress, was shown also as living 'near the Green.' She was one of the few villagers who became friends with Marianne Foyster. The electoral roll included five Scriveners, all of whom were related to one another and five Theobalds, to whom the same comment applied.

What this document tells us is that not much changes in a small hamlet such as Borley. As we have said before, the place is not isolated, it is only two miles away from Sudbury and Long Melford and by the middle of the 1930s both private and public transport were operating at a reasonable level. Yet despite these facts, there seem to have been very little movement of the population. Broadly speaking, Borley people appear to have continued to live in Borley and to have married each other, presumably.

By the late 1930s, the church authorities were trying to sell Borley Rectory and the Rev Alfred Clifford Henning was acting as an estate agent, probably unpaid, on their behalf. He managed to let it to Harry Price for a year, but by 1938 the Ecclesiastical Commissioners had decided that the place was becoming a liability and that it should be disposed of as quickly as possible, if necessary by auction. They instructed a local surveyor, Stanley Moger, of the Estate Office, Halstead, Essex, to prepare a report on the condition of the rectory. We have a copy of it and it has an ethos about it which is as depressing and gloomy as the building which it described.

Moger's report is dated 26 May 1938 and is addressed to the Ecclesiastical Commissioners, 1, Millbank, Westminster, London, SW1. The document commenced:

'Gentlemen, re Borley Rectory, Essex. Acting upon your letter of the 4th inst to the Rev A C Henning, Rector of Lyston and Borley and at his wish, I have inspected the above property for the purpose of ascertaining and advising as to the figure which should be placed as Reserve if an Auction Sale is held in the near future.

'Description and Condition.

'Rectory. The property comprises a well-built red brick and slated residence standing close to the road with the church on the north side across the road. The drive is of a semi-circular nature with gates in and out, but the trees on both sides of the road render the building somewhat dark.

'The exterior of the fabric is in fair structural condition, with the exception of the verandah on the east side which is much dilapidated, part down and dangerous, the same remarks apply to the greenhouse, heating and potting sheds on the south side.

'The interior is roaming and quite out-of-date, requiring much expenditure in refitting and modernising. The decorative condition is decidedly old and of cold appearance and would undoubtedly have to be completely and thoroughly done out before occupation.'

The report went on to describe the various rooms in the rectory. All of those on the ground floor had a ceiling height of ten feet, nine inches; they were very lofty and it must have been difficult to keep the place warm. There were an entrance porch and an inner hall, the dining room, the study (known also as the library and which was the base room for Harry Price's observers), the drawing room, two storerooms and a pantry, the servants' hall, the kitchen, the larder, the dairy and the scullery. There were three staircases leading to the first floor. The upper rooms, all of which had a ceiling height of nine feet six inches, were listed as the main landing with two side corridors, ten bedrooms, a dressing room, a chapel (with a stained glass window) and a boxroom over it and at the top of the small tower, a bathroom and a lavatory. In the courtyard were another lavatory, a knife house, a coal store, a refuse pit and a geared hand pump for forcing water up into the storage tanks; the pump was said to be of a 'very old pattern and quite out of date.' It was recommended that the various fixtures should be included if possible in the sale as they were 'old, poor conditioned and today practically valueless.'

The report referred to a number of outbuildings, including the rectory cottage, which was described as a garage or coach house with a first floor flat and which was situated in what was called the stable yard. These buildings, like the rectory itself, were brick-built and slated and were said to be in fairly good condition externally, but 'the interior sadly needs bringing up to date;' there was reference to a number of forcing pits (that is cold frames), which were without lights, in a poor state of repair and 'hardly worth the cost to put it right.' Drainage discharged into a cesspit in the garden some distance from the main building, which arrangement 'appeared to be satisfactory.' Water was 'derived from a deep well, was believed to be pure and to provide an ample supply;' we can hope only that there was no connection between these two 'facilities.'

After brief descriptions of the garden and nearby farm buildings, both of which were said to be in a neglected state, the report concluded:

'Assessment. The whole of the Rectory Property is Rated at £24 gross with a Rateable value of £17. This is undoubtedly a sympathetic valuation owing to being a Rectory, but from my knowledge of over forty years, I do not think the value would be put more than £35 gross and £26 rateable, which shows that the Property is not looked upon with favour.

'Local Rumour. The Rectory is supposed to be HAUNTED and a few years ago was the Hunting Ground of many hundred of Spiritualists and Inquisitive persons, in fact, so many visited the site that the Police had to handle the matter. This, as you may imagine, is a considerable detriment to selling, as many view but turn away on this account.

'Future. If not disposed of within a reasonable time, I fear the end will be unfortunately as is the case today with large, out-of-date Residences - Demolition for the value of the Materials after cost of pulling down, which in this case would be merely the Bricks, Slates, Doors and Windows. The site value would be very little and most difficult to dispose of.

'Reserve. Taking everything into account, I regret that I cannot recommend a higher reserve than Four Hundred and Fifty Pounds, although possibly a private sale may bring more, but that an Auction be held at the end of August or early September if an acceptable offer be not received in the meanwhile. I am, Dear Sirs, yours faithfully, Stanley Moger, OBE, FAI, FCIA.'

It would be quite impossible to accuse Moger of indulging in the technique known as 'hard selling' and it must be rare indeed for a surveyor's report to refer to an alleged haunting. Once again, we have mention of the number of visitors to Borley and the need for the police to be there as well on at least some occasions. Not all was doom and gloom, however, regarding the property. Although the rectory was consumed by fire less than a year after the report was written, James Turner converted the cottage into a reasonably comfortable dwelling and he did his best to tidy up the old rectory grounds. In fact, as recently as 1984, a firm of auctioneers and estate agents in Sudbury was advertising what they called 'Borley Rectory Cottage' for the price of £79,000 freehold. Despite all of the rowdyism which is said to occur at Borley, the firm described the property as 'An interesting detached Victorian residence situated in an enviable rural position opposite the village church.'

We have two letters in front of us written by Alan Gregson, one of the two sons of Capt William Hart Gregson, who was the owner of Borley Rectory when it was burned down in 1939. These interesting letters were written from Australia and throw a completely new light on some of the events of the late 1930s. Obviously, Gregson was in correspondence on a fairly regular basis with the recipient of his letters. The first of them was dated 16 July 1985:

'It was a pleasant surprise to have your letter of the 1st July regarding Borley rectory and I shall endeavour to contribute my factual recollections.

'In 1938 the Church of England was retrenching and combining parishes and one could buy a really substantial redundant rectory for well below its worth. We had lived for years in various cottages and bungalows which my father owned in urban Essex and then the prospect of a 'proper' house was appealing; we were offered Radwinter Rectory (a charming place) and Borley. In those days we saw no need for daily access to a school, college or place of employment.

'Borley and Liston parishes had been merged; the rector was the Reverend A C Henning and he lived with his wife and a small black dog in the more compact Liston Rectory about a mile away. On the C of E behalf he showed us around Borley. As you will have gathered, this 21-roomed house, built in 1860 by the clerical family of Bull (*Dum Spiro Spero*) had been empty for some years. At one point Mr Henning said, 'I think I have to warn you, Capt Gregson, that this house is supposed to be very haunted.' We laughed.

'Because of its beautiful wooded grounds, excellent construction, secluded location, attractive coach-house (and three wells) we elected to purchase at £350 and we took possession in autumn 1938. We never actually slept or ate in the rectory, but in the quarters above the coach-house. A bachelor family.

'My father's considerable library and all his furniture, memorabilia etc, were stored in some ground floor rooms of the rectory. I remember that we furnished the middle front downstairs room sufficiently for the rector's one or two vestry meetings.

'. . . . . Needless to say, the fire itself in 1939 was (a) a sad loss of irreplaceable family possessions and a costly building and (b) a pure mischance not attributable to Poltergeist, Marianne, elemental or any mortal person. I could dwell more on that post-fire summer but it was widely reported at the time; our feeling of loss was partly obscured by the stream of sightseers, media people, souvenir hunters and amateur psychists (a diversion not entirely unwelcomed by us; my father received 3 guineas, I believe, for a 3-minute BBC broadcast) . . . . .

'We occasionally attended matins, my father considering it 'the proper thing' and we three would have lifted the congregation to 5 or 6. But it was during that time that Anthony and I had our preparation for Confirmation. You will have viewed the ponderous Bull tomb or monument inside the little church. I remember occasionally giving a hand pumping the organ . . . . .

'For what it's worth, I can verify the episode of the dogs; our original dog, Peter, was a spaniel-retriever cross, black (from Bill Bendall, plasterer, of Maldon). Peter was a happy, reliable, uncomplicated dog until the day when he panic'd in the Borley courtyard and ran howling away down towards Long Melford and was never seen again. Searches and enquiries yielded nothing. Some weeks later we obtained a young dog and I'm sorry to say that fairly soon afterwards the same thing happened to him.

'The heavy well-cover: why, I wondered, would the dark cellar contain a circular well going down 40 feet or more utterly devoid of any protection, not even a kerb? That was why we covered it with a door which had been lying somewhere on the property (a good old-fashioned framed t and g[1] door as I recall, weighing at least 70lbs).

'Not only footprints in overnight snow, but the tracks of ironshod wheels, as of a carriage, certainly ran from the front of the rectory, down the lawn past the cedar tree and they seemed to lift-off at the shrubbery one winter's morning. The thing to remember is that no physical access for anything bigger than a wheelbarrow led to that part of the grounds.

'Later in the summer of '39 we were holidaying in the Lake District when the war began. So we vacated the Borley property, occupied one of our Maldon cottages and it was some years before we found a buyer for Borley . . . . .'

In all probability, readers will have noticed that there are two minor errors in this otherwise most informative letter. First, the rectory was built in 1863, that is three years later than indicated and second, the large monument in Borley church is dedicated to the memory of Sir Edward Waldegrave and his family, not to the Bulls. Readers will note also that Alan Gregson said that his father purchased the rectory 'for £350;' it had been reported elsewhere that the price was £500, but presumably the family should know what they paid for the place. However, the most interesting part of the letter is that which deals with the fire and the effect which it had upon Capt Gregson's position and reputation. According to Robert Wood, the author of *The Widow of Borley*, the captain had burned down the rectory in order to obtain the fire insurance money and he was therefore an arsonist and a fraudster. This blunt statement was made without any qualification and in one sense without any evidence, because the matter was never tested in a court of law. The insurance company, which was represented by such formidable sounding individuals as the lawyer Mr (later Sir) William Crocker and the loss adjuster Col Cuthbert Buckle, refused to meet what they described as an 'impudent claim' for £7356 and maintained that Capt Gregson had started the fire himself quite deliberately. Eventually an out-of-court settlement in the sum of £750 and costs, was reached. We are aware, of course, that blood is thicker than water, but the contents of Alan Gregson's letter do not indicate that his father was, or indeed needed to be, in any way dishonest. It is clear that Capt Gregson was the owner of several properties in 'urban Essex' (presumably in the Maldon area) in addition to Borley Rectory. Furthermore, he had lost his library, his furniture and other valuables in the conflagration. If he had been in the business of committing arson and fraud, then surely he would have seen to it that his valuable and irreplaceable possessions would have been in store elsewhere. To borrow Robert Wood's favourite cliché 'it just won't do' and we feel that the issue of the fire is not as simple as he would have us believe; the reality is that the matter is clouded in doubts and uncertainties.

The question of the two dogs which became terribly agitated in the rectory courtyard and then tore away never to be seen again, has been referred to in the other books about Borley. Harry Price felt that the behaviour of the animals, on separate occasions of course, was yet another mystery and the three authors of the highly critical *The Haunting of Borley Rectory* suggested that these canine antics were due to the presence of worms or to having eaten too much white bread. The sceptics could have said that some household pets are very aware of, and responsive to, psychic activity; we feel that these authors may have done so, but their problem was that the alleged haunting at Borley had not been 'their' case. Finally, we note with interest the account of the carriage tracks in the snow in an area of the rectory grounds where such a vehicle could not have gained access.

Alan Gregson's second letter was dated 18 October 1985 and it is clear that he had been asked to supply more information about the fire and its consequences. He wrote:

'. . . . . You wanted to hear more about the fire itself; well, although we'd bought the property and taken possession in late 1938 we lived initially in the flat above the coach-house, pending re-decoration and furnishing of the rectory (not all 20 rooms of it though). A great deal of our furniture, etc, was stacked in the entrance hall and stairwell temporarily. There being no electricity or gas, our lighting was by oil lamps, which were not pressure lamps. One of these was an argand-type[2] brass table-lamp which was carried into the rectory any evening when we required to fetch one of our books or other articles. On one such evening my brother and I were in the flat, it was about bedtime and my father wanted a book or document from the rectory; apparently he stood the lamp on a table or box while he rummaged about and then a stack of books suddenly keeled over onto the lamp, overturning it, breaking the glass and spilling kerosene which then caught alight and speedily ignited surrounding articles. Like most households, this one didn't have ready-use firefighting equipment and so my father immediately sent us boys to the nearest telephone (Borley Green) to call the fire brigade from Sudbury . . . . .

'The apparitions seen at the height of the fire: it was widely reported (possibly as a result of a verbal account which gathered weight and credibility) that a human-like form was seen inside an upstairs window silhouetted against the blaze, at a place where the upper floor was already burnt; the captain of the fire brigade asked if it was certain that nobody was inside the burning rectory and when he was so assured, he is said to have drawn attention to the mysterious figure at the window which had been visible apparently for a few seconds. Later, another person reported the same sighting. But I don't know how much subjective thinking may have prompted that belief. Who were the 'man and lady' seen in the grounds just outside the burning building? Neither of these visions was seen by me personally . . . . .

'The annual Church Fete of Borley *cum* Liston was held in 1939 and the Revd Henning and my father arranged for it to be in the grounds of the ruined rectory; it was billed as a Psychic Fete with guest appearance,

I believe of Harry Price . . . . .

'The fire was centred on the main staircase and so it destroyed rooms of the main block; the two wing-ends at right-angles were spared, though heavily scorched and their roofs damaged. Subsequent high winds made the parapet gable-ends unsafe, in fact all was unsafe inside and this was why we were at some pains to keep visitors from climbing in. Many of these were really welcome and pleasant people - but also the inevitable few vandals, thieves and pranksters who seemed annoyed that we were still there at all.

'We started a visitors' book — some quite interesting persons — and a firm called British Films Ltd filmed some footage at the rectory and later invited us to Wardour Street to see it on screen; its eventual fate is buried under the more exciting happenings of September 1939. (With a cast of us three, you can be assured that it would not have changed the course of cinema history) . . . . .'

Alan Gregson was asked to provide further details of the night of the fire and we are very grateful that he did so. The reference to various figures being seen in the blazing rectory had been made by many people, but Gregson was quite definite to the effect that he had not witnessed these alleged phenomena. One person who did claim to have seen the figure of a woman dressed in blue at an upstairs window of the ruined building in a room where no flooring remained, was Rosemary Williams, of Borley Lodge. She stated that she had seen the figure on the night of 26 March 1939, that is exactly one month after the date of the fire. She was accompanied by Charles Browne, of Pound Hall, Long Melford, who claimed that he saw the figure as well, but for a shorter duration of time. The alleged sighting came to the attention of the Rev Henning, who reported it to Harry Price. The latter wrote to Miss Williams, who replied to the effect that she was prepared to make a statement in return for a fee of one guinea. Critics of the case noted that her report was among Harry Price's files and they assumed that this modest business proposal had been agreed to. They assumed incorrectly, because Price refused to pay Miss Williams; he was not a parsimonious man, but he argued quite properly that statements given in return for remuneration were virtually worthless. Presumably the lady backed down and her report finished up in Price's Borley dossier without a payment having been made to her[3].

By and large, the burning down of the rectory and the outbreak of the war in the following September marked the end of the involvement of the Gregson family with Borley. Capt Gregson was placed in charge of an open-cast mining operation in Scotland and his two sons went eventually into the armed forces. Before they did so, the captain had approached various coach companies with a view to regular trips to Borley being organised to his own profit. We see nothing devious about this and neither do we feel that it indicates in any way that he may have set out deliberately to defraud his insurers. After all, he had lost his largest property (and we remember that he owned others in Essex), his furniture, his library and other valuables and there was no reason at all as to why he should not have tried to make good his losses at least to some extent in whatever way was possible. Perhaps he failed to take into his calculations the influence that Adolf Hitler would be bringing to bear on the situation in the near future. Interestingly, Capt Gregson wrote to Harry Price on 23 January 1940 and stated that he and his sons would like to go back to live at Borley, '. . . as we need a lot of room and definitely like the atmosphere . . .' Whether he was thinking of extending the rectory cottage, or perhaps of having the main house rebuilt we do not know. It is a matter of history now that the Gregson family did not return to live at Borley.

We have found these documents to be absolutely fascinating and their importance should not be under-estimated. In addition to the documents, we have seen dozens of newspaper articles about Borley dated from the late 1930s onwards. We shall quote from just one of them, which appeared in a national newspaper[4] on Christmas Eve 1954. The journalist[5] had seen in advance the report on the alleged haunting which was commissioned by the Society for Psychical Research entitled *The Haunting of Borley Rectory*. This work was highly critical of Harry Price and his methods of investigation and this aspect of the matter formed the main thrust of the article. The writer stated that the Society's report would be available 'early in the New Year' but in fact it did not appear in book form until January 1956. This particular work seems to have been leaked to the press well ahead of schedule and we cannot help wondering if this was done with a certain element of glee in view of the rancour which had existed between the Society for Psychical Research and Harry Price, who had died in 1948. In fairness to the journalist who wrote the article, he concluded it by quoting the words of the wife of the then rector of Borley. Mrs Henning said: "My husband and I think that this investigation is a dastardly attack on Mr Price when he is no longer here to defend himself". We cannot avoid drawing attention once again to the unfortunate fact that so much has been disputed about the Borley case and its principal researcher. Because of his love of publicity Harry Price may have had difficulty in a competition designed to discover 'the most honest man' but we feel that many readers will find themselves in agreement with the sentiments expressed by Mrs Henning.

CHAPTER TWELVE

What is the truth?
Summary and conclusions

Harry Price claimed that the Borley case was unique. He based that assumption on his statements to the effect that the alleged phenomena were reported over a very long period of time (several decades, in fact) and that the poltergeist activity in and near to the rectory was on at least some occasions extremely violent. This was his most famous investigation and at the time of his death, he was in the process of preparing a third book on the subject; it is almost certain that it would have been a best-seller, as the first two had been. With all due respect to Harry Price's claim, it is certainly true to say that many other priest's houses were alleged to have been haunted; indeed in *The End of Borley Rectory* there is a reference to the well-known belief that the Wesley family had a lot of problems resulting from poltergeist activity at Epworth Rectory in Lincolnshire. However, we are able to describe another example of a haunted rectory which is much nearer in place and time.

Approximately ten miles from Borley, over the county boundary in Suffolk, there is yet another isolated hamlet called Polstead. The former rectory there is now a private residence, but this large building, which is 400 years old and is set in approximately four acres of garden and paddock, has also a lengthy history of alleged paranormal disturbances. Nobody knows precisely when those disturbances commenced to manifest themselves, but we are told that the Rev John Whitmore, who lived in the rectory from 1795 to 1840, carried out a service of exorcism at the beginning of the 19th century. What is not clear is what form the phenomena took, but in view of the length of time that this particular priest remained in residence at Polstead, we have to assume that either they were not too violent or that he was prepared to tolerate them anyway. Certainly it seems to be the case that many of these Victorian clergymen remained in post for very long periods indeed, haunted rectories notwithstanding. To bring the case up to date, Mrs Mary Neads, whose late husband was the rector of Polstead from 1963 to 1976, was quoted as saying that she was aware

Fig 88. The old rectory at Polstead

of 'unusual but not unpleasant spiritual activity.' However, the wife of Mr Neads' predecessor, the Rev Paul Biddlecombe, told *The Church Times* in 1978 that she used to feel that she was being pushed out of bed by an unseen force and that her young daughter used to wake up in considerable distress because of screaming noises which appeared to emanate from the hearth and flue in her bedroom.

The alleged phenomena seem to have become far worse when the last clergyman to reside at Polstead rectory moved into the place, together with his family. They were the Rev Hayden Foster, his wife Margo and their son Gerard and they remained at the house for precisely five days and nights. All was quiet during the first four days, but on the fifth day, which was the day before the new rector's induction ceremony, Mr and Mrs Foster moved into a smaller bedroom in order to make room for some guests who were coming to stay with them temporarily. At about three o'clock in the morning Mrs Foster was awakened by the sound of screaming, but it was not her son having a nightmare. Then she saw that the appearance of the room had changed; in fact it had been decorated quite recently, but it took on the appearance of a dreary room with dirty and peeling wallpaper. Worst of all, the rector's wife had a terrible feeling of being strangled and suffocated. The following morning, the Fosters packed their bags, moved in with friends and refused to return to the rectory. Unlike the Borley case, in this instance the Church Commissioners decided to take speedy action and to put the house on the market. The then archdeacon, the Ven Jeremy Walsh, commented to the effect that the rectory was being sold primarily because of its size and the consequent high maintenance costs, but he added that the history of the haunting and the recently reported phenomena had hastened the decision to dispose of the property. The then bishop of the diocese, the Rt Rev Leslie Browne, said that he was unaware of the rectory's reputation and that he would not have moved the Fosters into it if he had been informed about the matter. Apparently, the bishop talked to Mrs Neads about the haunting after the Fosters had left and she told him that she and her husband got used to the phenomena, which included, interestingly, the sounds of footsteps when nobody was about.

To their great credit, the church authorities 'played the game' and the estate agents were instructed to mention in their brochure the fact that the rectory was reputed to be haunted. Eventually it was sold as a private residence and the final comment came from archdeacon Jeremy Walsh. He said that 'as Christians believe that there is a spiritual dimension to our lives, then they should not be surprised if they find that spiritual forces break through occasionally;' with which statement we find ourselves in full agreement. He added that in the event of the new occupants being disturbed and requesting that a service of exorcism be held in the house, then that request would be considered very seriously. The Polstead case came to a head in 1979, 40 years after Borley Rectory was destroyed by fire. The Church Commissioners had learned much from the latter affair; it would appear that they acted far more decisively and quickly in the disposal of Polstead Rectory and one can conclude reasonably enough that they did not wish to have another 'Borley' on their hands.

We return to the question of Harry Price's claim to the effect that the features of the haunting of Borley Rectory were unique. We think that it is true to say that in terms of broad outlines there are similarities between the two cases, although on points of detail there are differences. To be fair to Price's statements, the probability is that he was unaware of the disturbances at Polstead. Although they appear to have gone on for a very long time, it seems that the attention of the media was not focused upon them until the late 1970s, 30 years after Price's death. Certainly, it seems strange that there should have been mysterious occurrences at these two country rectories which were not situated far away from each other.

Before leaving the Polstead area, we feel that we should mention that this small place was the scene of a particularly gruesome 19th century killing. The case has attracted a lot of attention over the years and a number of books and many articles have been written about what has become known as 'the Red Barn murder'[1]. Basically it was a story of love and passion and the outcome of it was that the young lady who was involved in the drama, one Maria Marten, joined the ranks of the 'missing persons army.' Not long after Maria vanished, her stepmother dreamed that she had been murdered and that her body had been buried in the earthen floor of a local barn. Maria's stepmother told other people about her dream and it was decided that the floor of the barn should be excavated. Tragically, the young lady's corpse was discovered and it was quite clear that she had been killed. In due course, a young man called William Corder was arrested and tried and he paid the supreme penalty. It could be argued that there was a psychic dimension to this case, but it does not appear to be linked with the alleged haunting of Polstead Rectory. We remember that the Rev John Whitmore deemed it necessary to carry out a service of exorcism in the house 'at the beginning of the 19th century.' It is virtually certain that this must have taken place well before the date of the murder in the barn, which was committed in 1827.

We turn now to the subject of the so-called ley lines which may have a bearing on at least some of the phenomena which have been reported at Borley[2]. First of all, what are ley lines? They were discovered, or to be more precise, re-discovered in 1921 by a gentleman called Alfred Watkins. He lived in Herefordshire and was a local business man. He was also a keen amateur student of archaeology, rural landscapes and photography. He knew well the area in which he lived and during the course of one of his outings up into the local hills, he took a rest and surveyed the panorama in front of him. It was a scene with which he was already very familiar, but he noticed a new feature for the first time. He observed that in very many cases ancient monuments such as churches, bridges, crossroads, barrows and stone circles were in alignment with each other. This led him to spend a great deal of time making a detailed study of the possibility that this state of affairs was the result of patterns which had been constructed deliberately and purposefully and not due to accident or chance.

Eventually Watkins wrote and had published some books about what he called ley lines. By this time he had become convinced that he had stumbled upon an early form of planning and that the siting of ancient structures on straight lines was definitely not the result of happenstance. In addition to the position of these ancient buildings, he noticed that a remarkably high number of places with names ending in 'ley' or 'leigh' were to be found also on the lines. These suffixes indicated that a clearing, a field or a pasture had been created in the woods and forests which covered the country many centuries ago. Such clearings were not natural features of the landscape; they were man-made and this must have meant that at least small communities were responsible for them. Alfred Watkins laid down guidelines which help students of the subject to locate the position of the ley lines. He stated that if at least five ancient monuments and/or places were in alignment with each other and were situated within a total distance of 25 miles (from the first point to the last one) then it could be assumed reasonably that the imaginary line was indeed a ley line.

An obvious question is, who was responsible for these patterns? Alfred Watkins believed that neolithic men were the originators, although much later other peoples made unwitting use of them. He argued that neolithic men needed three commodities which had to be conveyed sometimes over very long distances. They were flints, salt and clay. The first items were essential for making weapons for hunting and creating clearings in the woods, the second was for the preservation of food and the third was used for making pots and other primitive artefacts. In view of the fact that in neolithic times the whole country was covered in forests, these early surveyors saw no reason to depart from the well-known principle that the shortest distance between two points is a straight line. Later on, other peoples would make use of and develop these ancient routes. The Roman invaders were great road builders and their famous streets followed therefore the direction of the ley lines, assuming of course that Alfred Watkins' theories are correct. It is certainly true to say that the Roman roads were very straight and there are only a few examples of deviation in order to avoid natural obstacles such as hills and rivers. In such instances, the road would go over the hill or a bridge would be built over the river and then continue on its course in a relentless straight line. Gradually the early and small settlements expanded into larger communities and monuments were erected along the routes. To summarise the position the tracks were constructed first and the early travellers, their settlements and their marks followed later. Of course this is a simplification; there were exceptions and eventually communities were established elsewhere.

The second important theory to do with the ley lines is that they are said to follow lines of magnetic force. It is argued that such magnetic lines exist and that the early peoples were aware of them. Perhaps like migrating birds who know instinctively which direction to take, they possessed a sixth sense about such matters. We have to make two comments about the magnetism theory. First, it is accepted without question that the north and south poles are centres of magnetism and it is assumed that other parts of the earth's surface have similar properties, albeit to a lesser extent. Second, if the early surveyors were really aware of such lines of magnetic force, then they may have felt impelled to construct their ancient ways along them in order that the necessary quantities of flints, salt and clay could be moved about.

It has to be said that not everyone agrees with Alfred Watkins' theories. One such person was the late Dr Simon Broadbent, whose death on 15 March 2002 was marked by a lengthy obituary in *The Times* a month later. Broadbent was primarily an advertising statistician but he had also a lifelong interest in megalithic monuments. In a paper read to the Royal Statistical Society[3] he argued against claims made for the existence of ley lines, emphasising that the number of alleged lines was fewer than would be expected from a random distribution of locations between which lines could be drawn. There was no reference in the paper to the other alleged property of ley lines, that is that they are also lines of magnetic force. Dr Broadbent was using his professional skills to try to disprove the beliefs of Alfred Watkins. However, other people have reservations about statisticians and will quote Disraeli's sardonic comment: 'There are three kinds of lies; lies, damned lies and statistics.' It would appear that Queen Victoria's favourite prime minister was not amused.

What has all this to do with the alleged haunting at Borley? A writer called Frank Smyth contributed a chapter about Borley to a book entitled *Ghosts*. He quoted freely from Trevor Hall's critical book about Harry Price, but concluded that on balance there did seem to be grounds for believing that the hamlet, especially the church, was the location of some genuine paranormal phenomena. Towards the end of his piece it is stated that two ley lines intersect at Borley and that this may have something to do with the phenomena there[4]. With the aid of a large-scale map of East Anglia and a transparent ruler, we think that we may have found two more ley lines which run through Borley. Certainly all of the four imaginary lines meet the criteria suggested by Alfred Watkins: within a total distance of 25 miles at least five places are in alignment and there is a fair sprinkling of names ending in 'ley' or 'leigh' including, of course, Borley itself. One such line runs roughly from west to east and goes through Sturmer, Wixoe (almost), Stoke-by-Clare, Borley, Hadleigh and Chattisham. Another line runs in a north-west to south-east direction and cuts through Cavendish, Pentlow, Foxearth (almost), Borley, Great Cornard, Honey Tye (a crossroads), Nayland, Boxted Cross, Ardleigh and Little Bentley. There appear to be two more lines running in a south-west to north-east direction. One of these passes through Great Saling, Church End, Sible Hedingham, Gestingthorpe, Borley, Rodbridge and Thorpe Morieux. The other goes through Belchamp Walter, Borley, Rodbridge, Lavenham (almost), Preston St Mary and Stowmarket. Students of local archaeology and geography may disagree with us; we claim no expertise in the matter, but we maintain, as stated above, that these four imaginary lines meet the requirements laid down by Alfred Watkins.

The point is that if a number of ley lines do intersect at Borley and if it is true that they are associated with with magnetic force, then there could be consequences, to say the least of it. Many people have claimed that when they have been at Borley they have experienced difficulties with electrical and mechanical appliances and furthermore that those same appliances have worked perfectly well after they had been removed from the place. We have recorded already the experiences of Dr Ritchie in the early 1930s and on a separate and later occasion his son Ted, both of whom had problems with their cars; in 1954, Godfrey Thurston Hopkins of *Picture Post* took a photograph of the rectory gates and when the picture was developed it included a shadowy figure for which he could not account; many people have reported that the organ in the locked church 'played itself' and this was after an electric pump had been fitted to the instrument (they include Thomas Musk and his colleagues who noted the phenomenon in 1987); our friend Paul Kemp told us that his tape recorder refused to operate properly at Borley when there was nothing mechanically wrong with it. Geoffrey Croom-Hollingsworth and his psychical research group from Harlow spent a lot of time at Borley in the 1960s and claimed to have kept the spectral nun under observation for 12 minutes (see chapter nine). On another occasion they set up a tape recorder in the porch of the church and kept watch from a distance. Nobody entered the porch, but the group heard a loud noise emanating from it and then found their recording equipment in a dreadful mess[5]. The tape was removed from its reel and lay in a tangled heap on the floor of the porch. In 1974, a film director called Denny Densham obtained permission to set up tape recorders in the church on a number of occasions and some of his recordings were used in a BBC television programme. One night, Densham and his team found that one of their recording machines had jammed, the tape was removed from it and was tangled up[6]. At the time, the equipment was under observation and nobody except the engineers was present. This is exactly the same problem which the Harlow psychical research group had experienced approximately ten years earlier.

It is of interest to note that Thurston Hopkins was not the only person to have had difficulties with his photographic equipment at Borley. Some seven years earlier in March 1947, Dr C Hilton-Rowe, a former Bank of England official, visited the hamlet in order to take some photographs in the church and churchyard (this was done at the request of Harry Price)[7]. All went well until Hilton-Rowe walked across the road to take a picture of the gate at which the carpenter Fred Cartwright claimed that he had seen the spectral nun on four separate occasions in 1927. The doctor produced a meter in order to test the light, but the needle failed to move. He gave the meter a sharp tap and the needle jumped to another position, but then it refused to move again. Hilton-Rowe reported that the needle would not behave as it should have done whilst he was near to the gate. When he moved away from it, the meter performed normally and gave no further trouble. So we have two photographers endeavouring to take pictures of exactly the same point outside the rectory grounds; the one had problems with his light meter and the other produced a picture which included a shadowy figure which should not have been there.

It would be the height of absurdity to suggest that electrical and mechanical appliances behave frequently in an eccentric fashion at Borley. We have driven to and through the hamlet on hundreds of occasions and have taken many photographs there. At the risk of tempting providence, we have not experienced any difficulties, so if any readers decide to drive to Borley in order to have a look round, all the chances are that no ills will befall them. Nevertheless, the above

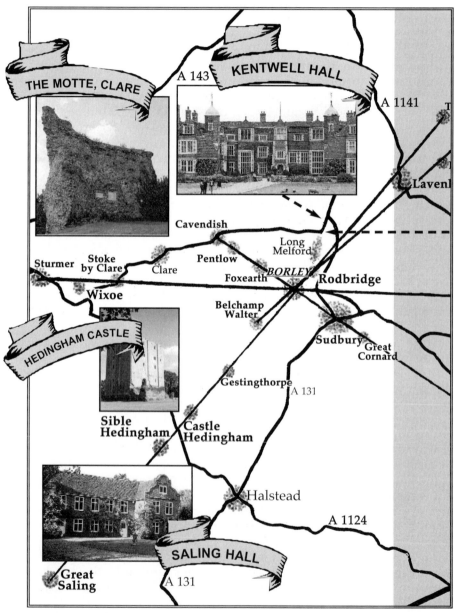

Fig 89. Map of the Essex-Suffolk border showing connecting . . . . . .

catalogue is made up from a few examples, of which there are many more. What we are suggesting and with very great caution, is that if a number of ley lines intersect at Borley and if they possess the magnetic properties ascribed to them, then this state of affairs may account for some of the minor phenomena and/or problems which we have just mentioned. We feel that it is unlikely that they would be responsible

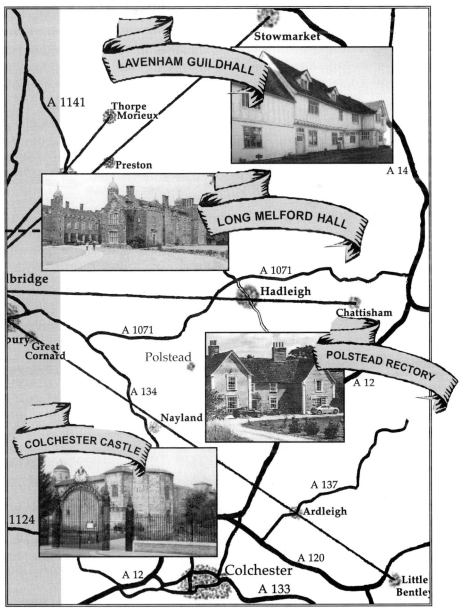

...... *points which could be ley lines.*

for the apparitions and the sometimes violent poltergeist activity which so many intelligent people claim to have witnessed at Borley. Surely if these latter phenomena are genuine, then they are much more likely to be a psychic echo of a former tragedy or unhappiness.

The time has come to turn our attention to the philosophical aspects of the paranormal in general and then to see if they have any bearing on the alleged haunting of Borley in particular. Psychical research and official science have never been very comfortable in bed together, the main problem being that although some phenomena can be and have been tested stringently when they occur, they cannot be reproduced at will like an experiment in a chemistry or physics laboratory; either they will happen or they will not happen. In a similar fashion, the reality of such phenomena cannot be 'proved' in a court of law. However, any person who finds himself involved in a court hearing has to take an oath and swear on the Holy Bible that he 'will tell the whole truth and nothing but the truth.' Yet this ancient collection of books contains reports of perhaps the most famous apparition of them all. During a period of approximately six weeks between the crucifixion and the ascension, first of all the body of Jesus Christ vanished mysteriously from the cave in which He had been laid to rest and then He was seen by many witnesses. It is recorded that there was nothing wraith-like about the figure, it was quite solid in appearance, and He spoke to those who saw Him. So we have the perhaps contradictory situation in which people who are about to give evidence in a court of law have to swear to be truthful whilst holding a copy of the Holy Bible, which is all about faith and then they will be questioned and cross-questioned, often in an aggressive manner, by lawyers who will be concerned mainly with scoring points over each other in their search for what they consider to be 'proof' and 'the truth.'

The whole point is that when one is considering the paranormal it is really a matter of belief rather than 'proof' and we are inclined to add rather cynically, whatever the latter may be. What may be acceptable as proof to some people will not be acceptable to others and as we have indicated above, religious beliefs are a matter of faith rather than proof. It is very easy to become involved in circular and unending discussions about what really constitutes proof; other people who are far more qualified than ourselves in such matters do so frequently, but we have no intention of going down that route. We venture to suggest, however, that neither scientists nor lawyers should be too rigid in their attitudes. With regard to the former group, despite all of their dissertations about big bangs and black holes in the universe, they have yet to explain satisfactorily the long-term implications of time and space. We repeat that it is perhaps unfortunate that psychical research does not slot conveniently into the grooves of orthodox science, but we feel that this is no justification for closed minds. Happily, many scientists do take a deep interest in the paranormal and we have noted already that several universities in various countries have established departments of parapsychology. With regard to lawyers and their concept of proof, there have been so many instances in which fiercely argued cases and rulings by brilliant legal experts have been overturned, or have been found to be 'unsafe' — or to put it in the vernacular, 'they got it wrong.' All of us, get it wrong sometimes and it is essential to try to keep one's attitudes flexible[8].

However difficult and unco-operative paranormal phenomena may be, nevertheless it has been possible to carry out some experiments and tests and we shall refer to two of them. The Society for Psychical Research was founded in 1882 and one of its early projects was the carrying out of a mass survey. This was done with the assistance of the media, which in those days meant newspapers and magazines only. The Society announced that they would be pleased to receive details from members of the public who claimed that they had seen an apparition. Seventeen thousand replies poured in and when they had been collated some most surprising features emerged. The majority of such alleged sightings were not of the dead, rather they were of people who were still alive, but who could not have been present at the places where the figures were seen; the 'real persons' were either abroad or some considerable distance away. Second, the common factor in nearly all of the cases was that there was an element of considerable stress and / or emotional crisis, such as danger, illness or impending death at the time of the sightings. We realise, of course, that it is almost certainly the case that some of the people who contacted the Society were not telling the truth about their alleged experiences and were motivated by the thought that there may have been the possibility of extracting some money or publicity out of the situation. No doubt, the same uncharitable thoughts had crossed the minds of officials of the Society for Psychical Research. Quite rightly, they were and they continue to be very cautious people. However, we do not feel that a probably small percentage of false or inaccurate reports would have invalidated the rather surprising results of the survey.

One area in which it has been possible to carry out some controlled tests is that of thermal variations. It is the very essence of sensational ghost stories that people's hair will stand on end when a phantom appears, or that the great hall will become icy cold when the spectral knight in armour clanks his way through it. In fact there is an element of truth in all of this. On a more serious level, many intelligent and responsible people who claim to have seen apparitions have reported that they have felt cold; this was not necessarily due to fear, rather it was a question of a sudden drop in the temperature being noticed. However, as such alleged sightings take place so often out of doors, or perhaps in draughty and unoccupied properties, it is difficult to be precise about these variations. And of course there is always the problem that apparitions are not in the habit of making appointments; they will appear or they will not appear. Nonetheless, it is possible to record precisely any variations in temperature when mediums (mental and physical) are being tested under strict conditions and in carefully planned and controlled environments. Harry Price carried out many such experiments at his well-equipped National Laboratory of Psychical Research and reported his findings to the members of that organisation. Frequently it was found to be the case that when phenomena occurred, then the temperature dropped and the differences and duration of any such variations were noted with great accuracy. It is reasonable to assume and it is generally accepted by those supervising such experiments, that this is an indication to the effect that psychic activity (like any other form of activity) requires energy and that this energy is extracted from the immediately surrounding atmosphere.

Now let us consider what relevance these general tenets may have to the alleged haunting at Borley. There were (or are, perhaps) three main spectres: the nun, the Rev Harry Bull and the old-fashioned coach. Notwithstanding the rather surprising results of the survey carried out by the Society for Psychical Research, we think that it is virtually certain that of these three phantoms, two were of people no longer alive and the other was clearly some sort of echo from the past. The famous nun-figure, whom so many people claim to have witnessed and who may or may not have been the shade of 'Marie Lairre', seems to have been the victim of some early tragedy according to the planchette and seance messages (and there is very little else to go on with regard to her misfortunes). The spectre of the Rev Harry Bull, attired in a favourite plum-coloured dressing gown and carrying some documents, was said to have been seen in the rectory after his death. There is no record of him being involved in a tragedy, but he believed that he was psychic and he seems to have had a morbid streak in his mental make-up; certainly his late marriage caused considerable disapproval and stress within the large Bull family, not to mention the hostility of his step-daughter (see chapters three and eight). We cannot comment further on the alleged sightings of the coach, other than to reiterate the point that obviously the vehicle is to do with the past.

With regard to the matter of thermal variations, with two possible exceptions, no detailed and controlled experiments were carried out, so that it is possible only to make general comments. Many people claimed to have felt suddenly very cold when they maintained that they had seen apparitions or witnessed poltergeist phenomena at Borley. We are not implying that those claims were (or are) incorrect or mistaken, but we have to say that most of the hamlet is located on high ground and is a windswept place, that everybody who remembers the rectory reports that it was always a cold building and that the same complaint is made today about the church. The two possible exceptions were described in chapter five. The first of these was the experience of Alice Reid at Borley Rectory in 1937 and the second was the 14th visit of the Cambridge Commission on 19 January 1943 when temperature variations were recorded on the so-called 'cold spot' on the landing and at another nearby point in the building, which was by this time open to the elements. In concluding this brief discussion about thermal variations and psychic phenomena, we feel that we should refer to poltergeist activity, of which there was said to be a very great deal during the Foyster incumbency at the rectory. To the best of our knowledge no records were kept of any changes in the temperature during outbreaks of poltergeist activity, which is not in the least surprising for the obvious reason that poltergeists, like apparitions, do not arrive by appointment. The only comment that we can make in this respect is that in cases of spontaneous combustion (one of which was witnessed at Borley Rectory by Sir George and Lady Whitehouse — see chapter four), presumably the temperature will rise; it would seem, therefore, that there are exceptions to every rule.

We have to consider now the crucial question as to whether or not the alleged haunting at Borley was (or is) genuine. We have quoted many witnesses whom we have interviewed and who are reliable and responsible people. They gave to us their testimonies voluntarily and willingly after we had explained to them that we were not prepared to make payments for any statements. In most cases, these people have reported experiences which have not been published previously and in the few instances where we have referred to matters which have appeared in print already, then for the most part we have done so either because one of us (CM) knew personally the individuals involved and/or because the earlier versions did not include details of which we are aware. We have tried wherever possible to concern ourselves with first-hand reports only, although there are a few exceptions to the rule. One matter which we did not refer to was the fact that a distant relative of the other of us (EB) was employed as a resident domestic at Borley Rectory in the early part of the last century (before the first world war). She was so frightened by what she saw and heard that she left after only a few days. As she died many years ago, we did not have the opportunity to interview her and consequently we are unable to be precise about any details.

In addition to the many testimonies which we have recorded, there are so many others in the earlier Borley books. With regard to the two books on the subject written by Harry Price sceptics have claimed that because of his love of publicity, he altered statements to suit his own purposes, in other words, to make them more sensational. There is an element of truth in this, but it is no argument for dismissing the entire contents of his Borley books as nonsense. Many letters were printed verbatim and many of the reports were made by people who would not have allowed their imaginations to run away with them. For example, Sir George and Lady Whitehouse witnessed poltergeist phenomena at Borley Rectory during the Foyster incumbency in the early 1930s, including the spontaneous outbreak of fire in one of the empty bedrooms (see chapter four). This happened when the unreliable Marianne Foyster had not had the opportunity to slip away on her own for a few minutes. As we know, the Whitehouses were so concerned about the safety of the Foysters and the two small children that they insisted that they should stay at their house (Arthur Hall) for several days and in fact this arrangement was repeated on subsequent occasions. The best that Robert Wood, who wrote *The Widow of Borley*, could make of the situation was to suggest, without any evidence whatsoever, that Marianne Foyster may have endeavoured to seduce the Whitehouse's nephew, Edwin. Perhaps she did, but we doubt if she would have been successful. The reality is that one of us (CM) knew Lady Whitehouse well and she remembers her as being a very sensible and shrewd person who would not have been fooled easily by any trickery.

In chapter five we referred to the lecture which Kathleen Goldney gave to the Society for Psychical Research in 1975, her subject being 'the haunting of Borley Rectory.' She was one of three authors of the book of the same name which was highly critical of Harry Price's investigations. She concluded that lecture by stating that there were three and only three, hypotheses which would account for the alleged phenomena at Borley: first, such phenomena were genuine; second, they were produced fraudulently by Harry Price; third, they were produced fraudulently by other parties. In fact the book of which she was part author concluded by laying down the same three hypotheses, from which we may deduce that she was primarily responsible for that section of it. One of us (EB) was present at the lecture and during the lengthy period of question time allowed after the speech, suggested that there had to be a fourth hypothesis, that is that a very reasonable explanation of the alleged events at Borley was that there could have been some sort of mixture of the first three hypotheses. In other words, some of the phenomena were genuine and some were not (one cannot ignore the unreliability and untruthfulness of Marianne Foyster). It is remembered clearly that this suggestion appeared to throw the lecturer off of her balance; it was accepted reluctantly by her and enthusiastically by most of the audience. Also present at the packed meeting was Dr A J B Robertson, who had organised the series of visits to Borley during the late 1930s and early 1940s which became known as the Cambridge Commission. He too disagreed with Mrs Goldney's emphatic views on the lack of genuineness of the Borley haunting and it was quite clear that the majority of her audience did so as well.

One of the advantages which we may have over the authors of the other Borley books is that one of us (CM) lived nearby at Liston for over 12 years and knew well so many of the 'members of the cast' of the drama. We are in the position, therefore, to comment briefly on local attitudes. Quite simply, some of the former and present residents of the hamlet believe that the haunting was (or is) genuine and others do not. With regard to the former group, many of them claim to have witnessed phenomena, some of which have been recorded in earlier books and some of which we have reported for the first time. We were impressed by our witnesses who, after all, were describing events which should not have happened, according to what is accepted as being normal; but we would not have used any material which we felt was suspect. It is our opinion that these people 'saw what they saw' and 'heard what they heard' and we have not embellished their accounts. With regard to the latter group (the 'non-believers'), they are entitled to their view, but we must emphasise the point that it is necessary to be careful at all times not to allow rigid disbelief to interfere with logic. It is unsafe to postulate that because Mr A has neither seen nor heard at a certain location anything which cannot be explained normally, then the same will be true of Mr B. One has to beware of the type of person who says 'I did not see the ten o'clock bus go past my house this morning, therefore it cannot have done so.' And we have to remind ourselves of the fact that some people are psychically aware, that some are not at all sensitive in such matters and yet others are the possessors of hyperactive imaginations. The debate about the genuineness or otherwise of the Borley haunting is not a clear-cut and simple one; it is a very complicated one.

At the risk of adding to the complications, we have to look at the possibility that perhaps Borley was much haunted at one time and for a long time, but that this is no longer the case. When we were discussing the question of temperature variations in relation to psychic activity, we referred somewhat flippantly to the spectral knight in armour clanking his way through the great hall and causing the place to become icy cold. If the writers of sensational ghost stories are allowed a free rein, then all the odds are that the poor chap will have to keep making his dramatic appearances for centuries on end. The reality is that in the vast majority of reported cases of psychic phenomena, be it the appearance of phantoms or poltergeist activity, they are not usually of any great duration; rather it is a matter of weeks and months, not years and centuries, although as ever there are exceptions to the general rule (and the Borley haunting may be one of them). It seems to be the case that psychic activity not only needs energy which may be drawn from the immediate atmosphere, but also that in time the flow of required energy (whatever the source) will run out. If this theory is correct, then Harry Price was justified in claiming that the Borley haunting was most unusual with regard to its duration and of course, phenomena have been reported long after his death in 1948. The rectory was demolished totally by 1944 which put an end to any alleged phenomena in the building itself, but reports have continued to be made of such experiences in the general locality and we have recorded some of them for the first time. Nevertheless, those reports have become gradually less and less frequent and we feel that it is possible that this haunting, like most others, may have run out of steam. However, in view of the fact that the Rev Henry Dawson Ellis Bull claimed to be well aware of the ghostly nun in his garden and of the occasional appearances of an old-fashioned coach (as did his son, the Rev Harry), then Price's statement was fair enough; also, it does not seem to conflict with the general rule, described above. We have, perhaps, a long haunting, but one which may have petered out.

There is another point which should be considered with regard to the alleged haunting at Borley. If we accept, for the moment at least, that some of the phenomena were (or are) genuine, then the question arises as to whether or not the famous hamlet is any more or less haunted than anywhere else, or has this impression been created by the massive publicity which this particular case has received? The coverage has been massive indeed. After decades of local rumour, the balloon went up finally when the Rev Guy Eric Smith wrote to a popular and non-intellectual newspaper in 1929, asking to be put in touch with a psychical research group who could assist with the problems of his haunted rectory. It was a most extraordinary step to have taken and we cannot help feeling that the seemingly nervy Mabel Smith had a hand in this and that the motivation was to gain publicity to assist with the successful launch of her novel *Murder at the Parsonage*. This led to the arrival on the scene of Harry Price, who could and did investigate cases most thoroughly, but who was also a very publicity conscious individual. He wrote two full-length books on the subject and six more have been written since his death (three of them were critical and the other three were supportive). Price wrote also many articles about Borley, some of which were published abroad and consequently the case has attracted world-wide attention; he gave many lectures and broadcasts about the alleged haunting. Since his death in 1948, Borley has continued to be the subject of further writings, broadcasts and in recent years, television programmes. Other cases have received a lot of publicity from time to time (the Polstead Rectory affair was one of them and was reported widely in the national press), but we doubt if any of them could compete with Borley in this respect. All of this makes it extremely difficult to answer the question which we posed at the beginning of this paragraph; nevertheless we felt that it should have been put and no doubt it will lead to considerable discussion and debate in the future.

We have endeavoured throughout to present a balanced and impartial view of the Borley haunting, but now we will climb down off of the fence. We believe, to put it at its very lowest, that at least some of the phenomena were (or are) genuine, although there has been exaggeration, and at certain points along the trail, trickery as well. We feel that we cannot do better than quote again the statement made by archdeacon Jeremy Walsh in respect of the Polstead case: "As Christians believe that there is a spiritual dimension to our lives, then they should not be surprised if they find that spiritual forces break through occasionally".

Appendix A — The rectors of Borley
with their dates of induction

Peter de Cachepore	1236	William Cooper	1561
Robert de Walmesford	1295	Stephen Luskyn	1565
Peter de Guldeford	1298	William Louther	1569
Richard de Henley	1313	Robert Warren AMSTP	1607
Hugh Aumfray	1317	John Deeks (Intruder)	1642
Robert de Stokes	1335	Robert Warren AMSTP	1660
Regnerus de Aston Sommervill		William Playne	1661
	1340	Thomas Muriell MA	1680
Thomas de Cottingham	1343	Robert Goodwin MA	1709
John Grimesby	1348	Perry King MA	1719
Simon de Dullingham	1348	Humphrey Burrough MA	1722
Walter Sweyn	1348	Robert Moreton MA	1758
William de Woketon	1369	William Stevenson	1771
William de Shelton	1370	William Herringham	1807
William Wigor	-	John Herringham	1819
William Hyndell	1397	Henry Dawson Ellis Bull MA	
William Heyward	1399		1862
John Aleyn	1400	'Harry' Foyster Bull MA	1892
John Taylor	1429	Guy Eric Smith	1928
William Ingland	1441	Lionel Algernon Foyster MA	1930
Thomas Fox	1444	Alfred Clifford Henning	1936*
Thomas Massenger	1454	Edward Lanfranc Morgan	
Thomas Fenn	1460	Mathias MA	1955
William Maliard	1473	James Henry Leslie Pennell	1967**
William Norfolk	1482	Keith Finnimore	1973
Roger Smith	1488	Ernest Frederick Leonard Brown	
Nicholas Talbot (Kt)	1503		1977
Robert Fyrmyn	-	Christopher Cook	1984
John Dawe	-	Joseph Thomas Davies (Father	
Rad Metcalf	1552	Aquinas)	1989
Thomas Randelson	1556	Captain Brian Sampson	1996

* It was at this point that the parishes of Borley and Liston were combined.

** It was at this point that Borley and Liston were combined with two more nearby parishes, Foxearth and Pentlow. Further changes were in progress as at 2003.

Fig 90. The background picture is a 2002 photograph of Borley church

Appendix B — Chronological record of salient events, 1862 to 2002

1862 The Rev Henry Dawson Ellis Bull becomes the rector of Borley.

1863 Borley Rectory is built on the site of the former Herringham Rectory.

1875 A new wing is added to the rectory, creating an almost totally enclosed courtyard.

1892 The Rev Henry Dawson Ellis Bull dies and is succeeded by his eldest son, The Rev Harry Foyster Bull.

1900 Four of Harry Bull's sisters claim to see the phantom nun in the rectory grounds during the evening of 28 July. Later in the year, Ethel Bull and a servant see this apparition again.

1911 The Rev Harry Bull marries and lives in Borley Place.

1920 The Rev Harry Bull and his family move into Borley Rectory.

1927 The Rev Harry Bull dies, ending the Bull incumbencies. Both father and son, and many other people, claimed to have witnessed various phenomena (sightings of the spectral nun and the coach, and much poltergeist activity in the rectory) and by this time the legend of the haunting is well established. The rectory is sold to the Ecclesiastical Commissioners.

1928 The Rev Guy Eric Smith becomes the rector of Borley.

1929 Mr and Mrs Smith claim to have witnessed phenomena in and around the rectory and write to the editor of *The Daily Mirror*, asking to be put in touch with a psychical research society. The editor sends a reporter to Borley and contacts Harry Price, one of the best known psychical researchers of his day. On 12 June, Price and his secretary visit the rectory for the first time; they witness considerable poltergeist activity and an eventful seance is held late at night. On 14 July, the Smiths leave Borley Rectory, as the newspaper publicity leads to the arrival of hordes of sightseers who create a considerable amount of disturbance. The Smiths run the parish from an address in Long Melford and keep Harry Price informed of events.

1930 The Rev Guy Eric Smith resigns as the rector of Borley and obtains a post as a curate at Sheringham in Norfolk. On 16 October, the Rev Lionel Algernon Foyster becomes the rector of Borley; he, his 'wife' and an adopted daughter move into the rectory. He and Marianne claim that the poltergeist activity becomes much more serious and violent than hitherto and includes the appearance of the mysterious writing on the walls and spontaneous outbreaks of fire. Sir George and Lady Whitehouse and their nephew Edwin have some personal experiences of the phenomena and invite the Foysters to stay with them from time to time, as they consider that the rectory is unfit and unsafe to be occupied.

1931 Ethel Bull and one of her sisters visit Harry Price at his National Laboratory of Psychical Research and inform him of this further alleged psychic activity. On 13 October he visits Borley Rectory with some colleagues, who come to the conclusion that Marianne Foyster could be responsible for at least some of the phenomena. On being told this the Rev Foyster becomes very angry and Price does not go to Borley again until 1937. Foyster writes about the alleged phenomena and circulates the details around his family.

1932 The Marks Tey Spiritualist Circle, including Guy L'Estrange, a local medium, spend a night at the rectory in an attempt to exorcise the house; this appears to be reasonably successful. Marianne Foyster is absent frequently from Borley Rectory, due partly to her interest in a flower shop at Wimbledon, and partly to other activities.

1935 The Foysters move from Borley because of further and serious deterioration in Lionel Algernon's health and the rectory is never occupied again by a family.

1936 The Rev Alfred Clifford Henning becomes the rector of Borley and Liston and he and his family move into Liston Rectory.

1937 The Ecclesiastical Commissioners decide to try to sell Borley Rectory and offer it to Harry Price at a very low figure. However, he decides to rent the house for one year and establishes his team of 48 observers there on a rota basis. Various phenomena are reported there by some of them. The Glanville family experiment with a planchette board and are told that the spectral nun is 'Marie Lairre,' that she was a young novice from a convent at Le Havre, that she was deceived into going to Borley by a member of the Waldegrave family and that she was murdered there by him in 1667.

1938 During a further experiment with the planchette board on 27 March, members of the Glanville family are told by 'Sunex Amures' that he will burn down Borley Rectory 'tonight'. In May, Price's tenancy of the rectory ends, his team of observers is disbanded and he removes his equipment from the house. In the autumn, the rectory is purchased by Capt William Hart Gregson; he and his two sons occupy the cottage, but store much of their furniture and possessions in the main house. The Gregsons report various phenomena in the vicinity of the rectory.

1939 On 27 February the rectory and contents are destroyed by fire. Dr A B J Robertson MA establishes a rota of observers known as the 'Cambridge Commission'. In all, they visit Borley 25 times, the last occasion being in 1944. Various phenomena are reported and unusual thermal variations are recorded.

1940 The Rev Guy Eric Smith dies on 3 August. *The Most Haunted House in England* is published and Harry Price is inundated with information and theories about the alleged haunting.

1943 Urged on by Canon Phythian-Adams, Harry Price and some colleagues excavate under the cellars of the rectory and discover human remains, which are identified as those of a young woman; at a later date they are interred in Liston churchyard.

1945 The Rev Lionel Algernon Foyster dies. A letter above the name of Mrs Guy Eric Smith is published in *The Church Times*, stating (incorrectly) that neither she nor her late husband considered that Borley Rectory was haunted.

1946 *The End of Borley Rectory* is published; Harry Price receives yet more correspondence and plans a third book about the alleged haunting.

1947 The author James Turner purchases the rectory cottage and most of the grounds. He and his wife live there for nearly four years and report various phenomena.

1948 Harry Price dies on 29 March. Some months later, Charles Sutton, a journalist, alleges that when he was at Borley Rectory with Price, he accused the latter of being responsible for fraudulent phenomena.

1949 The Rev Alfred Clifford Henning writes and publishes his *Haunted Borley*. Throughout the 1940s, the hamlet continues to attract large numbers of visitors.

1951 The Bacon family purchases and occupies the rectory cottage, remaining there for over 20 years. Members of this family claim to have paranormal experiences at Borley, including sightings of the phantom nun.

1954 Excavation of the cellar floors of the former rectory is recommenced and continues for about three years; traces of earlier buildings are found, but nothing of relevance to the alleged haunting.

1955 The Rev Alfred Clifford Henning dies in January and the Rev Lanfranc Mathias is inducted as the new rector on 28 July. He and his family occupy Liston Rectory.

1956 *The Haunting of Borley Rectory* is published; the three authors (leading members of the Society for Psychical Research) are critical of Harry Price's investigations.

1957 One of the legendary tunnels is discovered by a firm of contractors to Halstead Rural District Council. The tunnel is ancient but well constructed and is located under Hall Lane and near to Borley Place. During the 1950s, a number of radio and television programmes about the alleged haunting are transmitted (some abroad). Many people continue to visit Borley and paranormal phenomena are reported.

Early 1960s The Bacon family sells most of the old rectory gardens for development; today four bungalows occupy the former garden.

1967 The Rev Lanfranc Mathias resigns as the rector of Borley and Liston and takes up his last living at nearby Gestingthorpe. Canon Leslie Pennell, already in post at Foxearth and Pentlow, becomes the rector of Borley and Liston as well. He is the first of several priests to be responsible for the four parishes, which arrangement is still in force at the time of writing (2002).

1970 Many visits are made to Borley by a psychical research group from Harlow, Essex. The members manage to record on tape the sounds of music and voices in the empty and locked church. On 20 June three members claim to witness simultaneously the appearance of the spectral nun. They report that the figure moves about and is kept under observation for twelve minutes before disappearing. The Harlow group investigate the case for the next two years.

1973 *The Ghosts of Borley — Annals of the Haunted Rectory* is published; the book contains much previously unpublished information.

1974 Tape recordings are made of footsteps in Borley church (at night and when the building is empty and locked) and are used in a BBC television programme. During the remainder of the 1970s research groups and many individuals continue to visit Borley.

Early 1980s The visits by groups and individuals are maintained. One local group keeps the case under permanent review (their visits are spread over a period of 15 years).

1988 On 6 July, five members of the above-mentioned group discover the entrance to the crypt of Borley church; it consists of a flight of stairs which is hidden under a bogus grave in the churchyard. Access to the crypt itself is prevented by a locked and barred door, on which is etched 'HFB, 1921.'

1992 *The Widow of Borley* is published.

1993 *The Ghosts of Borley* is published; this booklet contains some previously unpublished photographs and is quite separate to the work of the same name which was produced 20 years before.

1994 A television crew goes to Borley; their film is used as the basis of a programme which is transmitted some months later. The hamlet continues to receive many visitors.

1996 *The Enigma of Borley Rectory* is published.

1998 *The Borley Ghost Society* is published on the Internet. This magazine is organised by Vincent O'Neil, adopted son of the late Marianne Foyster.

2000 *We Faked the Ghosts of Borley Rectory* is published (see Appendix G).

2001 *Borley Postscript* is published

Appendix C — The extendible Bull family

Fig 91. Borley church circa 1910. The Edwardian gentlemen are said to be Walter Bull (left) and John Coker, a local farmer

The Bull family of Borley Rectory was a very large one by the standards of today and even by the standards of the late Victorian era. The general consensus is that there were 14 children who survived and one (Cyril) who did not.

However, there are problems. Some people have said that there were as many as 17 children and we find ourselves now in the position in which we have to speak plainly. The founding father of the Borley Bulls, the Rev Henry Dawson Ellis Bull, enjoyed the reputation of being the typical hunting and shooting squire parson. Less happily, there are persistent legends to the effect that he was a philanderer and that he was very free with the housemaids and the village girls, some of whom he impregnated. It has been alleged even that one of his domestics, Kate Boreham, went into labour in the rectory kitchen and was removed hastily to an address in Sudbury in order to avoid a scandal[1]. This may be so, but also it may be grossly unfair to the Rev Henry Dawson Ellis Bull and it is quite impossible to be certain at this distance in time; we are considering, after all, events which may have taken place over a century ago.

Another difficulty concerns the position of Walter Bull, who has been mentioned in several of the other books to do with the alleged haunting at Borley[2]. Some of our informants who knew the family well cannot recall him at all and we are aware of the fact that Basil Bull's second name was Walter. We have seen a letter written by Geoffrey Croom-Hollingsworth (who studied the case in great detail over a period of many years) in which he lists the family and their dates and he states that Basil Walter Bull died in Belgium in 1917. He was a victim of the first world war. On the other hand, Harry Price claimed to have interviewed Walter Bull about the alleged haunting, which meeting must have taken place in 1929 at the earliest and the latter was reported as having visited the Foysters on many occasions at Borley Rectory during the 1930s and as having been very unimpressed with the integrity of the rector's 'wife.' Another complication is that Harry Price said that Walter Bull spent most of his life at sea and if this is the case, then clearly he would not be remembered by many people who knew his siblings well.

Fig 92. Tennis at Borley Rectory circa 1890.

Appendix D — Dodie's diary

Caroline Sarah Elizabeth Bull was the eldest daughter of the Rev Henry Dawson Ellis Bull and the second child of his large family. She was born on 18 February 1864 and baptised on 17 April of that year[1]. As her names were the same as those of her mother, she was known as Dodie to avoid confusion,

During the course of local research, the Harlow group (see chapter nine) discovered a diary kept by Dodie, covering the period 1 January to 28 October 1885. We wonder if some of the document was lost or whether she became tired of what presumably should have been at least a year long project. Geoffrey Croom-Hollingsworth, the leader of the group, claimed that he found the diary in a second-hand shop in Sudbury. He offered it to the Harry Price Library for £1000 [worth about £9500 in 2002] but the authorities were not prepared to pay this amount for it.

The first page of the diary is reproduced as Fig 93 but for reasons stated in the caption, we doubt if the handwriting is Dodie's. A possible explanation is that Croom-Hollingsworth was in contact with the late Mrs C C Baines; he may have lent the diary to her and she may have copied it out in longhand. This lady wrote a book about Borley Rectory which was not published. However, one of us (EB) has what appears to be the first draft and there are frequent references to Dodie's diary. Whatever the case, we have a copy of the diary and it makes fascinating reading. It gives a wonderful insight into the life style of the Bull family and an energetic lot they seem to have been. By today's standards, being the rector of a very small parish would not seem to qualify as a full-time post but we remember that the two Rev Bulls, father and son, were typical examples of that Victorian and early 20th century phenomenon, the 'squarson.' They owned the rectory farm at Borley (it is still there at the time of writing) and they had another farm at Lavenham. They attended the local hunting and shooting activities.

Life for the female members of the family seems to have been one long round of dances, tennis parties, taking tea and 'leaving cards.' For example, Dodie tells us that she attended a 'Fancy Ball' at Liston Hall on 7 January. She went off at 8.50pm and did not return to Borley Rectory until 3.45 am on the next day. Part of the preparation for the ball involved Dodie and her sister Winifred (Freda) walking to Long Melford in order to borrow a high comb for Mrs Bull's *mantilla,* which is a lace shawl covering the hair and shoulders.

On the following evening (8 January), Dodie, her mother and some of her brothers and sisters attended another dance at the home of the Martyn family at Long Melford. Dodie records that she danced several times with Harry Martyn and she seems to have been rather keen on him.

Harry's father was the Rev Charles John Martyn, the rector of Long

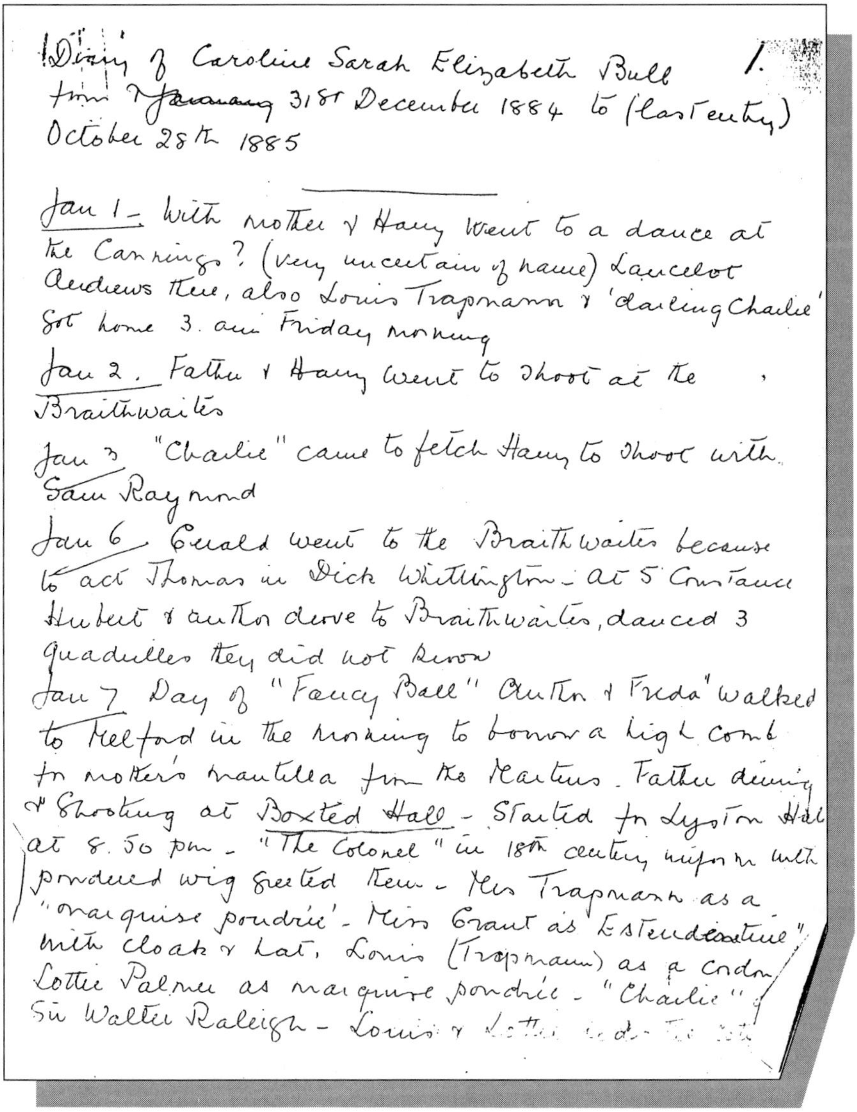

Diary of Caroline Sarah Elizabeth Bull / .
from ~~January~~ 31st December 1884 to (last entry)
October 28th 1885

Jan 1 - With mother & Harry Went to a dance at
the Cannings? (very uncertain of name) Lancelot
Andrews there, also Louis Trapmann & 'darling Charlie'
Got home 3. am Friday morning
Jan 2. Father & Harry Went to shoot at the
Braithwaites
Jan 3 "Charlie" came to fetch Harry to shoot with
Sam Raymond
Jan 6 Gerald went to the Braithwaites because
to act Thomas in Dick Whittington - at 5 Constance
Hubert & author drove to Braithwaites, danced 3
quadrilles they did not know
Jan 7 Day of "Fancy Ball" author & Freda walked
to Melford in the morning to borrow a high comb
for mother's mantilla from the Martins. Father dining
& Shooting at Boxted Hall - Started for Lyston Hall
at 8.50 pm - "The Colonel" in 18th century uniform with
powdered wig greeted them - Mrs Trapmann as a
"marquise poudrée" - Miss Grant as 'Estendentine'
with cloak & hat, Louis (Trapmann) as a condor
Lottie Palmer as marquise poudrée - "Charlie"
Sir Walter Raleigh - Louis & Lottie ... ...

Fig 93. This is said to be a photocopy of a page from Dodie's diary. However, it is difficult to believe that she set out to keep a diary from 1 January until precicely 28 October and had the foresight to predict the 'last entry.' The diary itself is now believed to be in the United States

Melford from 1869 until 1892 and an important local figure. During his incumbency a large amount of restoration work was carried out at Holy Trinity church, which is of cathedral proportions, and he had built a smaller church (St Catherine's) in the village as a memorial to his wife who died in middle age. He attempted to exert a calming influence in the potentially dangerous Melford riot of 1885[2]. Martyn

Fig 94 . The former rectory at Long Melford from the churchyard

was another typical squire-parson and, fairly predictably, he too lived in a huge Victorian rectory. The building exists still and it was here that Dodie danced the night away with young Harry who was four years her junior.

On 11 January, Freda had her 20th birthday party and Dodie wrote in her diary: 'How old one begins to feel. What a crop of old maids are growing up.' She was not yet 21! At least she managed to find a husband in due course, although he was not one of the local young men upon whom she had her eye. He was a (non-local) clergyman called Hayden.

On 13 January, there was another dance at nearby Cavendish Hall, from which Dodie returned at 3.15am. Next evening yet another dance was held, this time at Borley Rectory. The diarist tells us that 'the nursery was intended for spooning' and that she had 'a hot flirtation with Charlie'[3]. The last guests left at 1.00am which was probably just as well.

On 22 January, 'lessons started' and the party-going slowed down somewhat. As was often the case in Victorian families, the sons were given a formal education and Harry Bull and his brothers attended the prestigious Felstead School near Dunmow in Essex. However, his sisters were taught at home and Dodie and Freda gave the younger girls a basic education. And so life went on in the big country rectory; through her writing Dodie gives the impression that she found it rather stifling and that she wanted to spread her wings.

Dodie made only one reference to the paranormal. One evening when her father had gone out, she, her sister Freda and a guest decided to hold a seance. The diarist acted as the medium and they attempted to make chairs move of their own volition; the whole affair was probably very amateurish. Dodie commented: 'I seem to have a lot of electricity in me' but perhaps not as much as when eligible young men were in the vicinity. She appears to have been more interested in landing one of them than in the supernatural.

And then eventually came the evening of 28 July 1900 . . . . .

*   *   *

When this book was in an advanced stage of preparation, a diary kept by the Rev H D E Bull was discovered at the Essex County Records Office, Chelmsford and one of us (EB) has inspected it. It covers the period 25 May 1858 to 1 August 1860 although it appears that later pages have been torn out; there is no reference to Borley nor to Bull's forthcoming incumbency in the existing pages. It is possible that he kept a later diary; one of the witnesses whose statements appear earlier, the late Marie Poore, was definite that she saw a diary kept by his daughter Ethel, which referred to sightings of the nun in the garden (see page 126). Are there more Bull diaries awaiting discovery?

Appendix E — Marianne's marriages

In *The Ghosts of Borley* (published 1973) and *The Widow of Borley* (published 1992) it was stated that Marianne Foyster was married on four occasions and that all the marriages were illegal. We felt that the position should be clarified, our initial thoughts being that her first marriage (to Harold Greenwood) was not only illegal but also perhaps void in view of the fact that she was only 15 years old at the time. Had this been so, then her marriage to the Rev Lionel Algernon Foyster would have been in order. The matter has been investigated legally and this is not the case. Surprisingly, the age of consent was not

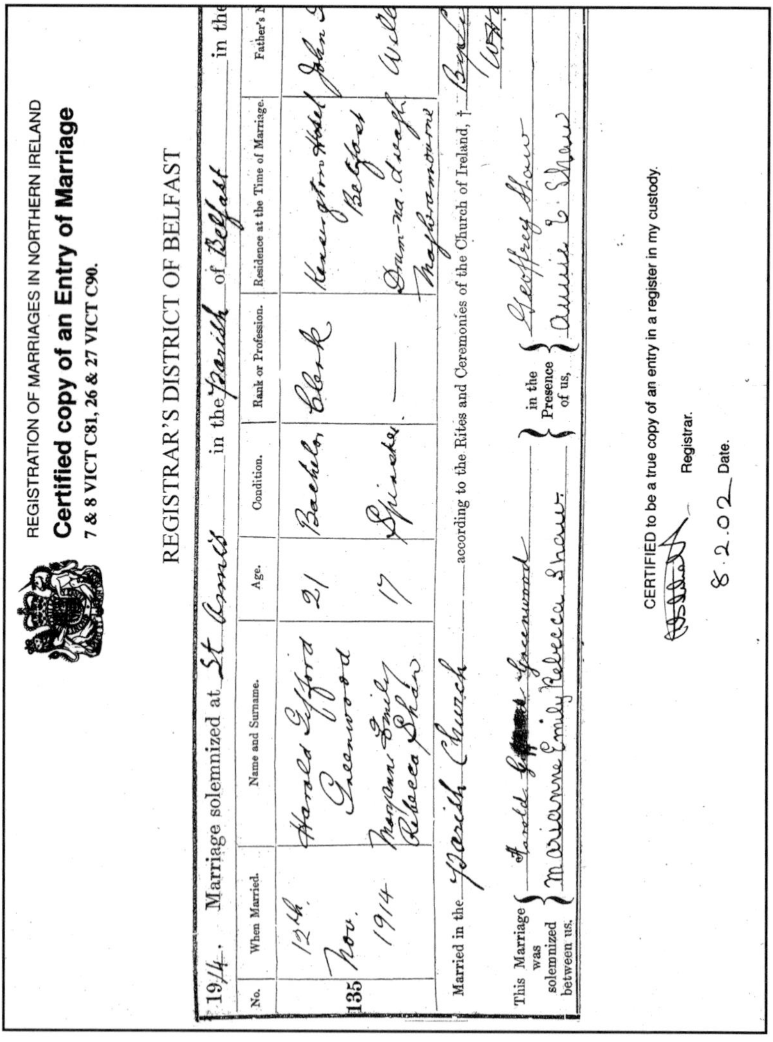
REGISTRATION OF MARRIAGES IN NORTHERN IRELAND
Certified copy of an Entry of Marriage
7 & 8 VICT C81, 26 & 27 VICT C90.

REGISTRAR'S DISTRICT OF BELFAST

1914. Marriage solemnized at St Anne's in the Parish of Belfast in the [illegible]

No.	When Married.	Name and Surname.	Age.	Condition.	Rank or Profession.	Residence at the Time of Marriage.	Father's N[illegible]
135	12th Nov. 1914	Harold Gifford Greenwood	21	Bachelor	Clerk	Kensington Hotel Belfast	John [illegible]
		Marianne Emily Rebecca Shaw	17	Spinster	—	Dun-na-dreagh [illegible]	Will[illegible]

Married in the Parish Church according to the Rites and Ceremonies of the Church of Ireland, by [illegible]

This Marriage was solemnized between us, Harold [illegible] Greenwood, Marianne Emily Rebecca Shaw; in the Presence of us, Geoffrey Shaw, Annie E. Shaw

CERTIFIED to be a true copy of an entry in a register in my custody.
[illegible] Registrar.
8.2.02 Date.

Fig 95. The certificate for Marriane's marriage to Greenwood in Belfast

raised to 16 until 1929, when the *Age of Marriage Act* came into force on 10 May of that year[1]. Previously the age of consent was 14 for a male and 12 for a female. Marianne's marriage to Harold Gifford Greenwood took place on 12 November 1914 and was therefore legal. She gave her age incorrectly as being 17 but this does not alter the position. We presume that she was concerned that Greenwood might have been put off the whole idea of marriage had he known how young she was. We note that the witnesses were Annie and Geoffrey Shaw; they were Marianne's mother and brother and they must have been aware of the deception.

After Harold Greenwood vanished (never to be traced again) Marianne's father had a legal separation drawn up by a solicitor. However, under English law such an instrument has never terminated a marriage and no doubt the solicitor would have made that clear.

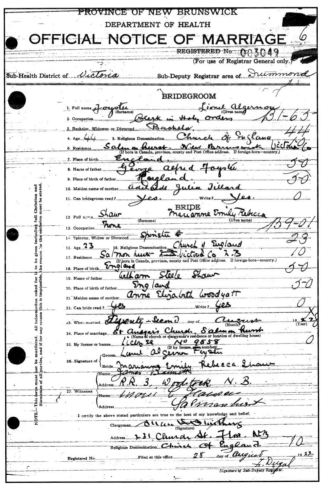

Fig 96. Certificate of Marianne's marriage to Foyster

Another aspect of the matter is that there was an interval of more than seven years between Greenwood's departure and Marianne's marriage to Foyster on 28 August 1922. In such circumstances one cannot assume that the missing person has died. It would have been necessary to have applied to a court for a presumption order to the effect that Greenwood was dead; we and other researchers have found no evidence that this was done. Similarly, no evidence of divorces have been discovered so there seems to be little doubt that Marianne's marriage to Foyster was bigamous, as were her third and fourth marriages.

We realise that it could be argued that these unfortunate facts have no relevance to the alleged haunting of Borley Rectory and that we have been guilty of stirring up the mud for the purposes of sensationalism. This is not the case and for two reasons. First, had we not referred to the matter we could have been accused either of ignorance or of a 'cover up.' Second and more importantly, critics of the case do take and will continue to take the view that Marianne cannot be regarded as a reliable witness. It should be noted that such critics are not in the same position as jurors who are told that they must base their decisions only on what they hear in court and that no other factors, such as past misdemeanours, may be taken into account.

We realise also that these matters may well cause distress to Marianne's descendants and we offer to them our sincere apologies and understanding but sometimes unwelcome facts have to be faced. We are more than happy to record that during the latter part of her life (in America) she became a welfare officer. Her work was highly regarded and she received an award for it.

Fig 97. The Rev Lionel and Mrs Marianne Foyster in 1931

Appendix F — Price at Pulborough

On 1 August 1908, Harry Price married Constance Mary Knight[1], her address being given as Riverside, Pulborough, East Sussex. In fact Constance Knight came from South East London, as Price had done. Especially from Price's point of view, the marriage was successful; first, it lasted for the rest of his life and second, the Knight family was very wealthy.

The Prices moved into Arun Bank, which is next door to Riverside, and never lived anywhere else. Price spent the remaining 40 years of his life there and his widow, who outlived him by 25 years, stayed on there until her death in 1973. Constance Price seems to have been the complete homebody; she took no part in her husband's work and when interviewed shortly after his death, she said: "I myself have no interest in and could not carry on his work. In the past I have had too much to do about the house"[2].

That house and Pulborough in general seem to have been Price's anchorage and, to a large extent, his operational base. Apparently, he and his wife were devoted to each other and in view of their differing interests, they complemented each other. Also, given Price's temperamental personality, living next door to his mother-in-law could have been a recipe for trouble but it seems that all was well. Our statement that Arun Bank was Price's operational base needs

Fig 98. Arun Bank in 2002. The room to the left of the front door was Price's study where he was found dead at his desk

justification in view of the fact that his National Laboratory of Psychical Research was situated in London. However, that organisation, founded in 1926 and metamorphosing into the University of London Council for Psychical Investigation in 1934, lasted for barely a decade and then fizzled out as the war clouds gathered. As compared with this decade, Price lived and worked at Pulborough for 40 years. During the lifetime of the National Laboratory he commuted each day to London and was back in his house by late afternoon except on those occasions when there were evening meetings and/or functions.

Price did most of his writing at Arun Bank and, as we have seen in chapter six, his last four books, including the two about Borley Rectory were reprinted several times. He was also highly skilled at light engineering and he set up a workshop at his home. He designed and made many pieces of equipment to a very high standard and they were used to test mediums and alleged phenomena at the National Laboratory. During the war, Price employed an assistant and produced equipment for the national effort.

Harry Price was a keen and active supporter of the local church at Pulborough during the whole of the time that he lived there; he was a churchwarden and sidesman. His enthusiasm had an unfortunate outcome on one occasion and we felt that this should be recorded. Among his other interests, he was a collector of old coins amd trade

Fig 99. The view from Arun Bank to the river Arun and the Sussex Downs

tokens. He was a fellow of the Royal Numismatic Society and his early writings included two long series of published articles to do with the trade tokens of Kent and Shropshire[3]. In 1923 it was decided to hold an exhibition in Pulborough church and Price lent his collection of ancient gold coins as part of the exhibition. Regrettably the coins were stolen on 26 September; the church was unattended at the time. The coins were never recovered and it transpired that the organisers of the exhibition had neglected to insure them.

Pulborough has expanded considerably during the last half century but Arun Bank exists still (2003) and externally looks much as it did in Price's day. It is a large double-fronted house, set back about ten yards from the road. The long rear garden slopes down to the river Arun and beyond it are glorious views of the Sussex Downs. Arun Bank is divided now into two flats.

Fig 100. A formal portrait of Price taken in the late 1920s when he started his work at Borley

Appendix G — The hoax

In the autumn of 2000 a book called *We Faked the Ghosts of Borley Rectory* was published, written by the late Louis Mayerling. Before discussing the book we need to say a few words about the author. He claimed to be the son of an Austrian lady, that he was born in Vienna on 4 September 1913 (in his own words, ' . . . at an unusually early age') and that he came to London and assumed the name George Carter, the surname being that of the family which adopted him and which lived in Mayes Road, Wood Green. On consulting the Genealogical Society, a member ascertained that a George Carter was born at this address on the same date that Mayerling claims to have been born in Vienna. We do not believe that this is a coincidence.

The pseudonyms do not end there. Mayerling/Carter claimed also to have played the piano in London jazz bands under the name of Lee Lennox and the banjo in a wartime Berlin night club impersonating Marlene Dietrich! We consulted two long-time professional jazz musicians who had never heard of Lee Lennox, although it is possible that he was a fill-in pianist or the bands in which he played were so insignificant and transitory that they did not merit remembering. Regarding the Marlene impersonation, we are not told how 'Marlene' got into occupied Europe but we are asked to believe that he/she escaped from it by walking over the Pyrenees!

In his book, Mayerling/Carter claimed that when a boy and a young man he stayed frequently at Borley Rectory (under the name of George Carter) and that all the alleged phenomena there were fraudulent. We suspect that he was never there and we shall discuss a number of points in support of this view.

We have related how Harry Price visited Borley Rectory for the first time on 12 July 1929 and how he organised a seance in the early hours of the next morning in an upstairs bedroom called the Blue Room. Those present (Price and his secretary, the Rev Guy Eric Smith and his wife, two of the Bull sisters and the reporter, V C Wall) spent several hours asking questions aloud, the replies coming in the form of tapping sounds from the dressing table mirror. One can have reservations about the accuracy of such 'information' but the phenomenon has been accepted by those present as genuine. The Mayerling/Carter explanation is that the people in the Blue Room were making so much noise that they disturbed the tenants of the rectory cottage who retaliated by tapping on the bedroom window with a pole. This is absurd. First, participants at seances do not make a lot of noise; they sit quietly hoping for results. Second, even if there had been an element of noise it could not have been audible in the cottage which was on the far side of the rectory and a considerable distance from the Blue Room which looked out over the large grounds. Third, the tenants would not have known when to tap the window.

Fourth, the upstairs windows of the rectory were situated at a considerable height so that a long pole would have been necessary and all the chances are that the alleged activities of the tenants would have resulted in glass panes being broken. Finally, such antics would have been obvious to people in the Blue Room and no doubt the rector, who was in effect their landlord, would have told the tenants to go away.

Another phenomenon which Mayerling/Carter mentioned is that the rectory piano appeared to play itself sometimes and he took personal credit for this. His explanation was that part of the back of the piano was missing, that the instrument was placed over a grille in the wall and that it was possible to pluck the piano strings through the aperture with a stick. This too is absurd. The reality is that the instrument was located in the drawing room and to the right of the large fireplace. On the other side of the wall behind the piano was the library and Sidney Glanville's carefully drawn up plans of the rectory do not show a conveniently placed grille between these two rooms. Neither is it likely that the well-to-do Bull family would have neglected to have had the back of the piano repaired should it have been necessary. However, the most perplexing aspect of this matter is that none of the other books about Borley Rectory contains any reference to this alleged music, ghostly or man-made.

In passing we note that the drawing room and the dining room were the two largest ground floor rooms in the rectory. Both were huge, lofty and well-lit thanks to large bay windows. Yet Mayerling described the dining room as small and dark, which indicates a lack of knowledge of the house.

A high point in Mayerling/Carter's book concerns a seance which is supposed to have taken place in the early 1930s in the slimy and amphibian-infested cellars under the rectory. Those said to have been present were Mayerling/Carter, Marianne Foyster, Montague Norman (then governor of the Bank of England) George Bernard Shaw, Sir Bernard Spilsbury (chief pathologist at the Home Office) and Maurice Barbanell (later to be editor of *Psychic News*). We are asked to believe that Lawrence of Arabia was also there at the outset but he left hurriedly because he objected to the presence of Bernard Shaw! Having spent most of his book ridiculing the Borley phenomena, Mayerling/Carter tells us that towards the end of this seance there was a sudden flash of light which blinded him temporarily and left him with long-term visual problems. These problems could be associated with another condition from which Mayerling/Carter said that he suffered. In our opinion the whole episode is nonsense although we would have to award top marks for name-dropping.

We feel that one of the most serious criticisms of this book lies in the fact that some of our own witnesses really do remember Borley Rectory, the Bull family, the Smiths and the Foysters. They have no recollection whatsoever of a Louis Mayerling/George Carter ever having stayed there, nor is there any mention of him in any of the extensive documentation.

We turn now to the illustrations, most of which are of very poor quality and at least one of which is not what it is purported to be. The picture in question is said to be of the author's mother and the Rev Lionel Algernon Foyster. We cannot identify the lady but the man is definitely not Foyster who was a tall, thin, cadaverous type.

We are unable to account for the frequent spelling mistakes, the grammatical errors and the childish 'jokes.' In our opinion this poorly written and poorly presented book is either a badly conceived and executed spoof or is in the realms of fantasy. It could have done serious psychical research a considerable disservice and is not of the calibre we would expect from someone who claimed to have been a doctor of music.

A concise bibliography with comments

Banks, Ivan: *The Enigma of Borley Rectory* (Foulsham, 1996). This book investigates the very early historical aspects of the case.

Dingwall, Eric, Goldney, Kathleen, and Hall, Trevor H: *The Haunting of Borley Rectory* (Gerald Duckworth and Co. Ltd, 1956). The first, and sceptical, report commissioned by the Society for Psychical Research.

Downes, Wesley H: *The Ghosts of Borley* (Wesley's Publications, 61 Lymington Ave, Clacton-on-Sea, 1993). A fairly brief booklet which includes some unusual photographs.

Fuller, John G: *The Airmen who would not Die* (Souvenir Press Ltd, 1979). This book is mainly about the *R101* disaster, but includes much information about Harry Price's considerable involvement in the consequences.

Hastings, Robert J: *An Examination of the Borley Report* (London, 1969). A further study associated with the Society for Psychical Research, which reaches different conclusions to the 1956 publication (listed above).

Henning, The Rev Alfred Clifford: *Haunted Borley* (published privately, 1949). A lengthy booklet and now rare; there are frequent references to allegedly paranormal occurrences at Borley.

Myers, Frederick W H: *Human Personality and its Survival of Bodily Death* (London, 1903). A standard work by one of the founding members of the Society for Psychical Research.

Palmers, Bernard: *The Reverend Rebels* (Darton, Longman and Todd, 1993). An account of the theological battles of the 19th century; one chapter is devoted to Father Alexander Heriot Machonochie and St Alban's Church, Holborn.

Price, Harry: *The Most Haunted House in England* (Longmans, Green and Co Ltd, 1940). *The End of Borley Rectory* (George G Harrap and Co Ltd, 1946). The first two books about the alleged haunting.
    Search for Truth — My Life for Psychical Research (Collins, 1942). Price's autobiography, which includes frequent references to the Borley case *Stella C — An Account of Some Original Experiments in Psychical Research* (Souvenir Press Ltd, 1973). This re-issue of one of Price's early books includes a long introduction by James Turner, who describes some of his own experiences at Borley.

Tabori, Paul: *Harry Price — The Biography of a Ghost Hunter* (Athenaeum Press, 1950). This biography by Price's literary executor includes a chapter devoted to the Borley case.

Tabori, Paul and Underwood, Peter: *The Ghosts of Borley — Annals of the Haunted Rectory* (David and Charles, 1973). This book contains much previously unpublished information.

Toulson, Shirley: *East Anglia — Walking the Ley Lines and Ancient Tracks* (Wildwood House Ltd, 1979). The long introduction is a general statement of the principles and theories to do with the ley lines.

Turner, James: *Sometimes into England* (Cassell, 1970). The first two chapters of this autobiography describe Turner's four years at Borley Rectory cottage

Underwood, Peter: *Borley Postscript* (White House Publications, 2001). This book contains some additional material and later thoughts from one of the authors of *The Ghosts of Borley*

Wood, Robert: *The Widow of Borley — A Psychical Investigation* (Gerald Duckworth and Co Ltd, 1992). Biography of an extraordinary personality.

O'Neil, Vincent: *The Borley Ghost Society*, published on the internet at www.borleyrectory.com. O'Neil is the adopted son of Marianne Foyster.

NOTES

CHAPTER ONE *The geography and the history*

1. *The Imperial Gazetteer,* Vol 1.
2. Borley church records.
3. Original notes in the Harry Price Library, London University*.
4. *The Most Haunted House in England,* chapter 1.
5. *Ibid,* chapter 1.
6. Borley church records.
7. Family Records Centre, London; Registrars General, Belfast; Fredericton, Canada. Marianne went through a form of marriage in each case but invariably false information was given.
8. *Haunted Borley,* chapter 5.
9. *The Most Haunted House in England,* chapter 17.
10. Sidney H Glanville's *Locked Book* (microfilm), Harry Price Library, London University.
11. 'Sunex Amures' never 'came through' again. One writer, the late Ivan Banks, stated correctly that spellings are sometimes inaccurate in seances and that 'Sunex Amures' ought to have been 'Senex Taurus', ie, 'Old Man Bull,' but this is stretching things too far.
12. Alan Gregson's letter dated 16 July 1985 (see chapter 11).
13. *The End of Borley Rectory,* chapter 10 (contributed by the Rev Canon W J Phythian-Adams DD).

CHAPTER TWO *The trees for the wood*

1. *Search for Truth*, Chapter 10.
2. *The Reverend Rebels,* chapter concerning Father Alexander Maconochie.
3. It is not known what precautions, if any, *The Church Times* took in 1945 to ensure that correspondents to its letters columns were genuine. There would have been verification difficulties due to telephones being less common than in the 21st century. The correspondent gave an address in Sheringham, a remote village on the north Norfolk coast, which would probably not have been well endowed with telephones. The policy at *The Church Times* at the time of writing (2002) was to investigate correspondents only if the letter raised a query in the editor's mind.
4. Various articles by Harry Price in *The British Journal of Psychical Research* and *The American Journal of Psychical Research*.
5. In the UK, among others, Cambridge, Edinburgh, Northampton, Coventry, Hertfordshire and London (Goldsmiths); in the Netherlands, Utrecht; in the USA, Duke and University of California, Los Angeles. The SPR regards these establishments with respect.
6. *The Most Haunted House in England,* chapter 12.
7. *Ibid,* chapter 7.

CHAPTER THREE *The Bull family*

1. Booklet celebrating the 750th anniversary of the institution of Peter de

Cachepore, first Rector of Borley, 1236.
2. Authors' interviews with Alfred and Margaret Finch, 1994.
3. *The Most Haunted House in England*, chapter 5 and plate 1.
4. P Shaw Jeffrey's letter dated March 1942 to Harry Price.
5. Family Records Centre, London
6. Authors' interviews with Alfred and Margaret Finch, 1994.
7. Letter dated 27 September 2001 from Colchester Royal Grammar School to EB.
8. *The Most Haunted House in England*, chapter 10.
9. Original notes in the Harry Price Library, London University*.
10. *The Ghosts of Borley*, chapter 1.

CHAPTER FOUR *The Smiths and the Foysters*

1. Borley church records.
2. Original notes in the Harry Price Library, London University*.
3. Manuscript originally in the Harry Price Library but returned to Mrs Smith at her request after Price's death.
4. Original report in the Society for Psychical Research archive, Cambridge University*.
5. Family Records Centre, London, and Belchamp Walter church records.
6. *Rayden on Divorce*, chapter 6.
7. Registrar general, Frederictown, New Brunswick.
8. Family Records Centre, London.
9. EB and CM's interviews with Alfred and Margaret Finch, 1994.
10. *Ibid.*
11. Family Records Centre, London.
12. A supermarket was built on the site.
13. *The Most Haunted House in England*, chapter 12
14. *The End of Borley Rectory*, chapter 3.
15. Original notes in the Harry Price Library, London University.

CHAPTER FIVE *The Henning Incumbancy*

1. *Haunted Borley*, chapter 1.
2. EB's and CM's interviews with Alfred and Margaret Finch, 1994.
3. *Haunted Borley*, chapter 6.
4. *Ibid*, chapter 7.
5. *Ibid.*
6. *Ibid.*
7. *Ibid.*
8. EB's interview with Kathleen King (née Finch), 1998.
9. *Haunted Borley*, chapter 7.
10. Young jackdaws are very quarrelsome and frequently fly about squabbling noisily. Breeding birds start laying towards the end of April and the eggs hatch early to mid May. The young birds are therefore at their most obstreperous in June when Price made his visit. Coming from the manicured West Sussex countryside around Pulborough, he was probably not familiar with the habits of jackdaws.

11. *Haunted Borley,* chapter 7.
12. *The End of Borley Rectory,* chapter 9 (contributed by Doctor A J B Robertson MA PhD).
13. *Sometimes into England,* chapter 2.

CHAPTER SIX *The famous Harry Price*
1. Family Records Centre, London.
2. *Search for Truth,* chapter 10.
3. *The Most Haunted House in England,* chapter 1.
4. Original report in the Society for Psychical Research Archives, Cambridge University*.
5. *Ibid*.
6. *The Most Haunted House in England,* chapter 12.
7. *Ibid,* chapters 16 & 17.
8. Copy in the Harry Price Library, London University.
9. *The End of Borley Rectory,* chapter 9 (contributed by Dr A J B Robertson MA PhD).
10. *Ibid,* chapter 14.
11. *The Haunting of Borley Rectory,* chapter 7.
12. CM's interview with Olive Marshall, 1996.

CHAPTER SEVEN *The last rector of Borley and Liston*
1. Articles in *The Daily Mirror ,* 10 - 17 June, 1929.
2. Sidney H Glanville's correspondence with the Essex Archaeological Society, 1938.
3. *What's my Line,* transmitted on 12 April, 1953, and CM's observations.
4. Borley church records.
5. We do not know how deep the earth on the tunnel floor was.
6. EB's and CM's interviews with Leslie and Ursula Pennell, 1995.

CHAPTER EIGHT *The last widow of Borley*
1. Original notes in the Harry Price library, London University*.
2. *The Ghosts of Borley,* chapter 6.
3. CM's interview with Dr Margaret Abernethy *circa* 1960.
4. EB's and CM's interviews with Nancy Goodale, 1996.

CHAPTER NINE *The vanishing lady and other reports*
1. *The Ghosts of Borley,* chapter 7, and EB's and CM's interview with Mr and Mrs Mills, former Borley residents.
2. EB's and CM's interview with Marie Poore and Hilary Wright, 1995
3. *Ibid*
4. EB's interview with Dorothy Lane, 1995.
5. Navy, Army and Air Force Institute, the organisation devoted to looking after the welfare of rankers mainly through the sale, at subsidised prices, of strong tea and substantial cakes.
6. A pre-fabricated tunnel-shaped building of corrugated iron much used by the armed forces during World War II, invented by Lt Col Peter N Nissen, a British engineer.
7. Is time in this life relevant to those in the next?

8. EB's interview with Thomas Musk, 1995.
9. Suffolk County Archives.
10. EB's and CM's interviews with Paul Kemp (see preface), 1996.
11. EB's interview with Gillian Cook, 1995.
12. *The Ghosts of Borley*, chapter 7.
13. *Ibid*, chapter 7.
14. EB's interview with Russell Herbert, 1996.
15. EB's and CM's interview with Marie Poore and Hilary Wright, 1995.
16. Church Commissioners Enquiry, 1937.

CHAPTER TEN *Further experiences and an exciting discovery*

1. EB's and CM's interviews with Nancy Goodale, 1996.
2. *Ibid*.
3. *Picture Post*, 1 Jan 1955.
4. *The Ghosts of Borley*, chapter 6.
5. EB's interview with anonymous witness, 1995.
6. EB's interview with José Simmonds, 2002.
7. EB's interview with local clairvoyant, 2003.
8. Booklet celebrating the 750th anniversary of the institution of Peter de Cachepore, first rector of Borley, 1236.
9. *Search for Harry Price*, chapter 18.
10. *The Ghosts of Borley*, chapter 5.
11. Booklet celebrating the 750th anniversary of the institution of Peter de Cachepore, first rector of Borley, 1236.
12. EB's and CM's interview with leader of psychical research group, 1996.
13. Clairvoyant's report, 2003.

CHAPTER ELEVEN *The documents and what they tell us*

1. Tongue and groove. Planking with a projecting strip down one edge and a groove down the other so that planks fit together continuously without gaps.
2. The International Guild of Lamp Researchers (www.dapllc.com/lampguild) definition: 'Although *Argand burner* represents a rather specific series of inventions and improvements, today all round-wick, central draft lamps are generally referred to as Argand burners.'
3. *The Ghosts of Borley*, chapter 4.
4. *The Daily Express*.
5. Chapman Pincher, later well-known for his writing on espionage.

CHAPTER TWELVE *What is the truth? Summary and conclusions*

1. *Maria Marten — The Murder in the Red Barn*, Peter Haining, 1980.
2. *East Anglia — Walking the Ley Lines and Ancient Tracks*, Introduction.
3. Broadbent, Simon, 'Simulating the ley hunter,' *J Royal Statistical Soc A* (1980), **143,** Part 2, pp 109-140.
4. *Ghosts*, pp 91-106.

5. *Ibid,* pp 91-106.
6. *Ibid,* pp 91-106.
7. *The Ghosts of Borley,* chapter 7.
8. For a whole dictionary of regrettable quotations, see *They got it Wrong,* Guinness Publishing, Enfield, 1995.

APPENDIX C *The extendible Bull family*

1. Family Records Centre, London
2. *The Most Haunted House in England,* chapter 9.

APPENDIX D *Dodie's diary*

1. Family Records Centre, London, and Borley church records.
2. Underfed and underpaid agricultural workers in surrounding villages had to come to Long Melford to vote in the 1885 general election. Already disgruntled by their living and working conditions, some 1200 people went on the rampage in Melford. Soldiers and extra police were drafted in to re-establish order.
3. 'Darling Charlie' appears often in the diary. He seems to have made a considerable impression but we are not told his surname. He was not the late Rev Hayden. We can suggest two candidates, who are at least possibilities. Harry Martyn's elder brother, Charles, was an exact contemporary of Dodie. An outside possibility is their father, the Rev Charles John Martyn who was a 49-year-old widower in 1885. He was said to have been a most charming man and Dodie seems to have been a somewhat predatory young lady.

APPENDIX E *Marianne's marriages*

1. *Rayden on Divorce,* chapter 6.

APPENDIX F *Price at Pulborough*

1. Family Records Centre, London.
2. *The Evening News,* 30 March 1948.
3. *The Kentish Mercury,* and *The Wellington Journal* (Shropshire), 1902 - 1904.

*Apparently these documents have not been retained in the libraries at London and Cambridge Universities. It seems that they may have been removed at some juncture but not returned. Today (2003) strict security measures are in force as they are in most libraries with valuable documents.

INDEX OF PEOPLE, PLACES AND PUBLICATIONS